The Social Thought of
C. Wright Mills

Social Thinkers Series

A Pine Forge Press Series

Series Editor
A. Javier Treviño
Wheaton College, Norton, MA

Published
The Social Thought of C. Wright Mills
By A. Javier Treviño

Forthcoming

The Social Thought of Georg Simmel
By Horst J. Helle

The Social Thought of Karl Marx
By Justin P. Holt

The Social Thought of Erving Goffman
By Michael Hviid Jacobsen and Søren Kristiansen

The Social Thought of Talcott Parsons
By Helmut Staubmann

SAGE
SOCIAL THINKERS SERIES

The Social Thought of
C. Wright Mills

A. Javier Treviño
Wheaton College, Massachusetts

⑤SAGE | PINE FORGE

Los Angeles | London | New Delhi
Singapore | Washington DC

Los Angeles | London | New Delhi
Singapore | Washington DC

FOR INFORMATION:

Pine Forge Press

An Imprint of SAGE Publications, Inc.

2455 Teller Road

Thousand Oaks, California 91320

E-mail: order@sagepub.com

SAGE Publications Ltd.

1 Oliver's Yard

55 City Road

London EC1Y 1SP

United Kingdom

SAGE Publications India Pvt. Ltd.

B 1/I 1 Mohan Cooperative Industrial Area

Mathura Road, New Delhi 110 044

India

SAGE Publications Asia-Pacific Pte. Ltd.

33 Pekin Street #02-01

Far East Square

Singapore 048763

Acquisitions Editor: David Repetto

Assistant Editor: Maggie Stanley

Production Editor: Libby Larson

Copy Editor: Teresa Herlinger

Typesetter: C&M Digitals (P) Ltd.

Proofreader: Rae-Ann Goodwin

Cover Designer: Gail Buschman

Marketing Manager: Erica DeLuca

Permissions Editor: Karen Ehrmann

Printed in the United States of America

Library of Congress Cataloging-in-Publication Data

Treviño, A. Javier, 1958- The social thought of C. Wright Mills/A. Javier Treviño.

p. cm. — (Social thinkers)
Includes bibliographical references and index.

ISBN 978-1-4129-9393-7 (pbk.)

1. Mills, C. Wright (Charles Wright), 1916–1962—Political and social views. 2. Sociology–History–20th century. 3. Social structure. 4. Social psychology. I. Title.

HM449.T74 2012 301.092—dc22 2010054089

This book is printed on acid-free paper.

11 12 13 14 15 10 9 8 7 6 5 4 3 2 1

Contents

Series Editor's Foreword

The Pine Forge Press Social Thinkers series is dedicated to making available compact, reader-friendly paperbacks that examine the thought of major figures from within and beyond sociology. The books in this series will provide concise introductions to the work, life, and influences of the most prominent social thinkers. Written in an accessible and provocative prose, these books are designed for advanced undergraduate and graduate students of sociology, politics, economics, and social philosophy, as well as for scholars and socially curious general readers.

The first half of the series will be devoted to the "classical" thinkers—Karl Marx, Max Weber, Georg Simmel, Erving Goffman, Talcott Parsons, and C. Wright Mills—who, through their seminal writings, laid the foundation for much of current social thought. Subsequent books will feature more "contemporary" scholars, as well as those not yet adequately represented in the canon: Jane Addams, Charlotte Perkins Gilman, Harold Garfinkel, Norbert Elias, Jean Baudrillard, and Pierre Bourdieu. Particular attention is paid to those aspects of the social thinker's personal background and intellectual influences that most impacted his or her approach in better understanding individuals and society.

Consistent with Pine Forge Press's distinguished track record of publishing high-quality textbooks in sociology, the carefully assembled volumes in the Social Thinkers series will be authored by respected scholars committed to disseminating the discipline's rich heritage of social thought and to helping students comprehend key concepts. The information offered in these books will be invaluable for making sense of the complexities of contemporary social life and various issues that have become central concerns of the human condition: inequality, social order, social control, deviance, the social self, rationality, reflexivity, and so on.

These books in the series can be used as self-contained volumes or in conjunction with textbooks in sociological theory. Each volume will conclude with a Further Readings chapter intended to facilitate additional study and research. As a collection, the Social Thinkers series will stand as a testament to the robustness of contemporary social thought. Our hope is that these books on the great social thinkers will give students a deeper understanding of modern and postmodern Western social thought and encourage them to engage in sociological dialogue.

Premised on Newton's aphorism "If I have seen further, it is by standing on the shoulders of giants" (an aphorism, incidentally, that was introduced into sociology by Robert K. Merton, himself a towering figure in the discipline), the Social Thinkers series aims to place its readers on the shoulders of the giants of 19th- and 20th-century social thought. It is my hope that the inaugural volume for the series—the one you now hold in your hands, *The Social Thought of C. Wright Mills*—does just that.

Acknowledgments

This volume has been a long time "in the making." Through the years, it has benefited from communications with Richard A. Gillam, Glenn Goodwin, Irving Louis Horowitz, John Leggett, Frank Lindenfield, Robert J.S. Ross, and Joseph A. Scimecca. I am especially thankful to Daniel Geary and John H. Summers for reading earlier drafts of the entire manuscript and making valuable suggestions for its improvement. In addition, I express my gratitude to four anonymous reviewers whose comments helped to significantly improve what I had written. Grateful acknowledgment is given to *The American Sociologist* (vol. 28, no. 3, 1997, pp. 29–56) and *Sociological Imagination* (vol. 43, nos. 2–3, 1997, pp. 155–180) in which appeared earlier versions of Chapters 5 and 6, respectively. Finally, I am most thankful to Kathryn Mills and Nik Mills for their many kindnesses that made this book possible.

Photo Credit: Photo by Yaroslava Mills, by permission of the Estate of C. Wright Mills

Introduction

It is no exaggeration to say that by the mid-1950s, American sociology had come to be dominated by two men: Talcott Parsons and C. Wright Mills. They were the most eminent representatives of the professional and the populist styles of sociology, respectively. Parsons, the professional sociologist, developed a grand theoretical scheme in academic sociology's inner "scientific" circles. By contrast, Mills, the populist, delivered "sermons" about the moral uneasiness of the era to a nonprofessional audience of learned "publics," by which he meant various groups of politically active people. Clearly, by mid-century, both Parsons and Mills were regarded as the undisputed "titans of American sociology" (Martindale, 1975, pp. 4–5).

This book closely examines the writings of C. Wright Mills and his intrepid, if somewhat solitary, effort at influencing American critical thought. In stressing the critical aspect of Mills's sociology, the book focuses generally on two of his lifelong intellectual concerns: (1) the interrelationship between social structure and personality and (2) the bureaucratization of modern society and the power relations it produces.

The rationale for this book's organization is that it allows the reader to examine how Mills's penetrating scrutiny of the centralization of power in the hands of a few elites and the manner in which institutions shape the character of individuals enabled him to formulate a unique "radical" sociology. This form of social thinking constituted, first and foremost, a running critique—more, a despairing analysis—of the types of uninformed men and women and repressive large-scale bureaucracies that had come to prevail in American mass society during the middle decades of the 20th century.

Outline of the Book

This book does not attempt to present Mills's works by chronology of publication, given that he frequently moved from topic to topic and his progression of ideas is not necessarily temporally linear. Thus, while it appears that, unlike Parsons, Mills had no coherent theoretical framework toward which he was building, it is nevertheless the case that the two basic themes mentioned above—always couched in terms of the "sociological imagination" that he made explicit—frequently appear throughout most of his works.

In an effort to get at the roots of Mills's radical sociology, Chapter 1 begins by presenting a brief and general intellectual portrait of the man and his social thought. To accomplish this, we examine Mills's personal background and intellectual influences in sociohistorical context.

As with all social thinkers, Mills's views on individuals and society had a direct influence on his social thought. Chapter 2 presents his perspectives on the fundamental attributes of individuals and society, not only as he saw them predominating during his time (i.e., the middle of the 20th century), but also in reference to what he thought they could become. In addition, we will see how Mills's social views determine his empirical methodology, which utilized both quantitative and qualitative techniques of data collection, as well as his more complex conceptual methodology, which in essence involves adopting an approach to the social world that he described as "taking it big." At bottom, however, Mills's disposition toward individuals and society, as well as toward the methodologies he employed in understanding them, were motivated by a "humanist concern." This was a consideration that made it his moral responsibility to earnestly consider the troubles and issues in the everyday lives of flesh-and-blood individuals. Mills's humanist sociology thus required connecting the social, personal, and historical dimensions of people's lives.

Continuing with his stated goal of endeavoring to define and dramatize the essential characteristics of the society of his time, as well as to see individuals as actors in the social drama of the 20th century, Chapter 3 is devoted to a detailed discussion of Mills's social psychology—that is, his consideration of the character of individuals in the context of their social structure—as articulated in the book *Character and Social Structure*, which he coauthored with Hans H. Gerth. The social psychological theoretical framework that Gerth and Mills outline in this book is fundamental to understanding all of Mills's other major writings, including his so-called stratification trilogy.

Chapter 4, the longest of the chapters, offers a detailed analysis of Mills's most well-known books: his stratification trilogy that consists of *The New Men of Power, White Collar,* and *The Power Elite.* Generally speaking, these three books are an analysis of the class structure and power relations in the United States during the 1940s and 1950s. But more than this, these are also the books that established Mills as one of the leading social critics—in the manner of Thorstein Veblen—of American society.

If the stratification trilogy constitutes some of Mills's best-known works, his writings on Latino populations and on Latin America have been largely ignored by current sociology. Chapter 5 looks at these writings, which consist of four pieces published between 1943 and 1960 that consider the character structure of four Latino populations: Mexican American youth, Puerto Rican migrants, Cuban revolutionaries, and Latin American intellectuals. The social psychological approach that Mills formulated in *Character and Social Structure* is applied to understand his views on Latinos—their motives, moods, and self-images.

A running theme found throughout Mills's major and minor writings pertains to the role of the mass media in the context of mass society. Chapter 6 offers a systematic analysis of Mills's statements on the American mass media, which he made between the late 1940s and the early 1960s. In particular, the chapter looks at what Mills says about the power elite's monopolization and manipulation of media symbols; the media markets in mass society; the community of publics and the democratic ideal; the public of public opinion; and the media's effects on labor unions, the intellectual community, television Christians, Cubans in revolutionary transition, and Puerto Ricans in New York City.

Mills's writings invariably have a powerful effect on his readers. His insightful critiques of contemporary U.S. society and of professional sociology will either leave them with a deep sense of pessimism about the current state of affairs or more likely provoke them to organize, mobilize, and take action for change. Few are those who remain indifferent to his incisive and urgent declarations. Chapter 7 considers three of Mills's final works that have inspired several publics. *The Causes of World War Three,* which calls for a politics of responsibility, served to galvanize the peace movement in the United States. *The Sociological Imagination*—a book that is part primer, part polemic—has both instructed and inspired generations of sociology students to understand the meaning of their own epoch for their own lives as well as to help them become active participants in history making. Lastly, Mills's 1960 "Letter to the New Left" gave hope to young radical intellectuals in making a more democratic society. It is because of this "letter" that Mills became regarded as a "prophet of the New Left." In the end, however, it is Mills's persistent outlook of doom and gloom that cast him as a disillusioned radical.

Chapter 8, the final chapter, considers the sociological work, mostly unfinished, that Mills left at the time of his death. It also looks at those books that have been organized and published posthumously by his admirers. In addition, it discusses those retrospectives that have been written on Mills—some amicable, others less so—as well as those studies that have been explicitly influenced by Mills's ideas.

Each chapter ends with a set of "questions for thought." These are not intended as discussion questions, but rather are meant to have the reader reflect on them. They are not questions whose answers will (necessarily) be found in the chapter. However, the information discussed in the chapter should help readers consider the questions. In each case, one or two of them will reference how the information given in the chapter may apply to today's social world.

The purpose of this book is to acquaint the rising generation of interested publics—students, scholars, activists, intellectuals—with the social and political ideas of one of the leading critics of mid-20th-century American society, ideas that, over half a century later, remain crucial in better understanding the world of the early 21st century.

1

C. Wright Mills and Postwar America

C. Wright Mills begins his most famous book, *The Sociological Imagination* (1959b), by declaring that "neither the life of an individual nor the history of a society can be understood without understanding both" (p. 3). In order to properly understand the social thought of C. Wright Mills, it is necessary that we heed his directive and locate his ideas in his own biography and in that particular period in history and space in which he lived and worked: postwar America (on this point see Brewer, 2004, 2005). It is in this way that we can best render an intellectual portrait of the man and his ideas. This chapter thus considers Mills's personal background and intellectual influences in sociohistorical context.

Personal Background

A leading critic of post–World War II America and one of the most controversial figures in social science, C. Wright Mills was doubtless the most influential American radical social theorist since Thorstein Veblen. Although his career as a social critic spanned only a little over two decades, Mills, through his inflammatory writings, contributed significantly to the development of the radical intellectual tradition in American social thought. His work is commonly characterized as "critical" or "radical" sociology largely because he (1) persisted in revealing the underside of U.S. society in the hope of fomenting structural change and (2) relentlessly attacked the mainline and what he regarded as "complacent" sociology of the 1950s.

Beginning with the 1946 book he edited, *From Max Weber: Essays in Sociology* (Weber, 1946), and up to the posthumous *The Marxists* (1962), Mills worked at a fevered pace, ultimately producing 11 books and over 200 articles. As one of the foremost dissident intellectuals of the Cold War period, and a particularly harsh critic of American foreign policy and national security strategy, and of big business and mass society, Mills indelibly stamped his thinking upon several generations of dissenters in sociology and the other social sciences.

Biography

Charles Wright Mills was born in Waco, Texas, on August 28, 1916. The second child and only son of a middle-class family of mixed English, Irish, and French ancestry, Mills grew up in Sherman, Fort Worth, and Dallas, and spent a few years in San Antonio. Indeed, before Mills turned 12, his family had moved to five Texas cities and changed residences eight times (Summers, 2008d, p. 3). But even though he eventually left Texas, only to return infrequently, as Irving Louis Horowitz (1983) explains, try as he might, Mills was never able to completely escape his cultural roots. "More than once," writes Horowitz allegorically, "and even by associates, [Mills] was described as a Texas cowpuncher who headed north via pony express to carry the message of radical sociology" (pp. 13–14). Unfortunately for Mills, he was never able to live down his Texas background. Mills's ostensibly raw "backwoods" beginnings, of which he was always acutely self-conscious, and his futile efforts to escape its uncultured mystique by immersing himself in urbane high-brow surroundings, may partially explain why he saw himself and was treated by others as an "outlander" in various aspects of his personal and professional life. In effect, Mills lived on the cultural margins of two distinct worlds, that of the provincial Texas cowboy and that of the metropolitan New York intellectual, while never completely belonging to either.

Apparently Mills also rejected his parents' middle-class style of life. His father, Charles Grover Mills, had escaped poverty to become that most representative of white-collar workers, an insurance agent. The senior Mills was frequently away on business trips, for weeks at a time, during the period that his son was growing up. About his father's influence, Mills had this to say:

> From my father I absorbed the gospel and character of work, determination with both eyes always ahead. That's the part of the America he knows, and it is part of him too. There was a time when I thought he did not possess a feeling of craftsmanship. But I was wrong. It is merely that his line of effort is one I did not understand. Looking back, I see he always did a good job, that he never quit until it was finished. (as quoted in K. Mills & Mills, 2000, p. 41)

Mills's mother, Frances, with whom he had an ambivalent relationship, affected middle-class manners and imparted to her son many "feminine" sensitivities. "From my mother," Mills wrote, "I have gotten a sense of color and air. She showed me the tang and feel of a room properly appointed, and the drama about flowers. She gave me feel. She also tried to teach me manners, but I fear I have forgotten many of them" (as quoted in K. Mills & Mills, 2000, p. 41). Whether he indeed forgot them, or more likely self-consciously endeavored to root out middle-class pretensions and prejudices, what is certain is that Mills took on a working-class persona, or better yet, a political ethos that he constructed for himself, of the Wobbly, which is to say the antithesis of the bureaucrat. Admiring strongly the radical syndicalist union, the International Workers of the World, whose members were known as "Wobblies," Mills states, "I am a Wobbly, personally, deep down, and for good" (as quoted in K. Mills & Mills, 2000, p. 252). This, then, is how the nonconformist Mills described himself.

It is common lore that Mills wore inexpensive clothes, drove a small Nash automobile (and later, a U.S. Army jeep, and rode a BMW motorcycle) and that his home furnishings were nothing if not utilitarian. Indeed, he seems to have gone out of his way to look and act like a manual laborer—a kind of intellectual lumberjack. In his study at home, Mills worked, not at a desk, but at a draftsman's table (Form, 1995). In a word, he took pains to reject his parents' middle-class world—a world he regarded as one of artificial politeness and painted-on smiles.

His mother, a homemaker with deep Texas roots, was a devout Roman Catholic. In accord with her wishes, Mills was baptized Catholic and later attended a series of parochial schools and served as a choirboy in the Catholic Church of Waco. But Catholicism "never took" for Mills. "I was an Irish altar boy before I reached the age of consent," he wrote toward the end of his life. "I never revolted from it; I never had to. For some reason, it never took. It was all a bit too tangible and bloody," he explained (as quoted in K. Mills & Mills, 2000, p. 313).

Despite his mother's strong Roman Catholic faith and Mills's rejection of it, Rick Tilman (1984) maintains that at the root of Mills's sociology can be discerned, not a Catholic social justice, but a type of radical Protestant individualism, one with an intellectual style characterized by overtones of hellfire and damnation. This was a Protestantism with its heritage in Puritanism's tough-minded practical idealism of social perfectionism. Tilman writes, "In a characteristically Puritan way, although not in the literal doctrinal sense . . . Mills . . . viewed the world as a place for combat between the greedy and parasitical on the one hand and the men of genuine learning, industry, and morality on the other" (p. 195). Perhaps somewhat similar to

Durkheim's treatment of sociology as a vehicle for clarifying the great moral questions of fin de siècle France, Mills firmly believed that sociology could supply the moral guidance required by a society—post–World War II America—that had lost its way.

After graduating from Dallas Technical High School in 1934, Mills enrolled as an engineering student at Texas Agricultural and Mechanical College (A&M), which at the time was an all-male military institution of just under 3,000 students (Kerr, 2009, p. 3). It was there that he first came in contact with sociology in reading Robert E. Park and Ernest W. Burgess's classic textbook *Introduction to the Science of Sociology*. And it was in terms of these two thinkers' ideas of the social self that the young Mills "first came seriously to analyze" himself (K. Mills & Mills, 2000, p. 29). According to Mills, the relentless hazing that he received at the hands of the upper-class cadets served to transform him into a rebel and an outsider, the persona that he deliberately cultivated and retained throughout the rest of his life (Kerr, 2009). More than this, Daniel Geary (2009) maintains that, as a result of his particularly unhappy freshman year at Texas A&M, Mills developed an enduring "visceral negative reaction to militarism" (p. 61).

At the beginning of his sophomore year, Mills transferred to the much more cosmopolitan University of Texas (UT) at Austin where, in 1939, he concurrently earned a BA degree in sociology and an MA in philosophy. It appears, however, that just prior to graduating, Mills, in an effort "to confront the world in its hard social forms" (Horowitz, 1964a, p. 18), had already decided to dedicate himself to the study of sociology. Indeed, during his senior year at UT, Mills submitted three essays on the sociology of knowledge: "Language, Logic and Culture," which was published in the October 1939 issue of the *American Sociological Review*; "Situated Actions and Vocabularies of Motive," which was also accepted in that same prestigious journal; as well as "Methodological Consequences of the Sociology of Knowledge," which appeared in the *American Journal of Sociology*. It was on the strength of these early articles, published by the two leading journals of American sociology, that Mills, by the age of 25, first came to the attention of scholars working in the areas of sociology of knowledge, pragmatism, and social theory.

Given that UT had no PhD program in sociology at the time, Mills, in the fall of 1939, began doctoral training in sociology at the University of Wisconsin, where he received a $300 fellowship. While at Wisconsin, Mills continued his studies in the sociology of knowledge and pragmatism and, during his final year there, met and quickly became close friends with Hans H. Gerth.

An émigré, Gerth had fled Nazi Germany in 1937. In possession of a comprehensive knowledge of the work of Max Weber, Gerth first introduced

Mills to Weber's ideas. And in 1940, the two began a 13-year collaboration, which ultimately resulted in two books: *From Max Weber: Essays in Sociology* (Weber, 1946), the first English translations of Weber's specifically sociological writings; and *Character and Social Structure* (Gerth & Mills, 1953), the first social psychology textbook that earnestly considers the influences of institutional order in shaping individual character.

Three months before the attack on Pearl Harbor, in 1941, Mills took a position as assistant professor of sociology at the University of Maryland, even though he had not yet completed his dissertation, *A Sociological Account of Pragmatism*. Upon hastily completing the thesis—in which he interpreted the careers and publics of the pragmatists Charles Sanders Peirce, William James, and John Dewey—Mills was promoted to associate professor and continued to focus his energies on the Weber project. This latter effort necessitated that Gerth visit him in the Maryland suburb of Greenbelt, for about 3 weeks at the end of August 1941, to work on the book.

With the involvement of the United States in World War II, Mills tried assiduously to avoid being drafted. His strategy was to fail the military's preinduction physical examination by "fencing" with the examining psychiatrist and acting restless and nervous, making his eyes dance about rapidly (Form, 1995, p. 57). In May 1944, he was classified as unfit for military service, not for heady reasons of mental instability, but for his chronic hypertension as well as having too high a pulse rate—a condition likely exacerbated by his working 14-hour days (K. Mills & Mills, 2000).

So even though Mills did not have to face the question of conscientious objection, he was, in fact, adamantly opposed to U.S. involvement in the war on twin grounds. First, he was highly suspicious of Franklin Roosevelt's administration, convinced that the president was leading the United States into a permanent war economy. Second, Mills saw structural trends in America's political economy that he believed paralleled those of Nazi Germany. Thus, contrary to most intellectuals of the time, Mills did not see the war as a struggle for democracy; rather, for him, it was just another opportunity for the imperial powers to redivide the world. The upshot is that, for Mills, his following the events of World War II closely, and reflecting on them, greatly increased his interest in politics—and, he claims, this made a radical out of him.

His opposition to the war notwithstanding, Mills's contributions to the war effort were made on two fronts. First, in 1943, during the height of the war, he gave formal lectures in American history at Maryland, three times a week for four semesters and without compensation, to scores of army recruits. Second, he served as a social researcher for the Smaller War Plants Corporation, a federal agency that promoted effective utilization of small businesses producing war materials and essential civilian supplies. The purpose of the study Mills was involved in was to convince Congress to establish a national agency to aid small businesses (Geary, 2009).

At war's end, in 1945, Mills joined the Department of Sociology at Columbia University where he would remain for the rest of his life. Realizing an unusually high publications output during his years at Columbia, he would nonetheless not be promoted to full professor for another 11 years. Numbered among Mills's Columbia colleagues were the eminent sociologists Robert S. Lynd, Daniel Bell, Robert M. MacIver, Seymour Martin Lipset, Robert K. Merton, and Paul F. Lazarsfeld. Under Lazarsfeld's overall supervision, Mills served as director of the Labor Research Division of the Bureau of Applied Social Research (BASR) and completed his first book, a study on labor unions and their leaders, *The New Men of Power: America's Labor Leaders* (1948). He also worked on the immigrant research project *The Puerto Rican Journey: New York's Newest Migrants* (Mills, Senior, & Goldsen, 1950) and collected a good deal of data for what is typically regarded as his best work, *White Collar: The American Middle Classes* (1951).

Although he remained the quintessential American throughout his life, Mills had an ostentatious disdain of everything Made in America (Swados, 1963). He was especially indignant toward academic social scientists that were uncritically accepting of what he called the "Great Celebration" of American society without addressing its cultural deficiencies. Nevertheless, despite Mills's anti pro-America stance, it would be incorrect to see it as a simpleminded negativism. He was always critically concerned with the preservation of the democratic tradition in the United States. Indeed, up until his last days, Mills remained troubled by the fact that the "social structure of the United States is not an altogether democratic one" (Mills, 1959b, p. 188).

Mills achieved a certain notoriety in academia, in part as a result of criticizing social scientists for engaging in methodological self-indulgence and for his admonition toward intellectuals for blindly supporting the militarization of American society. From the mid-1950s until his death in 1962, Mills developed an international reputation as he traveled extensively throughout Europe, the Soviet Union, and Latin America without knowing a word of any language other than English. In 1956, he obtained a Fulbright lectureship at the University of Copenhagen. Three years later, he was a visiting scholar at the London School of Economics. In addition to journeying to France, Scandinavia, the Soviet Union, and Poland, Mills spent time in Brazil and Mexico and visited Cuba a few months after Fidel Castro took power. Doubtless these travels expanded Mills's humanist vision of sociology as a science concerned with people's life situation—their hopes, fears, penchants, and goals—within the context of the historical epoch of their time.

Those personally acquainted with Mills invariably point to his abrasive personality and temperament, an unconventional demeanor that earned him the animus of buttoned-down academics who treated him like an intellectual pariah. At a time when academic protocol, particularly in the Ivy League, dictated that professors wear the standard white shirt, tie, and jacket, Mills dressed as a lumberjack—in flannel shirts, leather jacket, and combat boots. Cultivating this persona, he commuted to Columbia astride his BMW R69 motorcycle while toting his books and papers in an army surplus duffel bag (Halberstam, 1993; Miller, 1987; Swados, 1963; Wakefield, 1971). Horowitz (1983) paints a rich, vivid picture of the man's physical and personal traits:

> Mills was an imposing physical specimen by any standards. He was tall (about six feet two inches); he spoke in a thundering drawl that marked him as a native American even if one did not identify his Texas origins; he smoked much, laughed easily, and angered many—although more often over abstract ideas than personalities. In fact, he heartily disdained professional shoptalk as "gossip." His carefully cultivated popular image notwithstanding, he remained throughout his career a hopeless academic, down to his pipe. He argued for the sake of scoring points, accepted eccentricities just within the boundaries of prevailing taste, and believed in the life of the mind even if he spiked metaphors with slang and curse-words. Mills presented himself as someone for whom mannerisms excluded manners, civic concerns excluded polite behavior, and personal style excluded conventional dress. (p. 4)

Thus, owing largely to Mills's unrefined manner and flamboyant style, his polemical writing, his moral-political "preachings," and the celebrity status he enjoyed outside academe, he frequently found himself at odds with many if not most of his colleagues. He was subsequently marginalized, and, in effect, ostracized, from the sociological community. Mills's response to this exclusion was to become an academic outlaw and adopt the now legendary "gruff, irascible, aggressive exterior toward anyone who he sensed was in opposition to him and his work" (Wakefield, 1971, p. 66). What is more, in contradistinction to most sociologists of the period, Mills, as a public sociologist, aimed to convey modern social science ideas to a broader audience outside the academy by employing a clear and vivid prose. Such were his ways of showing contempt for the routine canons of academe and what he referred to as "the higher ignorance" of the received sociology of the time.

When, at the age of 45, he suddenly and unexpectedly died of heart failure, on March 20, 1962, he was the most widely read and best-known sociologist not only in the United States but also in Europe, Asia, and especially Latin America. His popularity was due largely to the sale, in the hundreds of thousands, in inexpensive paperback form, of his highly provocative mass-market "pamphlets": *The Causes of World War Three* (1958) and *Listen, Yankee: The Revolution in Cuba* (1960d). Contrary to most academic sociologists, Mills had an extraordinary ability to communicate with a general educated audience. Indeed, toward the latter part of his career when he had become more of a political radical, Mills came to be seen as a spokesman—a secular prophet—for the New Left, the new generation of radicalized students, activists, and intellectuals. All this, despite the fact that prior to the late 1950s, Mills usually wrote, not for the apathetic and alienated masses—the politically passive populace—but for the small circle of politically alert publics. As we shall see in Chapter 7, Mills produced a soft-cover about the nuclear arms race, *The Causes of World War Three,* with the specific intent of inspiring a wider audience—but in particular the international peace movement—to revolutionary political action.

Intellectual Influences

Mills's thought has been described "as an intellectual salad, or as a marble cake (rather than a layer cake) in which it is often difficult to ascertain different intellectual sources" (Tilman, 1984, p. 18). To be sure, Mills's critical theory has its origins in a divergent and wide-ranging variety of intellectual strands: from the classic European tradition to the classic American tradition, from social psychology to the social structural level of analysis, and from the elite theories of the neo-Machiavellians to the radical theories of the Marxists. Mills's intellectual influences were many and sundry. Surely, such expansive erudition is embodied in the ideal of the character type that is the antithesis to the cheerful robot—the Renaissance man. We now turn to some of Mills's more significant influences on his social thought.

Thorstein Veblen

One of Mills's professors at the University of Texas in the late 1930s was the economist Clarence Ayers who had taught Talcott Parsons during his undergraduate years at Amherst. A former associate of Thorstein Veblen's, Ayers introduced Parsons, and later Mills, to Veblen's thinking. But contrary to Parsons, who appreciated Veblen primarily as a developer of social theory, Mills admired him for his trenchant cynicism, sardonic worldview, and incessant mocking of the American "leisure" class. Veblen's iconoclastic indictment of the upper classes, however, contained an element of humor that Mills seemingly failed to appreciate. Mills (1956) writes sarcastically, "Veblen laughed so hard and so consistently at the servants and the dogs and the women and the sports of the elite that he did not see that their military, economic and political activity is not at all funny" (p. 89). It was during the time that he wrote these lines that Mills was considering with the utmost seriousness the insidious power of the military, economic, and political elites.

Mills was particularly attracted to Veblen's insights about the competitive habits of thought and the dilettante modes of conduct of those occupying the top of the social stratum, the so-called "leisure class." He also took to heart Veblen's notion that there exists a close relationship between social analysis and social criticism. In addition, Veblen identified conflicts of interest in American society from a historically rooted macro-sociological perspective, an approach that Mills employed throughout his career. Finally, it is perhaps "in style and populist bias that Mills most resembles Veblen" (Wallerstein, 1968, p. 363). Indeed, these two scholars' incisive uses of oxymorons and polysyllabic vocabulary share many similarities owing to the fact that Mills adopted such Veblenisms as "conspicuous consumption" and the **main drift,** which is to say the historic character of a particular time period, the social changes that take place but which are not always known to the general public. In sum, then, we may say that in all likelihood Veblen had a greater impact on Mills's analysis of American society than any other thinker.

The Pragmatists

Another of Mills's mentors while an undergraduate at Texas was the philosopher George Gentry who had studied under George Herbert Mead at the University of Chicago. Gentry introduced Mills to the writings of the American pragmatist philosophers who believed that reason would serve as a guide to freedom. It therefore comes as no surprise that Mills's master's thesis, doctoral dissertation, and earliest published writings, especially those on the sociology of knowledge, reveal a persistent reflection on pragmatic themes.

Due largely to Gentry's academic guidance, Mills's first intellectual frame of reference as a young scholar was **pragmatism**, the American philosophical tradition elaborated by Charles Sanders Peirce; William James; John Dewey; and the person most responsible for developing the pragmatic approach in social psychology, George Herbert Mead. It was perhaps Mead's connection of the subjective with the objective—the notion of the person as a self in relation to, and interaction with, other selves—that most influenced Mills. To be sure, Mead's fundamental premise that there can be no self apart from society forms the basis of Mills's book on social psychology, *Character and Social Structure: The Psychology of Social Institutions* (Gerth & Mills, 1953). In this volume, Mills not only liberally employs Mead's concepts of the "generalized other," "significant symbol," and the "I/me" distinction, but also gives them a stronger structural focus by treating them as processes within particular social institutions. For Mills, the conditions affecting the chances for a generalized other to develop are themselves determined by social structural conditions.

In his doctoral dissertation, "A Sociological Account of Pragmatism" (1942), Mills investigates how pragmatism as a school of thought came to be accepted by American academics. Indeed, he always maintained a lively interest in the social and intellectual values of pragmatism, which was for him not just an abstruse doctrine, but a practical way of life and a set of propositions about the nature of the world (Horowitz, 1964a). Pragmatism emphasizes the fusion between theory and practice, intellect and craft. Mills was deeply influenced by Peirce's and Dewey's belief in the power of people's intelligence to control their destiny. Thus, in Mills's view, theory must, of necessity, always be oriented toward action. Although he personally seems to have had little appetite for involvement in practical political agitation, Mills nonetheless saw his sociology as a form of "craftsmanship" where knowledge is intrinsically related to social action. The fact that he acted through his written work does not make Mills a mere armchair intellectual; for him, knowing is itself a type of action and consequently sociology must cease separating theory and practice.

Hans H. Gerth and Howard P. Becker

Yet another person who significantly influenced Mills was his teacher at the University of Wisconsin, Hans H. Gerth, a refugee from Nazi Germany who had been a student of Karl Mannheim and in fact had assisted Mannheim in the preparation of *Ideology and Utopia* (1936/1968). Gerth possessed a deep knowledge of the German sociological tradition that includes Weber's social action theory and Mannheim's idea that all knowledge is class based. It was at Wisconsin, then, that Mills came in contact with European social thought, under Gerth's tutelage. Possessed by "the unusual power of his will to succeed" (Martindale, 1975, p. 65), Mills, upon his arrival at Wisconsin, wasted no time in forming an intellectual relationship with Gerth. Thus, it was not long before Gerth, the professor, and Mills, the graduate student, were collaborating on research projects that resulted in the publication of, first, *From Max Weber* in 1946, and then, eventually, following its 13-year compositional history, *Character and Social Structure* in 1953.

Though a much lesser influence than Gerth, Wisconsin social theorist Howard P. Becker also served as Mills's introduction to the "classic" tradition in sociology. This tradition, which was to have a permanent impact on Mills, was articulated primarily in the statements of 19th-century European social theorists (exemplified by Herbert Spencer, Karl Marx, Karl Mannheim, and Max Weber) as well as some 20th-century American sources (most notably Walter Lippmann, Thorstein Veblen, William I. Thomas, and Florian Znaniecki). "The classic sociological tradition is a central part of the cultural tradition of Western civilization," wrote Mills (1960a) later in his career. "The crisis of one is the crisis of the other; and of all the spheres of Western culture, the classic tradition of sociology is the most directly relevant to those areas where culture and politics come now to such a terrifying point of intersection" (p. 9).

Max Weber

Within the European classic tradition, it was German sociology, and more specifically Weberian sociology, that stands out as the dominant influence on Mills. In his anthology of classic works of sociology, *Images of Man: The Classic Tradition in Sociological Thinking* (1960a), which he considered as a kind of supplement to *The Sociological Imagination* (1959b), Mills contends that Weber and Karl Marx stood head and shoulders above the rest as the most important classic social thinkers. Mills valued Weber for several reasons. First, Weber's work is not confined to one academic knowledge field. As a result of his great ideas being truly eclectic, Weber was able to thoroughly analyze various social phenomena within the context of different cultures, at several periods in history, and at the subjective as well as the objective levels of social reality. Second, Weber holds certain moral values rather passionately. Indeed, in much of his work, Weber is concerned with the moral crisis affecting the humanist tradition of Western civilization, a tradition politically informed by liberalism and Marxism. Third and finally, Mills admired Weber for his attempts to blend his sharp analytic conceptions with an encyclopedic knowledge of history. Weber, to be sure, always makes it a point to analyze specific historical periods and events in an attempt to answer questions from religion, to law, to the city (Mills, 1960a). In *White Collar*, Mills (1951) graciously acknowledges his debt to Weber: "The technical vocabulary used, and hence in many ways the general perspective of this volume, is derived from Max Weber. Such concepts as class, occupation, status, power, authority, manipulation, bureaucracy, profession are basically his" (p. 357). Weber's theoretical impression on Mills reached its zenith with the writing of *White Collar* (Tilman, 1984).

As will be shown later, the majority of Mills's theoretical concerns focus directly or indirectly on the interrelationship between character, or those most intimate features of a person's self, and social structure, which is to say the structural and historical features of society. In considering this association, Mills relies particularly on Weber's analysis of the dominant social trend of modern society: the growing bureaucratization of all aspects of social life. Weber taught Mills not only to recognize the might of the bureaucratic apparatus in industrial society, but also to despise it (Horowitz, 1963). This focus on bureaucratic social structures is aptly illustrated in *From Max Weber* (Weber, 1946). In Part IV of the book, appropriately entitled "Social Structures," Gerth and Mills translate and edit those essays in which Weber discusses the ideal personality types of the Prussian Junker, the Indian Brahman, and the Chinese Literati. Weber's main thesis is that these personality types are unquestioningly inspired and molded by the various social structural contexts in which they emerge, a theme that Mills would return to time and again. In this regard, Weber contributes to Mills's social psychology by providing the means for going beyond the structureless social behaviorism of George Herbert Mead to an institutionally defined social structure (Scimecca, 1977). Lastly, in his studies on unequal power relations, Mills makes good use of Weber's three dimensions of social stratification—class, status, and power—and adds a fourth, that of *occupation*.

Karl Mannheim

Yet another significant influence upon Mills was an early founder of the sociology of knowledge, the Hungarian-born Karl Mannheim. From Mannheim's sociological analysis of knowledge, Mills appropriated two main ideas. First, like Mannheim, Mills came to formulate a crucial role in public life for the intellectual. By the early 1950s, Mills had become unwavering in his belief that intellectuals were the only persons capable of undistorted thought. Accordingly, Mills saw the intellectual as the most viable agent for changing the conditions of sociopolitical existence. For him, it was imperative that the radical political intellectual act to reconstruct reality for others. In this sense, Mills along with Mannheim advocated the pragmatist unity of thought and action, theory and practice.

Second, and again following Mannheim, Mills believed that every age develops a political philosophy and ideological credo that is uniquely its own. In the mid-20th century, the two predominant ideologies of the West were liberalism and Marxism. Indeed, Mills devoted much time to demonstrating how both of these interpretations of politics, history, and culture had become obsolete. For Mills, the classic liberalism of the Enlightenment, which had served as the dominant ethos of capitalist societies like the United States, had turned into a conservative force that was no longer effective in explaining the operations of the contemporary marketplace. Similarly, the Victorian Marxism of the 19th century had hardened into a statist dogma, as graphically demonstrated by the case of Stalinist Russia. Nevertheless, Mills (1962) was realistic enough to recognize that "[i]n their classic versions, liberalism and Marxism embody the assurances and hopes, the ambiguities and fears of the modern age. Taken in all their varieties, they now constitute our major, even our only, political alternatives" (p. 13).

The Neo-Machiavellians

In addition to being thoroughly versed in the works of Veblen, Weber, and Mannheim, Mills was well acquainted with the Franco-Italian elite theorists, the so-called neo-Machiavellians: Gaetano Mosca, Vilfredo Pareto, and Robert Michels. As indicated by his use of selections from their work in *Images of Man* (1960a), Mills considered the neo-Machiavellians an integral part of sociology's classic tradition. Indeed, Mosca, Pareto, and Michels were particularly important to Mills at the time that he wrote *The Power Elite* (1956). Mills, however, rejects their anti-utopianism, for he thought it was quite possible to eliminate economic inequality and social hierarchy and create an undifferentiated society. Contrary to Michels, who maintained that democracy inevitably leads to oligarchy, Mills believed that democracy and egalitarianism are feasible and desirable goals to achieve. Pareto's view of the circulation of elites, those "superior elements" who are most "fit to rule," is based on innate biological instincts. According to Pareto, elites are intellectually, morally, and physically superior to non-elites. Mills, by contrast, explains the circulation of the elites on the basis of social factors: their institutional position, their distinct socialization process, and the like. Finally, whereas Mosca surmised that there will always be a ruling class that will achieve preeminence in society, and that this omnipotent elite shares all historical events for all epochs of human history and in all nations, Mills (1956) states that his own "definition of the power elite cannot properly contain dogma concerning the degree and kind of power that ruling groups everywhere have. Much less should it permit us to smuggle into our discussion a theory of history" (p. 20). Thus, the influence of the neo-Machiavellians on Mills's sociology was largely in reaction to what they wrote, as he has little or no sympathy for them.

Marxism

Lastly, in order to clarify the long-standing misconceptions concerning Mills's ideological commitments, a few words must be said about the impact of Marxism on his thinking. Since the early 1940s, Mills had been exposed to the Marxist-Freudian theoretical emphasis of the Frankfurt School, and in particular the work of émigré Germans Theodore Adorno, Max Horkheimer, Herbert Marcuse, and especially Franz Neumann and Leo Lowenthal—both of whom were colleagues of Mills at Columbia. What is more, in the course of his travels, Mills became acquainted with other leading Marxist intellectuals in both the Communist and non-Communist world. Of special significance in this regard was Fidel Castro. Doubtless, all of these experiences had a significant impact on Mills's thinking, but at no point in his work does he explicitly adhere to Marxism. Clearly, he was haunted by mixed and unresolved feelings about Marx and Marxism throughout much of his career, but it was not until the last few years of his life that he earnestly confronted Marxism head-on, in a more systematic and rigorous manner than he had done before. He had not seriously considered Marxism prior to that time because his audience was not very interested in it or knowledgeable about it. As Tilman (1984) points out,

> Mills had assimilated most of the original work of Marx and Engels, much of the subsequent literature written in the Marxian traditions, and a vast amount of socialist writing of the non-Marxist variety. Certainly, aspects of Marxian doctrine were occasionally incorporated in his work. (p. 34)

For example, in 1951, at the height of McCarthyism, a period of rabid anticommunism in American politics, Mills (1951) writes, "I cannot fail, especially in these times when [Marx's] work is on the one side ignored and vulgarized, and on the other ignored and maligned, to acknowledge my general debt, especially to his earlier productions" (p. 357). It is important to note that despite his defense of Marxism, Mills never identified himself as a Marxist, at least not of the orthodox variety.

Ideological identification aside, Mills adroitly employs some of Marx's key concepts to great advantage. For example, he uses the notion of *alienation* to describe the public mood of moral uneasiness and malaise that he believed was afflicting the amorphous collection of white-collar workers. States Mills (1951),

> Estranged from community and society in a context of distrust and manipulation; alienated from work and, on the personality market, from self; expropriated of individual rationality, and politically apathetic—these are the new little people, the unwilling vanguard of modern society. (p. xviii)

Mills also utilizes Marx's notion of false consciousness, but in Mills's case he applies it not to the working class, but to the new middle class of dependent salaried employees: they who are the products of mass society and who follow like sheep, with little hope of achieving a "true consciousness." Mills repeatedly maintains that the middle classes' false consciousness, or their lack of awareness of objective self-interest, ultimately results in their political indifference. In sum, Marxism had a notable, if somewhat limited, influence on Mills.

The Sociohistorical Context

To fully appreciate Mills's ideas, it is necessary to consider some of the noteworthy social issues and trends that were salient during the years in which he did his most creative work, 1945–1960. Clearly, the post–World War II era was a unique period in the history of the United States. In one short sentence, social historian James Miller (1987) tersely captures the epochal events over which Mills agonized and which subsequently fueled his radicalism: "C. Wright Mills," remarks Miller, "wrote in the age of the atom bomb and Eisenhower, the Cold War and McCarthy, at the twilight of Stalinism and the zenith of 'The American Century'" (p. 79). Mills was the archetypal intellectual of his time. Indeed, he seems to have possessed an extraordinary, almost uncanny, understanding of the main cultural temper, the felt condition, of this particular period in history—the mid-20th century. This understanding is perhaps most evident in *White Collar* (1951), where he brilliantly and insightfully describes how the new middle classes of American mass society were experiencing the complacent postwar years.

Mass Society

Postwar America saw the emergence of a postmodern era—the **Fourth Epoch**, as Mills terms it—where production, administration, and violence were centralized within bureaucracies and where reason and freedom were threatened. It was also a time that spawned previously unknown social groupings and trends. Thus, it is hardly surprising that Mills was struck by the newness of it all, a newness to which he makes repeated reference in his works: "the new immigration" (the Puerto Ricans coming to New York), "the new men of power" (the labor leaders), "the new middle class" or "the new little people" (white-collar workers), the "new society" (a political economy in which political and economic affairs are intricately and deeply joined together), and "the New Left" (the 1960s leftist student movement that aggressively challenged the legitimacy of America's political institutions). And, like other scholars, Mills was also critically examining those social conditions that were beginning to create the drift toward what they described as a **mass society,** a highly bureaucratized and impersonal social structure whose culture is characterized by a uniformity and mediocrity—of goods, ideas, tastes, values, and lifestyles—that paves the way for the commercial and political manipulation of the mass of people.

Today, many sociology students are acquainted with the "McDonaldization of society" thesis as well as with the notion of "the globalization of nothing," both proposed by the sociologist George Ritzer (2010, 2007, respectively). In this regard, Ritzer makes two basic arguments. The first is that **McDonaldization**—the process by which society takes on the principles of systematization, standardization, consistency, scientific management, and methodological operation that characterize the fast-food restaurant—has not only affected various sectors of American life (such as the workplace, education, travel, and health care), but it is increasingly coming to dominate the rest of the world. The second argument, **the globalization of nothing,** is that as a consequence of globalization (the accelerated circulation of people, lifestyles, things, and ideas), societies throughout the world are moving away from "something"—which Ritzer defines as unique and distinctive indigenous social forms (e.g., a gourmet meal, handmade pottery, a community bank)—and toward "nothing"—which he defines as social forms that are centralized, dehumanized, and lacking in distinctive substantive content (e.g., fast-food restaurants, the Nike swoosh, and ATMs). While these two conceptualizations are unique in explaining contemporary social trends, they may nonetheless be seen as theoretical extensions of the 1950s idea of mass society. Social historians Andrew Jamison and Ron Eyerman (1994) have the following to say about the mass society of Mills's time:

> The society that emerged out of the Second World War was given many names, as it evoked powerful images of conformity, loneliness, homogenization, standardization, and mediocrity. Individuals had become faceless figures in gray flannel suits, working in anonymous organizations and living in little boxes made of ticky-tacky. . . . It was in the 1950s that long-term and nearly invisible changes in the structures of American society began to become visible and demand a name. While many names were cast about, one that stuck was "mass society." (pp. 34, 36)

Ranch wagons and ranch-style houses comprised the esthetic vapidity of the great packaged "instant" communities of the new suburbs that had sprung up outside American cities since the war. Urban planner and social theorist Lewis Mumford (1961) scorned these suburban developments, the "Levittowns," and their tracts of "little boxes," derisively describing them as a multitude of uniform, unidentifiable houses, lined up inflexibly, at uniform distances, on uniform roads, in a treeless communal waste, inhabited by people of the same class, the same income, the same age group, witnessing the same television performances, eating the same tasteless pre-fabricated foods, from the same freezers, conforming in every outward and inward respect to a common mold, manufactured in the same central metropolis. Thus the ultimate effect of the suburban escape in our own time is, ironically, a low-grade uniform environment from which escape is impossible. (p. 486)

Such, then, were some of the social images that marked the middle-class American scene during the mid-20th century. Along with Mills, two other critics, sociologist David Riesman and an editor of *Fortune* magazine, William H. Whyte, Jr., focused principally on one segment of people in mass society who had become rootless and amorphous: the "new middle classes." Let us briefly consider what Riesman and Whyte say about the new middle classes of the 1950s, for many of their comments relate directly to Mills's vision of postwar American society.

The New Middle Classes

In his popularly acclaimed book *The Lonely Crowd* (1950), David Riesman proposes a most insightful character typology of middle-class Americans during the postwar period. In exploring the relationship between the historical experiences of Western society and their pervasive effects on individuals' mode of conformity, Riesman produces a tripartite typification of cultures and **social character,** or "the more or less permanent socially and historically conditioned organization of an individual's drives and satisfaction" (p. 4). Accordingly, he marks the transition from "folk" to "industrial" to "mass society" as the transition from tradition-directed to inner-directed to other-directed personality types.

Because social change is minimal in the family- and clan-oriented traditional ways of life of folk societies, Riesman contends that these societies produce **tradition-directed** people who possess a conformist social character uncritically accepting of institutionalized roles that have endured for generations. Put slightly differently, in folk societies, conformity is secured by inculcating the young with unquestioning obedience to tradition. Then, with the emergence of the Renaissance and Reformation, Western societies became involved in the process of almost constant expansion through exploration, colonization, and imperialism. This resulted in the **inner-directed** type as the dominant mode of insuring conformity through internalized controls. During this expansive phase, the goal was to develop rational, individualistic attitudes for exploiting a hostile environment. Inner-directed people epitomized by the "old" middle class of the 19th and early 20th centuries—the banker, the tradesman, the small entrepreneur, and so forth—were inculcated, early in life, with the ambition to pursue personal life goals pertaining to money, possessions, power, and fame. The inner-directed personality type, which predominates in industrial society, is embodied by the rugged individualist who is driven by the Protestant work ethic to succeed through incessant production.

The most recent stage of social development—the mass society—that typified postwar America's highly industrialized and bureaucratic social structure was marked by material affluence and an insatiable consumption of goods, services, and information. In this centralized and bureaucratized social structure, large-scale organizations act as agents of social control by making people exceptionally sensitive to the actions and wishes of others. Thus, among the "new" middle class of urban-suburban America (in particular, among those engaged in white-collar work and the service trades), there was beginning to emerge an other-directed social character that valued, not individual achievement, but the acquisition of effective interpersonal skills.

Riesman (1950) relies on the didactic literature on success to illustrate this transition of character types. He notes that as Americans move from a period of inner direction to one of other direction, the inspirational success literature changes from that which is "directly concerned with social and economic advance, dealt with as achievable by the virtues of thrift, hard work, and so on," to that which "recommends self-manipulative exercises for the sake not only of business success but of such vaguer, non-work goals as popularity" (pp. 149–150). The common identifying trait of **other-directed** people is their overwhelming psychological need for approval and direction from their contemporaries. Consequently, Riesman maintains that the white middle-class, urban-suburban American of the middle years of the 20th century was "shallower, freer with his money, friendlier, more uncertain of himself and his values, more demanding of approval" (p. 19). Owing to their compulsion to continuously receive signals, far and near, from a multitude of rapidly changing sources such as the mass media, the other-directed people suffer from a diffuse characterological *anxiety*. In addition, they are afflicted by civic apathy and *political indifference*. Riesman posits that other-directed individuals (whom he calls "the new-style indifferents"), in their attempt at over-conformity, are neither morally committed to political principles nor emotionally related to political events. Instead, they "achieve a political and personal style of tolerance, drained of emotion, temper, and moodiness. But, obviously, this can go so far that deadness of feeling comes to resemble a clinical symptom" (p. 244). Along the same lines as Riesman,

Mills in *White Collar* (1951) argues that political awareness was at a low ebb among the new American middle class.

William H. Whyte's *The Organization Man* (1956) is a study of the ideology, the social norms and values, of the new middle classes, or those strata that form the first and second echelons of American organization life. In an age of organization, these middle-class individuals had become the dominant members of society and their values set the American temper. They include the corporation men, the junior executives, the physician working for the corporate clinic, the physics PhD in a government laboratory, the intellectual on a foundation-sponsored team project, the engineer in the huge drafting room, and the young apprentice in a Wall Street law factory. These people, says Whyte, not only work for the organization, they *belong* to it. They are deeply beholden to the organization even as they complain of the "treadmill," the "rat race," and their inability to control their own destiny. Indeed, most see themselves as objects more acted upon than acting.

Whyte (1956) maintains that with the growth of the organization society, the cultural norms, ascendant since about 1900, had become antithetical to the Protestant ethic, which had been at the heart of American achievement in the 19th century. The Protestant ethic had placed primary emphasis on rugged individualism, personal independence, and freedom. It prized the virtues of hard work, thrift, independence, and competition. In contrast, the big organization which, by the mid-20th century, had come to dominate the whole of American life, emphasized cooperation and getting along with people. An ideological drift had therefore taken place in organization life, and the Protestant ethic had now given way to what Whyte terms the "social ethic." The **social ethic,** which may be called an organization ethic, or a bureaucratic ethic, is that contemporary body of thought that morally legitimates the pressures of society against the individual and which places a high premium on scientism, belongingness, and togetherness.

Scientism, the practical part of the social ethic, involves a belief in the application of the methods of science to human relations in order to achieve "belongingness." Scientism promises that with the same techniques that have worked in the physical sciences, social engineers can create an exact science of human relations that, through its techniques, allows everyone total integration with the organization. The chief problem with scientism, warns Whyte (1956), is that it comes perilously close to demanding that individuals sacrifice their personal beliefs, initiative, and imagination in order to belong. **Belongingness** refers to the belief that the ultimate and most urgent need of individuals is to feel a part of a group. The organization presumably creates an environment where everyone is tightly knit with one another. The idea is that if you are loyal to the company, the company will be loyal to you. This manner of thinking is, in part, derived from the notion that in the rapidly changing world in which the company man or woman is always on the move, he or she desperately needs roots, and fealty to the organization is a logical way to develop them. **Togetherness** is a belief that people want to belong together. Because he or she usually works in groups—at the conference table, the workshop, the seminar, the skull session, the after-hours discussions, the team project, and so on—the **organization man** or woman has a growing preoccupation with group work. These groups, if they are internally harmonious, will allegedly bring out the best in everyone. Work groups are therefore seen as the vehicles of creativity. Whyte argues that in devoting so much attention to making organization work through scientism, belongingness, and togetherness, society had come close to deifying and worshipping the organization.

In Whyte's (1956) view, the social ethic, along with the bureaucratization of society, has produced the organization man. The organization man is epitomized by the young man in the middle, the practical team player. He is the junior executive, the middle manager. Above all, he is conservative since his inclination is to accept the status quo. Ruled by a spirit of acquiescence, he does not want to rebel; he wants to collaborate. And since the organization man does not question the "system," he is not interested in ends but in means, or methodology. Sounding very much like Riesman's other-directed personality type, Whyte suggests that the organization man is a product of the social-adjustment type of schooling. Thus, given his anti-intellectual vocational training, it is not the larger questions of what or why that concern the organization man, but the technical points of the how.

The organization man is more likely to be in engineering, business, or commerce, and involved in narrow overspecialization. And contrary to the individualist entrepreneur of the 19th century who, driven by the Protestant ethic, ventured to realize the American Dream, the organization man is a technician who just wants to join the big corporation and work for somebody else. In the case of the old Protestant ethic, the primary emphasis was on hard work, competition, and being goal-centered; the operative phrase was, "Anything is yours if you only want it hard enough." In contradistinction, the new social ethic places emphasis on managing others' work, on cooperation, and being employee-centered; the motto here is, "Adjust to your situation; don't change it." Thus, the organization man wants to work hard but not too hard. He is content with seeking the good, equable life,

> a nice place out in the suburbs, a wife and three children, one, maybe two cars (you know, a little knock-about for the wife to run down to the station in), and a summer place up at the lake or out on the Cape, and later a good college education for the children. (Whyte, 1956, p. 78)

Because the organization man is a transient, caught up in the mobility of organization life, he is, by definition, the person who left home. Having lost the geographical and family ties that had previously tied Americans to local society, the young organization man is now rootless. In the suburban communities that have become his dormitories, the organization man tries, quite consciously, to develop roots to replace those he had when he left home. In the loneliness of the new suburbia, he finds a new kind of roots by making a home away from home. "More and more," writes Whyte (1956), "the young couples who move do so only physically. With each transfer the décor, the architecture, the faces, and the names may change; the people, the conversation, and the values do not—and sometimes the décor and the architecture don't either" (p. 305). This, according to Whyte, Riesman, and Mills, was what life was basically like for the American middle classes of the postwar 1950s.

One other influential book, a novel published in 1955, deserves to be mentioned since it struck a nerve with the American middle classes at that time: Sloan Wilson's *The Man in the Gray Flannel Suit*. The novel's protagonist, the man in the gray flannel suit—that faceless and lonely everyman of mass society—was a fairly universal figure in the frantic middle-class world of mid-20th-century America. Four years earlier, this figure had been Mills's main subject of study in *White Collar* (1951). In Wilson's novel, the figure is quintessentially depicted by 33-year-old Tom Rath, who had been a paratrooper in the Army during World War II. Rath now works as an executive at Rockefeller Center in New York City and is attempting to adapt to the insecurity of postwar civilian life. Each morning, he leaves his home in the Connecticut suburbs to make a living in the big city. Each evening, his wife, Betsy, and their three children meet him at the commuter train station when he arrives home from work. The Raths came to symbolize the frustrations, tensions, restlessness, and discontent of the American middle classes. In his portrayal of the postwar generation that came of age during the early 1950s, film critic Richard Schickel (1991) writes,

"Alienation," a novel word that yet fell trippingly from our tongues at that time, was a preoccupying topic. *The Lonely Crowd* was anatomized in 1950, and the fear of drifting into its clutches was lively in us. *White Collar* was on our brick and board bookshelves, and we saw how the eponymous object seemed to be choking the life out of earlier generations. *The Man in the Gray Flannel Suit* stalked our nightmares and soon enough *The Organization Man* would join him there, though, of course, even as we read about these cautionary figures, many of us were talking to corporate recruiters about entry-level emulation of them. (p. 6)

The End of Ideology

Finally, in attempting to capture the sociohistorical mood during Mills's most productive and creative period, mention must be made of the ideological climate of the quiescent 1950s. At this time, sociologists like Edward A. Shils and Mills's Columbia colleagues Seymour Martin Lipset and Daniel Bell, all of whom were associated with the CIA-funded Committee for Cultural Freedom, began espousing their **end of ideology** thesis, or the assertion that Western civilization was no longer influenced by ideology, a "truth" idea demanding a commitment to action. These scholars argued that such political philosophies as fascism and socialism had become irrelevant in the postwar period. Bell (1962), in particular, maintained that the 19th-century ideologies and ideological debates that had previously inspired liberal and conservative intellectuals had now become "exhausted" by such calamities as the Nazi concentration camps, the Soviet suppression of the Hungarian workers, and the rise of the Welfare State. According to Bell, we find therefore

> at the end of the fifties, a disconcerting caesura. In the West, among the intellectuals, the old passions are spent. The new generation, with no meaningful memory of these old debates, and no secure tradition to build upon, finds itself seeking new purposes within a framework of political society that has rejected, intellectually speaking, the old apocalyptic and chiliastic visions. (p. 404)

The end of ideology movement in the 1950s was prematurely heralding the death of radicalism in America. Accordingly, Mills consistently and mercilessly gibed intellectuals like Shils, Lipset, and Bell for partaking in "The American Celebration"—an uncritical and flowery praise of the United States—a kind of national conceit and self-satisfaction that was no more than an excuse for political complacency. Mills, throughout his career, directed his spleen particularly at intellectuals who either upheld the status quo or retreated from what was happening in the world. By the early 1960s, however, the emerging New Left was becoming inspired by Mills's critical sociology and by his notions about individuals and society.

Conclusion

This chapter has endeavored to draw a rounded intellectual portrait of C. Wright Mills. As such, it has expressly considered his unique form of social thought, which examines, first, the interpenetration of personality and social structure, of agency and constraint, and second, the power relations, the social inequities, produced by a highly bureaucratized "mass" society. In an effort to get at the roots of Mills's radical sociology, we considered his personal background and intellectual influences in sociohistorical context.

Mills's biographical influences—ranging from his complex relationship with his parents, to his persona as an "outlander," to his extensive contacts and travels throughout the world—coupled with his intellectual influences, stemming from the ideas of Veblen, pragmatism, Weber, and Marxism, ultimately led him to produce a humanistic form of sociology. In the next chapter, we consider Mills's humanist social thought which, despite his biting critique of the complacent middle classes of self-satisfied mass society (which Riesman and Whyte depicted as the other-directedness of the organization man), at bottom, always contemplated their fundamental character; their very human hopes, fears, penchants, and goals.

But before we leave this chapter, and in consideration of Mills's critical analysis of postwar American society (1945–1960), a few reflective questions may be posed:

- What kinds of people were Americans in this period of U.S. history?
- What were the social and cultural factors that made this period in U.S. history unique—different from what had been before and from what followed?
- How is it that the postwar era was both a time of national celebration and of collective anxiety?
- Why was Mills's particular brand of critical social thinking important at the time?
- How can Mills's analysis be applied to today's social, cultural, and political situations?

2

A Humanist Concern

In one of his best-known passages, C. Wright Mills (1959b) states, "What social science is properly about is the human variety, which consists of all the social worlds in which men have lived, are living, and might live" (p. 132). We may deduce at least two guiding assertions from this statement. The first is that social science—as a humanist concern—must endeavor, first and foremost, to acquire a full understanding of the human variety of individuals' lives. In this sense, it is important to consider individuals' personal experiences—their self-image, conscience, and emotions—in the context of their social worlds. Second, social scientists must rely on their own personal experiences of the problems of contemporary significance and heed their moral imperative—their own humanist concern—in securing a more just society for everyone.

As this chapter will show, Mills had a rather bleak view of contemporary individuals and society. He does not mince words and, in characteristically critical fashion, repeatedly informs his readers that postwar American society had produced a corps of complacent and apathetic people who not only did not know, but did not care, about their place in the historical social structure. However, despite Mills's negative portrayal of individuals and society during the Fourth Epoch, in the end, he never quite gave up hope for the coming transformation and emancipation of both.

The sections that follow present Mills's views of individuals and society. The balance of the chapter will consider how these views influenced his methodology. In both his epistemology of individuals as well as in this methodology of social science, Mills never abandoned the humanist concern in his work.

Mills's Views on the Relation Between Individuals and Society

Mills's sociology begins with the premise that individuals are first and foremost social and historical actors. As such, he maintains that their motives and behavior are not to be explained by organicist conceptions alone. People cannot adequately be understood as isolated biological creatures, as a bundle of reflexes, or a set of instincts. If they are to be properly understood, people must be considered with sensitive reference to the social structure that is their context. Thus, Mills (1959b) instructs the student of sociology to

> try to understand men not as an isolated fragment, not as an intelligible field or system in and of itself. Try to understand men and women as historical and social actors, and the ways in which the variety of men and women are intricately selected and intricately formed by the variety of human societies. (p. 158)

However, despite Mills's commitment to the notion that people are inherently social beings, he, like many pragmatists influenced by utilitarianism, always put the interests of society above the interests of the individual. This collectivist emphasis has led Don Martindale (1975) to charge, perhaps unfairly, that Mills did not truly understand individuals. Since Mills frequently reduced individuals to categories—personality and character "types," "varieties of men and women," "publics"—Martindale contends that Mills ultimately cast out individuality as a chaotic principle.

However that may be, to the extent that Mills did consider individual persons in his sociology, he saw them as possessing a nature that is volitional and active and that gives them the potential to be free. For Mills, humans possess the ability, if not always the desire, to awaken from their political apathy, shake loose their feelings of fatalistic resignation, and engage in social action that makes a historical difference. As Horowitz (1963) states, Mills had a "vision of man as the essential revolutionizing agent in all social relations" (p. 5). Mills's conception of human nature suggests, therefore, that few limits can be placed on the capacities of human beings. However, in modern U.S. society, most people's **freedom**, which Mills (1959b) defines as their "chance to formulate the available choices, to argue over them—and then, the opportunity to choose" (p. 174), is constrained by power relations. Those with the power to make the larger decisions for their society are freer than those without the power. Mills draws two conclusions about individuals in their relation to the power structure of U.S. society. First, while all people are free, some, by virtue of where they are placed within the social structure, are more powerful and free than others to shape human affairs. Second, and subsequently, history is made behind most people's backs.

Coming from a pragmatist position, Mills ardently renounces such strict determinist doctrines as the Marxist notion of economic determinism. Rather, like the pragmatists Peirce and Dewey, he places his faith in the power of people's intelligence to control their own destiny. But while he accepts the pragmatist conceptualization that reason plays a pivotal role in freeing individuals from the constraints of their social structure, he does not assume that this emancipation is an automatic process. Mills vehemently maintains that individuals in a mass society must refuse to remain **cheerful robots**, apathetic automatons who blindly and complacently accept their life-chances as being determined by fate. A true democratic freedom, declares Mills, can be realized only when individuals become aware of, and want to do something about, the social forces that constrain their lives. More to the point, individuals, in order to secure their freedom, must have not only the power but also the desire to make decisions concerning their own lives and their place in history. The passive spectators, the cheerful robots of the mass society, must be transformed into a **community of publics**—scattered little circles of face-to-face citizens discussing their public business in the spirit of direct, participatory democracy. From this vision of individuals, Mills developed what he regards as the ideal, that is, the egalitarian and democratic society.

Before turning to what Mills sees as the ideal society, it is first necessary to say a few words about his notion of society more broadly. To begin with, Mills (1959b) considers sociology's most inclusive working unit, its intelligible field of study, to be, not society itself, but social structure. By **social structure**, he means "the combination of institutions classified according to the functions each performs" (p. 134). Thus, the broadest aim of sociology is to understand each of the varieties of social structure, in its components and in its totality. Further, because social structures are usually organized under a political state, the most inclusive unit of social structure is the *nation-state*. Indeed, it is within the nation-state that the political and military, cultural and economic means of decision and power are organized. So, too, are organized into one or the other of the nation-states all the institutions (political, economic, religious, etc.) and specific milieus (home, workplace, neighborhood, etc.) in which most people live their private and public lives. And so it is in reference to the national social structure that sociologists can most readily study the major problems of contemporary society: of stratification and of economic policy, of public opinion and the nature of political power, of work and leisure. What is more, it is within and between the nation-states of the world that the effective means of power, and hence of history making, are organized. But because all nation-states are not equal in their power to make history—or in their styles of life—we can, in this sense, distinguish between two types of society: the overdeveloped society and the properly developing society.

The Overdeveloped Society and the Properly Developing Society

Departing from the Weberian notion of objectivity and scholarly detachment, Mills argues that sociologists and other intellectuals must be motivated by a commitment to politics. Indeed, throughout his later writings (those involved with radical political analysis), he frequently charges scientists and artists, ministers and scholars to practice the "politics of responsibility" and act in a morally responsible manner. Mills (1958) sees it as the intellectuals' obligation, their moral imperative, to critique contemporary "overdeveloped society" and set forth general and detailed programs on how to attain the "properly developing society."

An **overdeveloped society** like the United States, explains Mills (1958), is an affluent industrial society where conspicuous production and consumption dominate and control the lifestyles of many individuals, but in particular those individuals of the middle classes. Here, the middle classes ignore their fundamental human needs because the technological gadgetry of the military and science dazzles them. Moreover, they are frequently preoccupied with competing for what is most important to them: status. Consequently, the main features characterizing an overdeveloped society are emulatory consumption patterns, overproduction, and the deadening of human sensibility. In contrast, the **properly developing society** is a democratic order where troubles, issues, and problems are open to inquiry. It is a society that provides forums and other outlets through which all momentous decisions are made into public issues and openly debated by intellectuals before a community of free and knowledgeable publics.

According to Mills (1956), a true community of free and knowledgeable publics can exist only under four conditions. First, there must be roughly the same number of people giving their opinions as those receiving the opinions. Second, there must exist the opportunity for listeners to reply freely and without fear. Third, there must exist the opportunity for publics to collectively enact their beliefs. Fourth and finally, the community of publics must be free from governmental authority. While Mills believed that the complete realization of a society of publics was within reach, he nonetheless feared that as a result of the increasing concentration of political and economic power in the hands of a few elites, the society of publics, to the extent that it did exist, was rapidly disintegrating into a mass society.

Methodology

Like his intellectual influences, or rather because of them, Mills's empirical and conceptual methodologies were also many and varied. His empirical methodology may be classed as being quantitative and qualitative in orientation. His quantitative research involved the use of statistics and questionnaires; his qualitative methods, on the other hand, consisted of interviews, content analysis, participant observation, and—perhaps most important for him—the historical-comparative approach. Later in his career, as he entered the stage of his political pamphleteering and came to disdain number crunching in sociology, Mills relied increasingly and sometimes solely on such unstructured and unconventional research techniques as his own everyday experiences and observations.

As concerns his conceptual methodology, Mills makes it clear that he has no use for either grand analytical schemes or, at the other extreme, the intricate technicalities of statistical analysis. Rather, Mills maintains time and again that sociology and sociologists must concern themselves with the "big questions." According to him, social scientists have a political responsibility and a moral imperative—a humanist concern—in considering the individual's personal troubles within the context of the larger, more pressing issues of historical social structures. Accordingly, Mills's conceptual methodology advocates considering problems at the macroscopic *and* molecular levels of sociological analysis. In addition, as will be discussed below, Mills makes use of four analytical tools: (1) the working model, (2) the ideal type, (3) the polar type, and (4) the cross-classification technique. Also considered will be Mills's conceptual strategy of intellectual craftsmanship and his social psychological approach. Finally, this chapter will close with a brief analysis of Mills's notion of sociological truth and his humanistic approach to sociology.

Empirical Methods

For about a decade, from 1945, when he began working at Columbia University's Bureau of Applied Social Research (BASR), until 1956, when he completed *The Power Elite,* Mills made extensive and intensive use of official statistics in his empirical research. For example, in his first book, *The New Men of Power* (1948), Mills, along with a team of researchers, conducted a 1946 survey of labor leaders affiliated with the American Federation of Labor (AFL) and the Congress of Industrial Organizations (CIO). This quantitative study involved administering questionnaires to 500 labor leaders—a representative cross-section of American labor leaders at the national, state, and city levels—in an effort to explain how it is that the institutions to which they belonged formed the leaders' social characteristics.

For *White Collar,* Mills (1951) and his research team interviewed 128 white-collar workers in New York City during the fall of 1946. These respondents, which included middle managers, professionals, secretaries, and sales clerks working in law firms, insurance companies, universities, government offices, and department stores, were asked to answer 73 set questions about various occupational-related topics. In addition, Mills encouraged interviewers to try to understand the respondents' deepest thoughts and feelings. This required that the interviewers ask intensive, probing questions, which meant that the interviews frequently lasted several hours (Geary, 2009).

In researching *White Collar,* Mills (1951) also relied on the fieldwork he undertook in 1945 when he examined the stratification and power structure of six middle-sized cities in the Midwest and New England. This information helped him to sketch the social psychology of the American middle class. In addition, while at the BASR, Mills tabulated a wide range of statistical data that he obtained from several government agencies, including the U.S. Census Bureau, the Department of Agriculture, and the Department of Labor.

In 1950, Mills and his BASR colleagues, Clarence Senior and Rose Kohn Goldsen, published *The Puerto Rican Journey,* a survey representing a cross-section of all adult Puerto Ricans who were born in Puerto Rico, had migrated to New York City, and were now residing there. This statistical research study involved interviewing a total of 1,113 respondents selected from 2,860 adult Puerto Rican homeowners in the core areas of Puerto Rican settlement of two New York boroughs: Manhattan ("Spanish Harlem") and the Bronx (the Morrisania district). The questionnaire consisted of 101 questions, many of them subdivided. The interviewers inquired, in Spanish, about the respondents' experiences in Puerto Rico and New York. Included were such probing questions as, "Would you tell me in your own words why you left P.R. and came to NY?" "What do you personally most want out of your own life?" "What occupation would you like your children to follow?" In the final analysis, *The Puerto Rican Journey* involved a triangulation of four research techniques: content analysis, intensive interviews, participant observations, and statistical data.

Mills's student and friend, Dan Wakefield (1971), recounts that shortly after completing *The Puerto Rican Journey,* Mills had become "increasingly impatient with the technical, impersonal, statistical side of sociology" (p. 68). Indeed, by the time he produced *The Power Elite* in 1956, Mills was beginning to eschew structured survey research and employ more unconventional methods of data gathering such as sorting out a collage of firsthand impressions, happenstance personal encounters, newspaper and magazine clippings, and other people's empirical findings (Horowitz, 1983). Mills demeaned the use of statistical models of verification that he regarded as little more than nose counting. Perhaps this was just as well, for by the mid-1950s, his readers were responding to what Mills's long-time friend, the novelist Harvey Swados (1963), called Mills's

> poetic vision of America; an unlovely vision perhaps, expressed with a mixture of awkwardness and brilliance, but one that did not really need statistical buttressing or the findings of research teams in order to be apprehended by sensitive Americans as corresponding to their own sense of what was going on about them, more truly and unflinchingly than any other contemporary statement. (p. 40)

By the late 1950s and early 1960s, the period referred to as his years of "pamphleteering," Mills had become almost completely disenchanted with empirical studies, preferring instead to take a broad critical analysis of his subject. Mills (1959a) candidly admits,

> Now I do not like to do empirical work if I can possibly avoid it. It means a great deal of trouble if one has no staff, and, if one does employ a staff, then the staff is often more trouble than the work itself. . . .
> In our situation, empirical work as such is for beginning students and for those who aren't able to handle the complexities of big problems; it is also for highly formal men who do not care what they study so long as it appears to be orderly. All these types have a right to do as they please or as they must; they have no right to impose in the name of science such narrow limits on others. (p. 35)

But if by "empirical work" Mills also meant conducting interviews, then he was being disingenuous in saying that it is only for those who are indifferent to their subject and concerned only about the tidiness of their research. Indeed, Mills made extensive use of interviewing, even toward the end of his career, as he traveled to Poland, Yugoslavia, the Soviet Union, and Cuba where he spent many hours intensively interviewing Fidel Castro, Che Guevara, and others in collecting material for his book *Listen, Yankee*

(1960d). As late as 1960, in his unfinished manuscript, *Contacting the Enemy*, Mills laid down specific rules for interviewers visiting different countries for a short period of time:

> 1. Don't try to cover a great range of topics and of people. . . . Focus on one or two problems about which you've read a good deal. . . .
> 2. Don't just converse at random, at least not all the time. Try to raise the same or very similar questions with each person interviewed. If you don't do this, you can't very well make comparisons between their views.
> 3. Don't try to find out the frequency . . . with which some opinion or some type of person prevails. You can't do it. That requires a technique of sampling beyond the [visiting interviewer's] means. Try instead to find out the full range of opinion on each of your chosen topics of concern. Try to get an interview with at least one or two people who represent each type or each outlook that you come upon. But how do you do this?
> 4. First select someone who is known . . . to represent one extreme of the range of opinion or of types being studied. Interview him, then ask him to refer you to someone else who might be able to give you an interesting or worthwhile view of the matter under discussion. . . . Now follow up the chains of these referrals from both extremes of the range. . . .
> 5. Sometimes it happens that the answers from everyone you interview are quite uniform. That can mean one of three things: a) Opinion on the point is official and everyone, regardless of their true belief, is putting out the same line. The only safeguards against this are skill in interviewing and playing off facts previously known by you against what the person is saying in the interview. b) You have not gotten hold of people who hold "extreme" views; you've not covered the range. In this case, all you can do is to try again to find the other end of the range of opinion. c) There really *is* uniformity on the point in question; the range is quite narrow. In that case, if you're sure, then you've made a finding, but be very careful about this point. (as quoted in K. Mills & Mills, 2000, pp. 300–301, emphasis original)

In sum, it may be said that Mills, as he matured in his sociological analysis, rejected statistical research because, as he saw it, its mechanical and dispassionate nature prevented social science from addressing the big issues of the human condition. But throughout his career, Mills not only favored, he frequently made use of, the technique of intensive interviewing. Mills believed that, if done properly, the social scientist could, through intensive interviewing, gain a humanist understanding of people's psychology—their deepest thoughts, strongest motivations, and most intimate feelings—in connection with the social and historical dimensions of their lives.

Conceptual Methods

A trenchant critic of the two major schools dominating mid-20th-century sociology, Mills scorns, on the one hand, the "grand theory" of scholars like Talcott Parsons and, on the other, the "abstracted empiricism" of researchers like Paul F. Lazarsfeld, who was Mills's supervisor at Columbia's BASR. This section looks at what Mills regards as the crucial shortcomings of these two main styles of work in 1950s sociology—grand theory and abstracted empiricism—and also considers the conceptual methodologies that he proposed in their stead.

As previously indicated, Mills was not always or completely opposed to using the survey data of interviews and questionnaires. His chief complaint is not that these research methods are inferior, unsound, or faulty in some intrinsic way. Rather, his concern is with the fact that many sociologists, having been trained primarily as research technicians, partake of the "fetishism of method and technique," that is to say, that they slavishly and unquestioningly follow research procedures and neglect the larger, substantive social issues (1959b, p. 224). By becoming self-absorbed with a particular research technique, methodologists cannot see, much less study, the major developments of the time. They are engaged in what Mills calls **abstracted empiricism,** an approach that converts the pressing social issues of the day into mundane statistical assertions. Mills remarks that in these assertions there is a pronounced tendency to confuse whatever is to be studied with the set of methods suggested for its study. He further contends that because the abstracted empiricists are too molecular, too focused on such atomistic facts of observation as public opinion and voting behavior, they are unconcerned with the "big questions"—questions, for instance, dealing with the legitimacy and use of the existing distribution of power. In so far as their interests lie with trifling, technical matters having no bearing on the larger issues of social structure, these practitioners of abstracted empiricism suffer from a sort of "methodological inhibition." The kinds of problems they chose to study and the way in which they are formulated are quite severely limited by the scientific method. Mills (1954) believes that the abstracted empiricists "are out to do with society and history what they believe physicists have done with nature" (p. 22). Among the most sophisticated advocates of this school, Mills singles out his Columbia supervisor Lazarsfeld, who saw sociology as no more than a methodological specialty and who regarded the sociologist as the exemplary methodologist of all the social sciences. Mills strongly condemns Lazarsfeld and other similar researchers for their trivialization of individuals and society and for neglecting problems of contemporary significance.

In a similar vein as Whyte in *The Organization Man* (1956), Mills blames the bureaucratization of research institutions for giving rise to the abstracted empirical style and the "new" applied social science. He maintains that for the sake of efficiency, research institutions had developed rationalized routines and thus created a social science that is exceedingly technical. This kind of procedural social science runs the risk of being transformed into a vehicle for what Mills terms the new **illiberal practicality,** or the idea that research is client-oriented and that social scientists have become mere technicians, co-opted by the powerful who buy their services and use their findings for bureaucratic and commercial purposes. The technical specialists promoting and practicing this style of research, says Mills, are frequently inclined to assume the political perspective of their bureaucratic clients and bosses.

Mills complains that due to their narrow vocational training, research technicians are incapable of seeing the big picture, of asking and pursuing questions about whole societies. In his effort to understand the big picture, Mills adopts an approach to the world that he calls "taking it big," by which he means considering issues in a grand manner (Wakefield, 1971, p. 66). Accordingly, Mills frequently urges social scientists to ask the big questions by analyzing smaller parts in relation to the larger structural wholes. This approach is wholly in keeping with the classic sociological tradition of the 19th-century European theorists that Mills so admired.

Rather than yield to the illiberal practicality of abstracted empiricism, Mills attempts to locate the problems, not of specific clients, but of the public, and not in the minutiae of statistical data, but in the trends of the historical social structure. Believing that the individual's private troubles can be properly understood only within the broader context of structural issues, he considers both the micro and macro levels of social analysis and the "molecular" and "macroscopic" styles of social science research. As will be discussed later in this chapter, Mills's analytic methodological approach examines how changes in "milieu"—the social setting directly open to people's daily personal, social experience (e.g., the home, the workplace, the neighborhood)—are affected by changes in social structure. Similarly, Mills (1953) urges sociologists to shuttle back and forth between *molecular* research, characterized by "small-scale problems and by its generally statistical models of verification," and *macroscopic* modes of inquiry dealing with historical social structures in a comparative and systematic way (p. 266). For only by considering the interplay between the immediate milieu and the larger social structure, by employing the molecular along with the macroscopic styles of research, can proper attention be given to the questions of theory formation and empirical measurement, while grounding research in the organization of society. In sum, for Mills, the object of research is not to continue tallying more quantitative data, but to explain the bigger questions pertaining to the main drift, the underlying forms and tendencies of the range of society in the middle of the 20th century that directly affect people's lives. Mills makes it plain, however, that this explanation cannot be realized through the theoretically abstruse and empirically disengaged program proffered by Talcott Parsons.

Parsons's **grand theory,** or his general conceptual scheme for analyzing the structure and processes of social systems, is severely attacked by Mills on several grounds. First, he accuses Parsons of engaging in the "fetishism of the concept"—of being so preoccupied with the semantic and syntactic aspects of his turgid prose, that Parsons cannot possibly define in a clear and orderly way the social problems at hand, much less guide efforts to solve them. So frustrated is Mills with Parsons's (1951) pretentious and verbose writing style, with his penchant for associating and dissociating concepts, that he threatens to translate the 555 pages of *The Social System* into about 150 pages of straightforward English. To be sure, Mills in *The Sociological Imagination* (1959b) does reduce the message of Parsons's ponderous book to four short, cogent paragraphs (see pp. 32–33). His purpose in doing so, Mills explains, is to help grand theorists, with their excessively high levels of abstraction, "get down from their useless heights" and compel them to observe problems in their historical and structural contexts. In *The Sociological Imagination,* Mills conveys his deep antipathy toward Parsons's vapory abstractions and lack of intelligibility.

A second charge that Mills levels against grand theory is that it presents a static and monolithic view of society that neglects many structural features fundamental to society's understanding. Mills (1959b) contends that "any systematic ideas of how history itself occurs, of its mechanics and processes, are unavailable to grand theory" (p. 43). He believes that because every social structure is differentially constituted, each society must be analyzed within its unique *historical* epoch. Social scientists must not only be concerned with the problem of order; they must also pay attention to the problem of *change.*

Third, Mills, in pragmatic fashion, sharply critiques grand theorists for their lack of empirical referents. For Mills, social theory, in order to be workable, must stop dealing in categories whose level of articulation is so general that it deprives them of all practical application. Mills charges that, like abstracted empiricism, grand theory also fails to shed light on substantive human problems and pressing social issues. Grand theorists, Mills maintains, have lost all touch with historical reality.

Next, Mills rejects Parsons's notion that a single theoretical framework can be used to understand the entire unity of the social structure—not that

Mills is opposed to all types of conceptualization; his aversion is only toward those conceptualizations taking the form of fantastic, one-answer, universal schemes. In his sociology, Mills (1959a, 1959b, 1962) prefers to utilize a less lofty but more pragmatic analytical tool, the **working model**—a more or less systematic inventory of elements that is neither true nor false, but useful and adequate to varying degrees, and to which we must pay attention if we are to understand something of social significance. For Mills, Marxism, when stripped of its ideological dogmatism and orthodoxy, has the potential to serve as a highly effective working model for sociology.

Finally, Mills contends that owing to Parsons's near-obsessive preoccupation with the problem of social order and his unwillingness to accept any radical analysis of society (but in particular, middle-class American society), Parsons's theoretical work ends up providing ideological support for the status quo. The ideological meaning of Parsons's grand theory, remarks Mills (1959b), tends strongly to legitimate stable forms of domination. It seeks, moreover, to maintain the established master social institutions—for example, the economy, the polity, and the family—as they are. While Mills does not consider grand theory to have practical political relevance, he insists that Parsons's view of society has an obvious ideological meaning associated with conservative styles of thinking. And for Mills, American conservatism is nothing more than the celebration of American life as supremely virtuous. In short, American conservatism is the ideological antithesis of the intellectual radical tradition Mills was trying desperately to cultivate in his sociology.

From the aforementioned discussion on survey research, abstracted empiricism, and grand theory, it is clear that Mills favors utilizing two methodological approaches in sociology: the quantitative-statistical and the historical-comparative. Marx and Weber's methodological influence is especially evident in Mills's use of the historical-comparative approach. In a rare statement of praise, Mills (1960a) writes of Marx and Weber,

> One reason why Marx and Weber are greater than, for example, Mosca or Durkheim is that every line they write is soaked in knowledge of history. . . . In their work, sharp analytic conceptions are blended with an encyclopedic knowledge of history. They go to specific periods and events with definite questions firmly in mind. For them history provides that which is to be explained, and the materials used in their explanations. (p. 13)

Mills's conceptual arsenal also includes the methodological classificatory approach that casts general ideas into two heuristic models: ideal types and polar types. In the manner of Weber, Mills frequently and consistently employs the **ideal type** as an analytical model that allows him to talk generally and abstractly about some specific and concrete phenomenon. Serving as a yard-stick that compares and contrasts empirical social phenomena, the ideal type helps to identify those cases that diverge or deviate from its stylized depiction. Examples of this conceptual methodology are demonstrated in Mills's self-conscious exaggeration of social-structural types (e.g., the Fourth Epoch, the mass society, the community of publics) as well as in his one-sided accentuation of certain character traits to produce personality and social types (e.g., the new men of power, the new middle classes, the power elite, the cheerful robot).

Similar to the ideal type is Mills's **polar type**, the methodological classifica-tion that contrasts opposites for the purpose of sorting their dimensions in terms of which the comparisons are made. As Mills (1959b) explains, "Often you get the best insights by considering extremes—by thinking of the opposite of that with which you are directly concerned. If you think about despair, then also think about elation; if you study the miser, then also study the spendthrift" (pp. 213–214). Like what he does with ideal types, he exaggerates slightly the dimensions of polar types in order to more clearly reveal their tendencies.

As methodological conceptualizations, ideal types and polar types require that the criteria of their classifications be made explicit and systematic. Put another way, the "dimensions" of each type—that is, their elements, condi-tions, and consequences—need to be made clear. The best way of doing this, says Mills (1959b) is through the technique of **cross-classification**. This ana-lytical technique, which Mills insists must become "an automatic procedure" and "a persistent habit of mind" (p. 213) for the sociologist, uses charts, tables, or diagrams of a qualitative sort and, in systematic fashion, casts general notions as *new* types. An example of cross-classification is found in a diagram in *Character and Social Structure* (Gerth & Mills, 1953; see Figure 2.1), dem-onstrating the presence or absence of the three functional demands of power-wielding in a leader's role: representation, legitimation, and decision making.

Figure 2.1

		Representation			
		Yes Legitimation		No Legitimation	
		YES	NO	YES	NO
DECISION MAKING	YES	1	2	3	4
	NO	5	6	7	8

Source: Character and Social Structure by Hans Gerth and C. Wright Mills. © 1953 Houghton Mifflin.

According to Gerth and Mills (1953), this cross-classificatory scheme allows for the sociological examination of eight types of leaders: (1) those who successfully combine all three functional role demands; (2) those who carry representations of power and wield power, but are not active developers of legitimations; (3) those who manage affairs and are active creators of legitimations, but do not employ or display the representation of power; (4) those who neither represent nor legitimate power, but who actively make decisions and manage their enactment; (5) those who do not manage decisions at all, but legitimate and display representations; (6) those who display representations and nothing else; (7) those who only legitimate, but do not display power or wield it; and (8) the non-leader who neither legitimates, displays, nor wields power (pp. 414–415).

The cross-classificatory technique producing this eightfold typology permits novel ways of thinking about what actions leaders may take. States Mills (1959a), "For the working sociologist, cross-classification is what making the sign of the cross is for a good Catholic, or diagramming a sentence is for a diligent grammarian. In many ways, the cross-classification is the very grammar of the sociological imagination" (p. 42).

Intellectual Craftsmanship

The foregoing discussion on method and theory brings us to one of Mills's most enduring statements concerning the conceptual strategy that he believed should inform the sociological enterprise, that of **intellectual craftsmanship**. Mills argues that, because the two are inextricably related, method cannot be separated from theory. Their difference lies in the fact that, whereas methods are methods for some range of problem, theories are theories of some range of phenomena. Mills (1959a) cautions sociologists to avoid the fetishism of method and concept: "[I]n actual practice, every working social scientist must be his own methodologist and his own theorist, which means only that he must be an intellectual craftsman" (p. 26).

Mills (1959a, 1959b) offers the beginning student of sociology practical advice on how to be an intellectual worker. He states that those who feel they are part of the classic sociological tradition should shun using received theories and research techniques in an unreflective manner. In order to ensure against methodological obsession and its mindless application, Mills advocates an unbroken continuity between what social scientists pursue intellectually and what they, as persons, observe and experience in their everyday lives. In social science, the intellectual's professional activities should always be fused with his or her personal life. Put slightly differently, Mills is proposing that social scientists learn to use their own personal experience in guiding their intellectual work. Such work may be properly described as a "craft," the manual or mental processes through which workers freely employ their capacities and skills in creating the products of their enjoyment and enjoying the products of their creation.

Mills uses the phrase "intellectual craftsmanship" in referring to a style of work as well as "to the joyful experience of mastering the resistance of the materials with which one works" (Gerth & Mills, 1953, p. 397). In order to engage in intellectual craftsmanship, Mills recommends that sociology students keep a "file," a journal of sorts, in which notes are habitually taken in an effort to join the personal with the professional, to record studies underway as well as studies planned. The file should consist of a continually growing collection of facts and ideas, from the most vague to the most finished: personal notes, excerpts from books, bibliographical items, outlines of projects, and so forth. At a later point in time, the sociologist rearranges the file by playfully combining previously isolated ideas and notes on different topics and finding unsuspected connections between them. Rearranging the file releases the imagination as the sociologist becomes receptive to unforeseen and unplanned linkages, all the while keeping in mind the several problems on which he or she is actively working. Then, through the use of ideal types, polar types, and cross-classification techniques, the sociologist attempts to systematically order the findings. On completing this, the findings are then paired down to essentials by relating them to one another in order to form a working model. Finally, the sociologist relates the working model to whatever he or she is endeavoring to explain.

The Social Psychological Approach

Another conceptual methodology that Mills employs is very clearly the *social psychological approach* as he analyzes people's character structure and psychic structure. By **psychic structure,** Mills refers to the integration of feelings, sensations, and impulses that are anchored in the human being as a biological organism. By **character structure,** he means the relatively stabilized integration of the organism's psychic structure linked with the social roles of the person (Gerth & Mills, 1953, p. 22). Mills, however, was sociologist enough to always attempt to link psychic structure and character structure to the **social structure,** the interrelation of various institutions and the ends they serve.

Mills's most obvious and detailed utilization of the social psychological approach is found in *Character and Social Structure* (Gerth & Mills, 1953). Here he posits that a well-articulated model of character structure can be developed with the appropriate integration and systematization of Sigmund

Freud's psychoanalysis and G. H. Mead's symbolic interactionism, and in particular, Mead's daring effort to anchor personal consciousness in the social process. Mills notes, however, that both these thinkers had an inadequate notion of social structure. They simply did not consider how institutions influence the character and conduct, the personalities and motivations, of individual men and women. Freud and Mead's theoretical shortcoming notwithstanding, Mills makes it clear that he is interested in the psychological features of people in society, in their innermost acts: in particular, their self-image and their conscience. He believes that even such intimate and subjective features of the person as emotions and actions are socially patterned. Mills (1959b), however, cautions against taking a strict psychiatric approach focusing solely on the individual case at the exclusion of macro-level analysis: "Many great public issues as well as many private troubles are described in terms of 'the psychiatric'—often, it seems, in a pathetic attempt to avoid the large issues and problems of modern society" (p. 12). Mills's point is that the psychology of the individual can only be adequately understood within the context of the larger social structure in history. Put another way, for Mills, there always exists an interrelationship among biography, social roles, and institutions. His objective, therefore, is to bridge the gap separating depth psychology and structural sociology.

We will consider Mills's social psychology in greater detail in the following chapter. But before leaving this discussion of Mills's conceptual methodology, two more issues deserve mention: his notion of what is "truth" and his humanistic view of sociology.

Truth

In Mills's sociology, "truth" appears to be a double-edged sword: It is, at once, subjectively constructed *and* based on objectively defined situations. In the form of models of empirical verification, truth is culturally constructed by the selective language of its users. That is to say, the accepted verification models are always ideological and therefore subject to social determinants. For Mills (1939, 1940a), knowledge—that is, reason and logic—is socially determined and relativized; it is conditional to the social context in which it flourishes. This approach helps us understand Mills's emphatic denouncement of absolutist ideological positions; be they from the Right or Left; be they inspired by classic liberalism or by orthodox Marxism.

In one of his more acclaimed essays, "The Professional Ideology of Social Pathologists" (1943a), Mills contends that the meaning sociologists attribute to their facts—that is, their ideology—is determined by the social contexts from whence they come. For example, he maintains that during the

1920s and 1930s, most sociologists working within the social pathological perspective shared a common style of thought, a similar conceptual framework, characterized by a low level of abstraction and lack of explicit systematization. In addition, the social pathologists considered only those problems that were practical, defined problems in terms of deviation from norms; approached problems as problems of individuals; and emphasized the "organic" structure of society. This theoretical orientation of the American pathologists reflected their relatively homogeneous, rural, Protestant, politically conservative, middle-class backgrounds. Mills's point is that the problems that pathologists (or, for that matter, any other type of sociologists) decide to study and how they conceive those problems are determined by their sociocultural milieu. Truth, for Mills, is relative.

Thus, in Mills's view, sociological inquiry is always relative in nature and comparative in time and place. Because sociologists of knowledge consider the social conditions under which ideas can be adjudged true or false, it makes the most sense for them to refer to *degrees* of truth. Mills sees it as the sociologist's job to disclose those conditions under which the degree of truthfulness can be assessed, as well as those conditions affecting the use of one verification model over another (Scimecca, 1977). Accordingly, he calls for a comparative conceptual approach that is necessarily historical and subjective.

Mills's notion of truth is also objective and pragmatic. American pragmatism, which, as already noted, greatly influenced Mills, holds that the most significant test of truth is found in its workability, that is, in the fruit ideas bear and the results to which they lead. Thus, for the pragmatist, a statement is true if it expresses a fact or describes a situation upon which people can act and secure the anticipated results. To be sure, Mannheim (1936/1968) himself had, in pragmatist fashion, proposed that "the ultimate criterion of truth or falsity is to be found in the investigation of the object" (p. 4). Gerth and Mills (1953) appear to share this view when they discuss the connection between stratification and political mentality:

> Often the "mentality" of strata is allowed to take predominance over the objective position. It is, for example, frequently asserted that "there are no classes in the United States" because "psychology is of the essence of classes." . . . But this is to confuse psychological feelings with other kinds of social and economic reality. . . . No matter what people believe, class structure as an economic arrangement influences their life chances according to their positions in it. If they do not grasp the causes of their conduct this does not mean that the social analyst must ignore or deny them. . . .
>
> "[S]ubjective" attributes must *not be used as criteria* for class inclusion, but rather, as Max Weber has made clear, stated as probabilities on the basis of objectively defined situations. (pp. 339–341, emphasis original)

Further on, Mills admits that psychological factors of subjectivity are likely to be associated with stratification. Thus, for Mills, as for Weber and Mannheim, sociological truth is at once based on the objective conditions of social life and is subjectively meaningful.

Increasingly, throughout his career, Mills began to hold a more objective notion of truth, one that was politically informed. This was a **politics of truth,** by which he meant that intellectuals had a moral and political obligation to tell the truth—to disclose the facts—about social reality, particularly since this reality was being distorted by the stultifying culture of mass society and the manipulation of the mass media. Thus, for example, in *Listen, Yankee* (1960d), Mills seeks explicitly to present to the U.S. public—a public that had access primarily to information from U.S. media sources—"the truth" about the Cuban Revolution. For Mills (1959b), therefore, one of the overriding political ideals inherent in sociology is the value of truth, of fact:

> The very enterprise of social science, as it determines fact, takes on political meaning. In a world of widely communicated nonsense, any statement of fact is of political and moral significance. All social scientists, by the fact of their existence, are involved in the struggle between enlightenment and obscurantism. In such a world as ours, to practice social science is, first of all, to practice the politics of truth. (p. 178)

Noam Chomsky, one of the leading intellectuals of contemporary times and a trenchant critic of U.S. foreign policy and the legitimacy of U.S. power, first read, as an undergraduate, Mills's comments on the role of the intellectuals. Some 20 years later, upon rereading these and other similar commentaries, Chomsky (1967) found that they had "lost none of their power or persuasiveness" (p. 323). Indeed, in his own celebrated essay "The Responsibility of Intellectuals" (1967), which he wrote during the time of escalating U.S. military involvement in Vietnam, Chomsky argues that intellectuals have a responsibility to speak the truth and expose the lies of governments. He claims that too often the intellectual community fails to respond to, indeed, tends to be quite tolerant of, the deceit and distortion undertaken "in the national interest." What is more, intellectuals, particularly those government experts with Washington contacts, are not only unwilling to analyze the causes and motives of objectionable political and military actions, but also their concern is only with whether the deceitful implementation of these actions can succeed in their deception. According to Chomsky,

A good case can be made for the conclusion that there is indeed something of a consensus among intellectuals who have already achieved power and affluence, or who sense that they can achieve them by "accepting society" as it is and promoting the values that are "being honored" in this society. It is also true that this consensus is most noticeable among the scholar-experts who are replacing the free-floating intellectuals of the past. (p. 348)

In a statement that is reminiscent of Mills's views, Chomsky writes, "If it is the responsibility of the intellectual to insist upon the truth, it is also his duty to see events in their historical perspective" (pp. 352–353).

Conclusion

As a concluding comment to this chapter, it may be said that Mills's overarching conceptual methodological approach—which subsequently informed his empirical methodology—is decidedly *humanistic*. Indeed, he repeatedly chides the abstracted empiricists and grand theorists for their failure to face up to the realities of human affairs. In order to attain excellence of clear and meaningful expression, Mills (1954) goads them to acquire "the humanist concern." For him, the humanist concern means focusing on the troubles and issues of the variety of individual human beings—"the human variety"—and the meanings these troubles and issues have for them. This humanist sociology of Mills's places science at the disposal of the popular welfare and is steered by a doctrine of moral responsibility. As Horowitz (1983) states, "Mills came to believe that social theory must contain a moral edge, and that such an edge was locked into the primal belief that change in human beings can be for the better" (p. 7). When the sociologist Alfred McClung Lee (1973) was presenting his humanist sociology (what he referred to as the "humanist-existential paradigm") in a textbook to undergraduates, he described its orientation in terms that closely echoed Mills's humanist concern:

When I say that I am an existential humanist, I mean only that my intellectual focus is upon what exists and upon what is most relevant to man. . . . [I]n such a view, first causes (or origins) and ultimate consequences, as well as absolutes and infinites, are irrelevant except as human artifacts to be considered as such. Methods and tenets useful in other sciences are to be treated as possibly helpful suggestions. Techniques of research and theories must serve human understanding of man's lot. (p. xii)

In the final analysis, it may be said, following Tilman (1984), that Mills's humanist concern aside, his premature death prevented him from achieving a conceptual methodological approach in which the conflicting intellectual crosscurrents of Marx and Weber, Freud and Mead, were more systematically and explicitly integrated with each other. The next chapters consider how these and other thinkers impacted upon Mills's major works. Before turning to those chapters, however, we consider the following questions as food for thought:

- How do Mills's views of individuals and society influence the ways by which he endeavors to study them?
- How realistic are his notions of what individuals and society should be like?
- What are the sources of the tensions between Mills's quantitative and qualitative methodological approaches?
- How is Mills's humanist sociology of individuals and society different from and similar to the sociologies of today?

3

The Social Psychology

The major works of C. Wright Mills may be subsumed under at least four general groupings. First, there is the book *Character and Social Structure* (Gerth & Mills, 1953)—the subject of this chapter—where he articulates the social psychological, theoretical framework that informs many of his other works. Second, there is the important trilogy on power and social stratification—consisting of *The New Men of Power* (1948), *White Collar* (1951), and *The Power Elite* (1956)—in which Mills critically discusses the American class system. These volumes will be the subject of Chapter 4. Third, in Chapter 5, we will examine Mills's disparate writings on Latinos and on Latin America, which consist of four items written throughout a 20-year period. Fourth, Chapter 7 briefly considers his polemical tract on the politics of responsibility, *The Causes of World War Three* (1958), as well as the now-classic *The Sociological Imagination* (1959b), in which Mills makes a declaration that has now become a familiar refrain to students of sociology throughout the world: Sociology must take into account the relation between biography and history and their intersection within particular social structures. Before turning to these works, it is worth quoting a statement made by Mills in 1955, by which time he had achieved global fame as a sociologist, explaining his philosophy of writing:

> As a writer, I have always tried, although in different ways, to do just one thing: to define and dramatize the essential characteristics of our time. Whether I have written of labor leaders or farmers, of business executives or Puerto Rican migrants, of office workers, housewives or workingmen, I have tried to see them as actors in the drama of the 20th century. I have often failed in this, and no doubt will again, but that is what I am trying to do. (as quoted in K. Mills & Mills, 2000, p. 279)

Mills's two main objectives noted in the above quote—to define and dramatize the essential characteristics of his time, on the one hand, and to see various populations as actors in the social drama of the 20th century, on the other—require that, in his writings, he consistently consider the character of individuals in the context of their social structure. It is for this reason that we begin with an analysis of Gerth and Mills's social psychology.

The Sociology of Persons and the Psychology of Institutions

As previously indicated, Mills coauthored the social psychological treatise *Character and Social Structure* (1953) in collaboration with his mentor at Wisconsin, Hans Gerth. In the book's foreword, Robert K. Merton aptly describes the volume as "an historically oriented psychology of social institutions" (p. vii). While it is certainly this, Oakes and Vidich (1999), who see a strong and distinct Weberian influence throughout, describe it more pointedly as the first sociology textbook that demonstrates how Weber's typologies, combined with his structural and historical analyses of institutional orders and cultural spheres, can be utilized to investigate the social bases of the formation of distinctive types of personality, character, and conduct.

Whatever else it may be, the work, to be sure, is a concise and systematic statement concerning the psychological nature of the five major institutional orders constituting the historically significant forms of social interaction: the (1) political, (2) economic, (3) military, (4) religious, and (5) kinship orders. Here, Gerth and Mills not only consider how types of personalities are variously anchored in each of the institutional orders, but they also discuss how the institutional orders themselves are variously integrated to form historical types of social structures. Their central aim is to build a working model of persons and society by combining the sociology of persons with the psychology of institutions. This synthesis produces for Gerth and Mills a "social psychology" through which they aim to achieve three objectives. First, they attempt to describe and explain the conduct and motivations of men and women in various types of societies and at various points in time. Next, they ask how the external conduct and inner life of one individual interplays with those of others. Finally, they seek to describe the types of persons usually found in different societies, and then to explain them by tracing their interrelations with their societies. In short, Gerth and Mills's social psychology provides a better understanding of social structures by showing how they shape the personalities of men and women as historical actors. In developing a social psychology that employs the macroscopic as well as the molecular modes of inquiry and considers the objective social functions of institutional orders alongside the subjective meanings of institutional members, Gerth and Mills are compelled to combine key concepts from the works of Mead, Freud, Marx, and Weber.

During the first half of the 20th century, none of the major schools of psychology (Gestalt, behaviorism, pragmatism, or psychoanalysis) possessed a well-developed notion of social structure. Attempting to rectify this conceptual deficiency, Gerth and Mills employ the Weberian approach to social psychology in considering the particular impact that social structure has on the individual's character. They diagram the major components of character and social structure in the following chart (Figure 3.1):

Figure 3.1

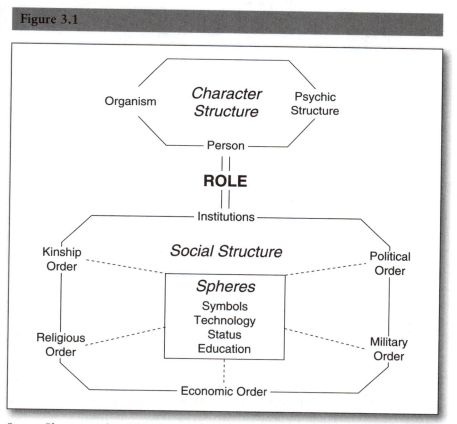

Source: *Character and Social Structure* by Hans Gerth and C. Wright Mills. © 1953 Houghton Mifflin.

Basic Concepts

As the casual reader is sure to note, *Character and Social Structure* can generally be regarded as a lexicon in social psychology. As such, it chiefly consists of an elaborate and precise presentation of myriad technical concepts that Gerth and Mills use as building blocks in developing their theoretical framework explaining their sociology of persons and psychology of institutions. They begin by defining the major components of **character structure.**

As noted in the previous chapter, **psychic structure,** or personality, refers to the integration of feelings, sensations, and impulses that are a fundamental part of the human organism. **Organism** refers to the human being as a biological entity. **Person** refers to the human being as a player of roles that involve reference to emotions, perceptions, and purposes. Thus, instead of explaining the person's behavior in terms of stimulus and response as did the behavioral psychologists, Gerth and Mills prefer to look at the subjective meanings that persons give to motives.

Since their primary objective is to bridge the social basis of character structure with the notion of social structure, Gerth and Mills (1953) begin with the pivotal concept of role. The term **roles** refers to "(1) units of conduct which by their recurrence stand out as regularities and (2) which are oriented to the conduct of other actors" (p. 10). Serving as the major link between character and social structure, role is the key term in Gerth and Mills's definitions of person and institutions. **Institutions** consist of an organization of roles, one or more of which is understood to serve the maintenance of the total set of roles. An **institutional order** consists of all those institutions within a social structure that have similar consequences and ends or which serve similar objective functions. In the modern Western world, five major institutional orders form the skeletal structure of the total society.

(1) The **political order** consists of those institutions within which people acquire, wield, or influence the distribution of power and authority within social structures. (2) The **economic order** is made up of those establishments by which people organize labor, resources, and technologies in order to produce and distribute goods and services. (3) The **military order** is composed of institutions in which people organize legitimate violence and supervise its use. (4) The **kinship order** is made up of institutions that regulate and facilitate legitimate sexual intercourse, procreation, and the early rearing of children. (5) The **religious order** is composed of those institutions in which people organize and supervise the collective worship of God or deities, usually on regular occasions and at fixed places.

Spheres are aspects of social conduct that characterize all institutional orders. Gerth and Mills identify the four most important spheres that may be used within any of the five orders: (1) symbols, (2) technology, (3) status, and (4) education. **Symbols** are visual or acoustic signs, signals, emblems, ceremonials, language, music, or other arts used in understanding the conduct of human actors. **Technology** refers to the implementation of conduct with tools, apparatuses, machines, instruments, and other physical devices and the skill employed in that conduct. **Status** is the sphere consisting of the agencies and means of distributing prestige, deference, or honor among the members of the social structure. **Education** is the sphere consisting of those institutions and activities concerned with the transmission of skills and values to those persons who have not acquired them. A **social structure** is composed of institutional orders and spheres; its unity depends on the relative importance of each institutional order and sphere, and their relation to each other.

The Roles People Play

Simply put, the main thesis of *Character and Social Structure* is as follows: In emphasizing the roles people play in various institutions, Gerth and Mills demonstrate how character structures—personality traits and conduct patterns—are molded by the institutional orders to form historical types of social structures. Accordingly, they begin with the premise that a person is composed of a constellation of organized social roles. Because persons are usually involved in several institutional orders, their character traits are shaped by the various roles they enact within these orders. Each of the roles, therefore, is a segment of the different institutions and interpersonal situations within which the person moves. Persons are related to society by the roles they acquire. Persons and institutions have reciprocal effects through the linkage of both by social roles. For instance, an individual may be simultaneously a mother, wife, and daughter, and hence involved with the kinship institution. As a voting Democrat, she is participating in the political institution, and as a physician working in a hospital, she is connected to the economic institution.

Institutions form persons by means of the roles persons internalize through language and other symbols of the symbol sphere, including the types of conversation typical of an institutional order. Language is crucial to the operations of institutions because it serves as (1) the most important mechanism of interpersonal conduct, (2) the major source of knowledge of our selves, and (3) the medium in which social roles are organized. In short, language and its symbols are used by institutions to coordinate the roles of their members as well as to justify the enactment of these roles. Through language—that is, conversation—we learn what others expect of us. Thus, much of our social conduct is enacted in order to meet the expectations of others. These expectations provide the basis for the development of our *self-image*, our idea of what kind of person we are, involving our relations to other people and their appraisals of us. According to Gerth and Mills, the self-image we possess at any given time is a reflection of the appraisals of self, significant others, and the generalized other.

Significant others are those intimates, encountered in a given institution, who matter most to us, to whom we pay attention, and whose appraisals—approbation and criticism—are reflected in our self-appraisals. The key mechanism by which institutions form persons involves the circle of significant others established by the institution. The evaluation of those who are significant to us determines the construction and preservation of our self-image. Character traits, therefore, are influenced by significant others. One of these significant others is the institutional leader who wields authority over the members of a given institution. In order to succeed in an institution, the person internalizes the expectations of the institutional leader, and this in turn acts as a means of social control. Institutional controls are patterns upheld by the institutional leaders and their agents. Parental authority, for example, guarantees the roles played by the children of a household.

Internalizing the attitudes of significant others like the institutional leader forms the **generalized other,** the experience of the appraisals of those who are not immediately present but who are authoritatively significant to the person. For Gerth and Mills, the generalized other refers to certain institutional orders in which the person is involved on a daily basis. Thus, contrary to Mead, Gerth and Mills advocate an institutionally defined generalized other, which is to say, the *institution,* and not necessarily the whole society, may represent the generalized other.

By internalizing the expectations of institutional leaders, as significant authoritative others, the persons who enact the institutional role come to control themselves, that is to say, they pattern and enact their roles in accordance with the constraints built into their characters. As they develop as institutional members, these constraints are often generalized and are thus linked psychologically with particular institutions. The institutional leaders attempt to justify their rule by linking it with moral symbols, sacred emblems, or legal formulas that are widely believed and internalized. When symbols are deeply internalized, they are usually not questioned. Operating as a conscience of sorts, a superego as it were, the appraisals and values of the generalized other sanction the person's actions and desires. The generalized other acting as a symbolic model appeals to the members' religious or moral duty in fostering attachments to the institution. In this case, the individual is expected to maintain institutional membership "for better or worse." When transgressing the appraisals and values of the generalized other, which are, in essence, the appraisals of many significant others that become internalized expectations of self, the person feels the pangs of conscience and experiences guilt.

Changes in the composition of the generalized other, or what Gerth and Mills term a "crisis of conscience," can occur in two ways: (1) through a person's growing up or maturing and (2) through the transformation of a generalized other that is typical of an entire stratum or an entire society. Persons grow up and mature through three interrelated lines of development: somatic, psychic, and biographical. *Somatic development* refers to the biological growth of the organism. *Psychic development* means psychological maturation. *Biographical development* has to do with the different roles a person takes up and casts off in the passage from one age group to another. The most important conditions favoring the chances for an effective generalized other to emerge are found in the childhood and adolescent phases of the life history. Consider, for example, that the period of adolescent upheaval (a crucial stage of life frequently experienced by middle-class teenagers in contemporary Western society) results largely from an intensified need for and awareness of the approval of others. This contradictory stage between childhood and adulthood, when the adolescent is not yet integrated with a durable mate and does not fulfill a regular occupational role, is usually fraught with frustrations, anxieties, and insecurities. A generalized other arises only with great difficulty when many contradictory or inconsistent expectations are exacted of the person. Social adolescence is over when the person is regularly expected to enact, and does enact with greater or lesser conformity, the roles that adults of his or her social position typically perform. The biography of a person consists of the transformations in character that result from abandoning the old roles and taking on new ones.

The second way in which a crisis of conscience occurs—transforming the generalized other of an entire stratum or society—involves changes made at the level of institutional orders. Thus, at this macroscopic level that considers the larger framework of social structure, *crisis* refers to a sufficient collapse of institutional orders resulting in either ecstasy or mass panic; in either case, people are "beyond themselves." For example, in political and economic revolutions like the French Revolution, the Bolshevik Revolution, and the various palace revolutions, the authoritarian other of public figures and political leaders may initiate a reappraisal of new values and loyalties. Parents and teachers may assimilate these reappraisals and present them to children of an impressionable age. Or, shifts in interpersonal circumstances may bring out such reappraisals, which will then be conveyed to public figures and political leaders, thus forcing profound structural and historical changes. In this period of transition when old institutions break down and new ones are not yet available, the norms of a society are smashed, new significant and authoritative others may emerge who define new values and new loyalties, and there is a crisis in every person's conscience as his or her authoritarian other changes. Persons are reappraised, and they reappraise themselves as well as the selves of others. Gerth and Mills (1953) contend that, as ideological movements, liberalism and socialism "have tended to operate in a total way: their goals and policies have to do with extensive modifications of the structure of all orders and spheres—religious and political, kinship and economic, military and technological, status and educational" (pp. 440–441).

In order to determine which character types can be deduced from the roles individuals play in institutions, Gerth and Mills attempt to understand the individual's *motives,* or subjective formulations of action. In developing a sociological approach to understanding motivation, Gerth and Mills explain how and why human conduct takes a specific direction. They propose that the center of motivation for persons is primarily located in the expectations of others that are internalized from the roles that persons perform. In other words, motivation results from the balancing of self-image and the appraisals of significant and generalized others. Gerth and Mills's general aim is to understand types of persons integrated with roles in various degrees and in various ways, by knowing something about the motives or intentions prompting the acquisition and enactment of these roles in various situations. For them, motives are terms that persons typically use in their interpersonal relations. As such, motives are viewed as social justifications for one's conduct, and as means of persuading others to accept and to further one's conduct.

Gerth and Mills examine **vocabularies of motive**, or those specific terminologies that individuals employ in given social situations to justify the past, sustain the present, or endorse intended future actions. Accordingly, they borrow from Weber's conception of the social function of motive: a term in a vocabulary that appears to the actor or to the observer to be an adequate reason for conduct. Vocabularies of motive become components of the generalized other; they are internalized by the person and operate as mechanisms of social control. Vocabularies of motive are used not only to persuade others of the moral rightness of our conduct, but also to motivate them to behave in a similar way. Although some vocabularies of motive are internalized during childhood, new roles in new social contexts require that new vocabularies be adopted at later stages in life. In addition, as institutional orders undergo historical transformation, vocabularies of motive must also change. During situations of crisis, however minor they may be, people tend to ask questions that involve alternative or unexpected purposes of conduct.

Turning again to the notion of role, Gerth and Mills maintain that the features of certain roles in various institutional orders are usually stratified according to the three analytically separate but causally interrelated dimensions of class, status, and power. **Class** is determined by wealth, property, and the occupational roles operating within the economic institutional order. In its simplest objective sense, class has to do with the amount and source (property or work) of income as these affect the chances of people to obtain other available values. The **status** sphere involves the successful realization of claims to prestige by certain individuals as well as others who honor the claim; it refers to the distribution of deference in a society. Status can be claimed in any institutional order, and because individuals enact roles in more than one order, their status usually rests upon a combination of roles. For example, a person's status may be based primarily on his or her military occupation, but the person may express his or her status claims in the educational sphere, and cash in on these claims in the political order. Consider the case of Dwight D. Eisenhower who, as an army general, also served as a college president (Columbia University), on the way to becoming president of the United States. Or consider the more recent, if relatively less clear-cut, career status trajectory of Lawrence Summers, who first came to public prominence in the education occupation (as an economics professor and later as president of Harvard University), then served in the economic order (as a part-time managing director of an investment and technology development firm on Wall Street), and was subsequently recruited into the political order (as director of the White House National Economic Council for President Barack Obama). Of the various interconnected dimensions of stratification, status is the most relevant to the psychology of the individual because it is directly connected to the person's self-esteem.

Third, **power,** or political influence, refers to the realization of one's will, even if this involves the resistance of others. Power is the most important dimension because it usually defines both class and status. In other words, the power position of institutions and individuals typically depends upon factors of class and status, often in intricate interrelation. And when we speak of the power of classes and status groups, we usually refer to power in the political order. By means of power, such groups attempt to influence or determine the policies and activities of the state.

Gerth and Mills explain that these three definitions of stratification—class, status, and power—are loose formulations of Weber's terms, and their intent is to make them more elaborate and precise. To these three dimensions, Gerth and Mills add a fourth: Veblen's emphasis on occupation. **Occupation** refers to a set of activities pursued more or less regularly as a major source of income. Occupations consist of economic roles and skills. As roles, they may be found in various institutional orders, but they are usually located in the economic institutional order. Occupations are skills that are marketable from the individual's standpoint and functional from the standpoint of society. The most decisive shift in occupations in the 20th century has been the decline of the independent entrepreneur (the "old middle class") and the rise of the salaried employee (the "new middle class"). The shift to a society of employees has made occupation and the educational sphere crucially important. Different occupations require different levels and types of education. In turn, the type and amount of education is an important basis of prestige. Further, in the United States, the enjoyment of prestige is often so disturbed and uneasy that the bases of prestige, the expressions of prestige claims, and the ways these claims are honored are now subject to great strain, a strain that often throws ambitious men and women into a virtual status panic.

The important differences among people, say Gerth and Mills, are those that shape their biographies and ideas. We should, therefore, expect certain psychological traits to recur among persons associated with the same **strata,** a grouping consisting of people who are characterized by an intersection of the dimensions of class, status, power, and occupation. Put another way, the probability that people will have a similar mentality and ideology, and that they will join together for action, is increased the more homogenous they are with respect to these four dimensions of stratification. As we will see in Chapter 4, many of these themes concerning social stratification form the conceptual basis of Mills's best-known works, *The New Men of Power, White Collar,* and *The Power Elite.*

The Unity of Social Structures

Gerth and Mills next turn their attention to the problem of structural unity or integration. Calling the functionalist assumption of social integration (that each unit of a society is related to every other unit and that society is in some manner a whole of busily interacting parts) "an uninformed truism," they contend that it is not an explanation at all but merely an abstract description. Instead of engaging in pure description, Gerth and Mills prefer to empirically explain, historically compare, and psychologically analyze the unity of social structures.

Gerth and Mills begin by identifying the most convenient "units" that prevail in a society. These units are the institutional orders and their corresponding institutions, spheres, and roles. They further maintain that relations between the institutional orders are causal and variable, which is to say that unit relations are not the simple input–output interchanges that Parsons imagined. Gerth and Mills are interested in tracing the "ramifications," or those activities which are ends in one order but which are used as the means of another institutional order, and in understanding how such ramifications may facilitate or limit activities and policies in other orders. They then propose that the institutional orders comprising a social structure are integrated through four ideal-type "modes of integration," or "principles of structural change." Gerth and Mills identify these as (1) correspondence, (2) coincidence, (3) coordination, and (4) convergence.

Correspondence means that a social structure is unified because its several institutional orders share a common structural principle that operates in a parallel way in each. For example, during feudalism there existed the structural principle of *vassalship* that was paradigmatically exemplified in the "exchange" between lord and serf. The serf swore personal allegiance to the lord in return for the lord's protection. Aside from the lord–serf relationship, the psychology of vassalship also found a correspondence in the political, kinship, and religious orders. In reference to the political order, the aforementioned exchange allowed for the coherent domination of large estates. In the kinship order, the principle of vassalship enjoined the knight to prove his love for his "occidental lady"—the noble wife of another knight. The principle of vassalship played itself out in the religious order as the Christian knight pledged his loyalty to Christ, the Lord in whose name he crusaded against the heathen and barbarian.

Coincidence means that different structural principles or developments in various orders result in their combined effects in the same, often unforeseen, outcome of unity for the whole society. Gerth and Mills admit that they are not aware of any society that is integrated solely in terms of coincidence. There are, however, many societies in which the partial operation of coincidence has served as a mode of integration. For a striking and detailed case of how various structural principles converge at a given time and place, Gerth and Mills look to Weber's work on Puritanism and its role in the character formation of the entrepreneur of modern capitalism. Puritanism motivates the believer to approach work as a "calling"—an ascetic exercise—pursued methodically for the sake of the kingdom to come. The consequence of such motivation is the emergence of a particular type of personality in the economic order: the entrepreneur as a psychological type who will not readily consume the profits he or she makes but reinvests them in the business for extended production. In addition, the structural principle of asceticism may also be found in the kinship order, where recreational sex is suppressed, and in the political and military orders, where the spontaneous release of aggression is prohibited. In other words, self-discipline and the absence of self-indulgence are fostered in each of these institutional orders. The importance of the entrepreneurial psychological type for modern capitalism is evidenced by the fact that even after society became increasingly secularized, emphasis was still placed on the ascetic character traits of hard work and self-discipline, traits that are essential to the continued existence of capitalism. Thus, the ramifications of Puritanism influenced the great economic transition from feudalism to modern industrial capitalism.

Coordination refers to the integration of a society by means of one or more institutional orders that become ascendant over other orders and direct them; thus, other orders are regulated and managed by the ascendant order or orders. But these societies also involve correspondence and coincidence. An example of this type of structural unity is found in Nazi Germany. In this case, the totalitarian party served as the organization through which certain high agents in the political, economic, and military orders coincide, and by which they coordinate their own and other orders and institutions. In other words, the Nazi Party became the dominant institutional order that imposed and defined substantive policy goals for all the other institutional orders. As a pervasive mechanism, it broke up or infiltrated—and so controlled—every organization, even down to the family. Further, with the partial exception of the religious order, the Nazi Party controlled the symbol sphere of all orders. Because it monopolized all formal communications, including the educational sphere, all symbols were recast for the purpose of legitimating the Third Reich.

Finally, the fourth type of structural integration, **convergence,** means that two or more institutional orders coincide to the point of fusion, thus becoming one institutional setup. In societies lacking functional specialization, as in the American frontier of the 19th century, certain institutional orders may blend. For instance, in the kinship-centered frontier, the church, police, and schools converged in, and its functions were carried out by, the family. Thus, the roles of women as wife and mother came also to include the nurse, the midwife, and the teacher; the roles of men as husband and father, came to include the lay religious leader and, if needed, the vigilante and militiaman.

Social-Historical Change

Correspondence, coincidence, coordination, and convergence are useful not only for analyzing the unity of social structures, but also the sequences of historical change; in fact, these modes of integration appear, in dynamic perspective, as principles of social-historical change. "Regardless of how unified a social structure may seem," write Gerth and Mills (1953), "its unity is part of history, and history is change" (p. 371). Thus, their examination of the unity of the social structure leads them to the problem of *social-historical change*. By social change, Gerth and Mills are referring to the emergence, growth, and decline of the roles, institutions, and orders comprising a social structure. When the role is taken as the unit of socio-historical change, we ask how many people play a given role and at what tempo is one role displaced by another. On the other hand, when the institution is considered as the unit, we ask how many institutions of given types exist and what types of institutions most generally prevail within an order. And when the institutional order is used as the unit of social change, we look at the shifting relations of this order to other orders within the social structure. Finally, the social structure itself can be overturned, as in total revolution or other epochal transitions. In this case, the orders comprising the social structure are recomposed so that a new social structure emerges. Most importantly, such revolutions mean that their legitimations and ideologies change. In understanding social change, we must see that the various institutions and roles are interdependent, say Gerth and Mills. They contend that an examination of this interdependence involves a detailed study of the political, economic, and military orders.

Master Trends

Gerth and Mills conclude by denoting what they see as the four "master trends," or basic transformations, characterizing mid-20th-century U.S. society. In their view, these master trends entail the "revolution of our time," and they are most readily discernible in the political, economic, and military orders. Indeed, Gerth and Mills (1953) regarded postwar America as a "political economy that is closely linked with military institutions and decisions" (p. 456). Thus, the first master trend involved the *coordination of the political, economic, and military orders*. This is what was meant by the Cold War that was characteristic of a world of nations polarized between the United States and the Soviet Union. Made powerful by their possession of nuclear weapons with enormous range and destructive capacities, these two superpowers centralized their political decision making by forming large bureaucratic structures that coordinated all of the major institutional orders. The key national decisions of the United States and USSR were of global scope affecting no less than the future of humanity. In the United States, these decisions, which were weighty and grave, and often frightful, tended increasingly to be "coordinated," as they were made by the top leaders in the highest echelons of the political, corporate, and military bureaucracies.

Mills continued to explore in greater depth this basic transformation of Cold War society in *The Power Elite* and *The Causes of World War Three*.

The second master trend had to do with the *psychological aspects of bureaucracy*. By this, Gerth and Mills mean that the increasing bureaucratization of modern society was accompanied by psychological stresses experienced by the individual in the form of frustration, despair, anxiety, and insecurity. The new middle classes were particularly affected. White-collar employees found themselves in a position that denied them the opportunity to take stock of their whole work situation. Their working environment became a mere fragment of the large-scale bureaucratic organization in which they worked. This resulted in their feeling increasingly alienated and powerless. What is more, as the bureaucratic organizations became more interdependent, a crisis in one produced a concomitant crisis in the others. For example, a crisis in the economic order resulting in unemployment led to the unemployed person giving up hope of finding any job; his or her former aspirations broke down, and with them the hope of the family of the breadwinner. Gerth and Mills (1953) state that

> [i]n modern society insecurity tends to be experienced not as a personal mishap or misfortune, nor as an irrevocable fate due to supernatural forces nor even to natural forces. And men, full of the tension of insecure positions correctly blame social factors for personal defeat. (p. 462)

Mills revisits these issues in *White Collar* and *The Sociological Imagination*.

The third main trend identified by Gerth and Mills is *the decline of liberalism*. In the classical or 19th-century sense, **liberalism** was an intellectual tradition, a political style of thinking, whose tenets emphasized individual freedom, egalitarianism, liberty, private property, fair competition, a laissez-faire market economy, and unlimited opportunities. Gerth and Mills contend that in the global context of the mid-20th century, with its total integration of institutional orders and the bureaucratization of organizational life, the incongruity of these liberal tenets had become glaringly evident. As an ideology, liberalism had turned into a political rhetoric that was increasingly meaningless and banal to large numbers of people. "Only the complacent and the uninformed," write Gerth and Mills (1953), "can feel assured of liberal and democratic developments in the world today" (p. 472). Mills launches a blistering attack on liberalism's role in the modern world in *The New Men of Power, The Power Elite*, and *The Marxists*.

Fourth and finally, Gerth and Mills (1953) analyze the *character structure in a polarized world*. Their concern was with the personality traits and conduct patterns that would emerge in an era polarized by the United States and the USSR's political, economic, and military struggle for the world. This struggle between the two power blocs has a portentous psychological meaning as "we witness and participate in an historic contest which will decide what types of men and women will flourish on the earth" (p. 480). Mills once again takes up this theme in *The Causes of World War Three*.

Conclusion

Joseph A. Scimecca (1977) maintains that *Character and Social Structure*, with its theoretical framework synthesizing the personality formation of the pragmatists with the emphasis upon the social structure of Max Weber and the German sociologists, is seminal to an overall understanding of Mills's works. In the next chapter, we shall see how the social psychological approach formulated in *Character and Social Structure* continued guiding Mills's writings throughout his most creative and productive period, 1948–1956. It is during these years that Mills published his most muscular and well-known sociological work, the stratification trilogy. First, however, a few questions may be entertained in reference to Mills's social psychological approach:

- Why is character structure an important component in social thought?
- How is Gerth and Mills's social psychology different from and similar to today's social psychologies as articulated in symbolic interactionism, dramaturgy, and social behaviorism?
- To what extent are the social emotions of pride and shame, anger and jealousy considered by Gerth and Mills in their social psychology?
- How relevant are the four master trends that Gerth and Mills identify to today's social world?

4

The Stratification Trilogy

*T*he *New Men of Power* (1948), *White Collar* (1951), and *The Power
Elite* (1956) constitute C. Wright Mills's stratification trilogy, or those
studies dedicated to analyzing the American class structure and power system. These studies attempt to relate the psychological characteristics of certain groups and their individual members—labor leaders; white-collar
workers; and the political directorate, the chief executives of large corporations, and the warlords—to the stratified American milieu of the 1940s and
1950s. These three volumes, which marked Mills as a scholar of the first
rank, "stand relatively alone as a comprehensive corpus of social criticism in
the decade following the Second World War" (Jamison & Eyerman, 1994,
p. 16), and through them Mills is able to express a unique vision of America
at mid-century, a time when social science readily accepted the pluralist
understanding of class and democracy, and subsequently attempted to blur
all social divisions.

Mills (1959b), in strong autobiographical tones, explains his motivations
for producing the three-volume series on social stratification:

> I wrote a book on labor organizations and labor leaders—a politically moti-
> vated task; then a book on the middle classes—a task primarily motivated by
> the desire to articulate my own experience in New York City since 1945. It was
> thereupon suggested by friends that I ought to round out a trilogy by writing
> a book on the upper classes. (p. 200)

Simply put, in each of these books—which are self-consciously written in
a new literary style, "sociological poetry," characterized by "an uneven mix-
ture of empirical social science and radical political analysis" (Geary, 2009,

p. 28)—Mills is chiefly concerned with power and the powerful: the elites, exploiters, and policy makers. Concomitantly, and to a somewhat lesser extent, he is also interested in the issue of powerlessness and in powerless populations. For example, in *The New Men of Power*, Mills analyzes the inability of labor leaders to exert power; while in *White Collar* he describes the essential powerlessness of the middle class; and in *The Power Elite* he examines the powerlessness and political acquiescence of mass society, which includes the bulk of the American people.

The New Men of Power

Based on a dozen or so articles on trade unions and their leadership that Mills wrote between 1945 and 1949, his interest during the 1940s was clearly with organized labor in the United States. The culmination of a research project on the characteristics of American labor leaders on which he had been working since 1941, coupled with the research he conducted as head of Columbia's BASR Labor Research Division, resulted in the publication of *The New Men of Power* (1948), the first volume in Mills's analysis of how the structure of power and stratification is maintained in U.S. society and how the ideology of liberalism legitimizes it. Here Mills focuses on the American labor movement and explains the ascendancy of union leaders and their role as a new elite. *The New Men of Power* is a study of the character of America's labor leadership—the positions they occupy, their career lines, and the traditions and anxieties that motivate them. In this monograph, which was the result of empirical studies conducted on 500 of the most powerful labor leaders in America, Mills maintains that the union leaders, by virtue of their occupation, and the prestige attached to it, had been recently thrust into positions of power.

Mills examines the values and background of the leaders of American labor and concludes that due to their similarity in occupation, class, status, and power, they could be expected to manifest a sameness of personality. However, given that their income was not high, an important distinction emerged between them and other powerful elites. Thus, while they were not members of the money elite—that is to say, labor leaders did not belong to the elite of class or prestige—they were nonetheless members of the elite of power. The labor leaders' power was bound up with the power of the union that they led; this power was based primarily upon the number of workers organized under them. In other words, labor leaders wielded power by virtue of their position in the union as representatives of the rank and file. As a consequence, and most regrettably to Mills, they became political opportunists wanting to realize small goals in short order. Hence, it was not political programs or ideologies that governed the decisions of the leaders of American labor; it was expediency. Labor leaders could not wait; they wanted the payoff of their policies to become immediately visible to the workers of limited memory and high expectation. Labor leaders, therefore, displayed the type of political mentality that lacked the capacity to develop a long-range substantive, economic, and political program, but that made many short-term demands in an agitated manner. Mills (1948) charges that, unfortunately,

> [s]uch piecemeal agitation is now the political substance of American liberalism. Like liberals in general, the labor leaders do not connect specific demands with general images of the kind of society they want, nor do they integrate immediate demands and general principles into programs. (p. 160)

Endeavoring to relate a type of social role to a particular social structure, Mills is interested in labor leaders not as individuals but as a social type formed by the roles they played in a political economy that was changing from laissez-faire to monopoly and a state capitalism with many corporate features. Accordingly, Mills attempts to paint a representative portrait of the "average" American labor leader, whom he sees as at once being an army general and a parliamentary debater, a political boss and an entrepreneur, a rebel and a disciplinarian. Mills finds that a negative image of union leaders prevailed in the mass public's view. The people interviewed by Mills believed that, in general, labor leaders lacked a social conscience and a sense of social responsibility—this, despite the fact that the public was largely unfamiliar with most of the leaders of trade unions. Moreover, several other sources, including the rank and file and the officials in both the unions and the corporations, also held certain images of the labor leader. Thus, according to Mills (1948), "[t]he labor leader acquires new mirrors in which to appraise his image from the angle from which others see him, and perhaps to conceive new images for himself" (pp. 105–106).

Composing a collective portrait of labor leaders led Mills to place them inside or outside one or both of the two big agglomerates of American unionism: the American Federation of Labor (AFL) and the Congress of Industrial Organizations (CIO). (At the time Mills was writing, the AFL and CIO were two separate union blocs; they became one unified organization a decade later.) Both affiliations helped their member unions in strike situations by supplying them with money and organizational talent. Mills, however, contends that the split between the two houses of labor ran deep: It divided different types of labor leaders. According to Mills, the two main differences between the leaders of the AFL and the CIO, and the two that are the most decisive and that carry heavy implications for other personal and opinion characteristics, were age and education. Simply put, young men (average age of 43) ran the CIO and older men (average age of 57) ran the AFL. In regard to education, the CIO leaders' median grade of formal schooling was 12.5 years; that of the AFL leaders was 9.3 years. Mills clearly prefers the younger, better-educated leaders in the CIO for one major reason: Ideologically, they were further to the left.

The Main Drift

Working from the premise that U.S. economic conditions since the Great Depression had been racked by the cycle of slump and war and boom, Mills's concern is with the **main drift:** those historical and structural forces that were moving American society toward "rationality without reason," or the use of rational means in the service of substantively irrational ends. As Mills sees it, the main drift in the postwar United States was toward the building of a war-oriented economy drawn into the bipolar Cold War conflict. Given the state of monopoly capitalism in the United States, unless there was a buildup to a war with Russia that brought profits to American businesses, the fiscal conditions during peacetime would result in an economic slump. Mills was well aware of the connection between slump and war, and the kind of social structure that prevailed. He knew full well that the two world wars had served to pull the United States out of economic slumps. Thus, Mills believed that those who monopolized the means of production (the business elite) and those who monopolized the means of violence (the military elite) had many interests in common. They, in effect, intended to "solve" the problems of slump with war, or by instigating a militarized form of capitalism.

Mills's thesis in *The New Men of Power* is that only the powerful force of labor unions as agencies of protest could stop this country's drift toward an expanding war economy, an economy that required spending large sums on munitions and other military items. As members of a strategic vanguard and the only potentially liberating mass force, the leaders of American labor—the new men of power—along with the labor intellectuals (i.e., the unions' lawyers, editors of the unions' newspapers, economists, statisticians, and research directors), could form an alliance of power and intellect to combat the social trend—the main drift—that was establishing the United States as a corporate garrison state.

Mills is also interested in the relationship of the labor leaders to the politically alert publics, or those groups that, to one degree or another, have the power to influence policy concerning labor–management relations. The distinct view each of these groups held of labor and of labor leaders helps Mills classify them as being on the political right, center, or left. While he identifies six such political "publics," our concern here is only with those four that Mills singles out for special consideration: (1) the liberal center, (2) the Communists, (3) the practical right, and (4) the sophisticated conservatives.

In social makeup, the *liberal center* was mainly middle class. It included salaried professionals, especially teachers and journalists, as well as many trade union officials. Because they identified labor with "the people," liberals were pro-labor. They saw trade unions as occupational and industrial pressure groups rather than as class organizations. The liberals generally believed that the labor leader was following a safe and sane policy, and they accepted the trade union status quo; that is to say, liberals would not use the unions for radical purposes. Finally, the liberals were the public that most reliably supported the policies pursued by the labor leader.

Not enough was known about the social makeup of the American *Communists* for Mills to describe them in detail. Suffice it to say that the Communists were the most important minor party in the union world and had already formed powerful cliques in several unions. Similar to the other political publics, the Communists also saw the unions as instruments for their aims. A mere 12% of the labor leaders holding general office in the unions were members of the American Communist Party (Mills, 1948, p. 196).

The *practical right* consisted of small businesspeople and constituted a well-organized segment of the Republican Party. The practical conservatives were the largest, most effectively organized, and the most respected of the political publics. They championed venture capitalism, and their goals were to make more money in business and to put down the labor leaders, the Communists, and other radicals who got in their way. The practical right was vehemently antiunion and fought labor because they resented labor's encroachment on their managerial activities. Mills contends that the apathetic masses, the politically passive people, were most aware of the political struggles between the liberal center and the practical right.

Lastly, the *sophisticated conservatives* were a shadowy group composed of the leaders of big business and finance capital who did not create political clamor, nor did they attempt to arouse the indignation of the mass public behind whose back the main drift was taking place. They left this task to the practical right. Instead, the sophisticated conservatives stealthily worked in and among the power elite, namely certain politicians, the chief executives of large corporations, and the military elite. As such, they tied in strongly with what Mills refers to as "the industry-armed forces-State Department axis." Believing that the main drift was in their favor, the sophisticated conservatives steered the nation toward a military economy as a way of avoiding an economic slump. In order to do this, they had to cunningly manipulate, and thus control, the labor unions and their labor leaders. They did so, first, by convincing labor unions that they were a stabilizing force and encouraging them to act as a counterforce against radical movements. Second, sophisticated conservatives took in the labor leaders as junior partners and used them as a front. In other words, they co-opted the labor leaders by having them join their personnel and public relations departments and, at the appropriate time, dismissed and replaced them with someone they perceived as more reliable. The object was to use the labor leaders to de-radicalize the workers, or to keep the Communists and other leftists away from them. The sophisticated conservatives reasoned that if they could handle the labor leaders and use their unions to keep the rank and file acquiescent, they could maintain their own until the war came again. In short, Mills sees the sophisticated conservatives and the practical right as strategic agents of the main drift.

Mills envisions the politics of American society in the middle of the 20th century as an engagement between the sophisticated conservatives and the liberal center, with the former getting the upper hand. This is the reason why Mills (1948) considers labor leaders to be part of a strategic elite. He believes they are the only ones who lead mass organizations that, during an economic slump, could organize the public and spark the beginnings of an egalitarian society built on the principles of immediate freedom and security. This would be a democratic society "in which everyone vitally affected by a social decision, regardless of its sphere, would have a voice in that decision and a hand in its administration" (p. 252). Ideally at least, such a society would be an arena in which politics would become so much a part of the lives of the workers, so connected with their daily work and their social routine, that political alertness would be part of their human consciousness as social beings.

As a way of achieving this society, Mills advocates that labor formulate democratic and egalitarian goals resulting in workers' control and social ownership of the economy. As such, he proposes a radical program of workers' control of industry that would halt the main drift toward the militarization of American culture. This program presents three alternatives: (1) shop-floor democracy, (2) economic planning, and (3) the formation of an independent labor party.

Shop-floor democracy requires increased union membership and solidarity so that workers could exert greater control over the social processes of their work. This means that in every workshop, plant, or office, the union workers would be involved in an independence of labor action, a self-regulation, which is to say that they would take over the tasks performed by owners of industry and their appointed managers and there would be no encroachment on shop organization by the state. The keystone of the democratic aim of unions, therefore, is control from below. The trade union would become the immediate political community of the workers, and within it issues directly affecting their daily lives would be posed for argument and decision.

Economic planning refers to the nationalization of the means of production and distribution in conjunction with the socialization—that is, the democratization—of the concrete organization of work. In Mills's view, socializing the means of production would further the humanization of the workers themselves. For it is in the workshop, more than in the electoral district, that the "new man" of a free society was to be developed.

The formation of an independent labor party is important to Mills for two reasons. First, the American labor movement had, since the 1930s—as a consequence of President Franklin D. Roosevelt's implementation of the New Deal programs designed to promote economic recovery and social reform—had its political power greatly restricted. Second, and related, without adequate political power, the alternative programs of shop-floor democracy and economic planning could not be implemented. According to Mills, the labor union had confined itself primarily to the role of mugwump (political independent) and lobbyist, pressuring the Republican and Democratic parties to guarantee labor's gains and secure more economic freedom. Thus, a labor party unaligned with either of the two major parties—that is, a party independent from the practical right and the liberal center—was needed to counteract the sophisticated conservatives' desire for a war-oriented economy. Labor's party would try to initiate, enlarge, and focus human autonomy beyond the sphere of production and the labor unions. It would be an agent in turning a collection of unions into a labor movement. For Mills, it was through the interlocking of the labor party and the union as a community that the political consciousness of the U.S. worker could be aroused. In sum, it was through these three programs—shop democracy, economic nationalization, and the creation of a labor party—that the trade unions would be taking political and economic action against the main drift.

The Economics of Cooperation and the Politics of Compromise

As Mills saw it, the labor leaders were tied to the structural changes occurring in American society, the sophisticated conservatives aligned themselves with the military, and America headed toward a social structure at once military and industrial that was integrated through the process of coordination. It will be recalled that in *Character and Social Structure* (Gerth & Mills, 1953), Mills views the coordination of the political, economic, and military orders as a master trend of postwar American society.

Labor leaders were caught between the drift toward a militarized capitalism and the oncoming of a complacent mass society. How the labor leaders would act in the face of these trends was the question Mills hoped to answer. According to him, a conflict arises when union leaders—despite professing a pro-labor ideology—increase their salary, change their lifestyle, gain prestige, and thereby go beyond the realm of their original reference group. These changes particularly affected their political behavior. What is more, labor leaders accepted the "rhetoric of liberalism," or the language common to political, business, and labor spokespersons that ensured their success. The liberal rhetoric, as applied to business–labor relations, has as its key word "cooperation." It states that if only labor and management manifested goodwill and showed intelligence in their dealings with one another, there would be no contradiction of interests but only cooperation, a sort of natural harmony between business and labor. This cooperative stabilization of the productive relations of the entire industry within the national economy implied a mutual goal for business and labor: to profit economically. Such success required compromise; that is to say, it necessitated adapting to the stability of commercial contracts and business deals. In short, the labor–management relationship was based on the economics of cooperation and the politics of compromise.

The formulaic chant of business leaders and union leaders was that, unless labor and management cooperate in the actual process of production and in the conduct of the monopoly economy as a whole, the Communists would take over. And while the mass public in the know-nothing atmosphere of the 1940s knew little or nothing about the Communists, they were nonetheless against them in the same way that they were against any radical or "un-American" idea, movement, or institution. The negative images of the Communists held by the mass public were obtained largely from the practical conservatives. Thus, in their cooperative efforts with business leaders, the labor leaders did not want to be stigmatized as Communist by their co-negotiators. Mills was convinced that the "coincidence of forces" between business and labor was the driving force behind the main drift.

Mills views the cartel-like arrangement between business and labor—a collaboration that was legitimized under governmental auspices—as being fueled by the slum–war–boom cycle and as leading the United States into a corporate form of the garrison state. The labor leaders did nothing to halt what Mills considered to be the coming establishment of a corporate state presiding over a permanent military economy. If anything, they had been taken in and misled by the liberal ideology and its rhetoric. Regrettably, "the liberal ideas which now prevail so widely are capable of leading those who take them seriously into a perilous adventure. Liberalism today often looks like a mantrap whose victims might well be collected in the hunting trips of the sophisticated conservatives" (Mills, 1948, p. 132). In order to counter the main drift, the union leaders would have to organize the white-collar workers into a coalition with the working class. Together they might arrest this trend toward a militarized economy.

Labor unions in the United States emphasized what Mills terms "business unionism." According to him, there was a basic affinity between business unionism and other types of established monopoly industry. Both had as their chief goal to do as well in a business way as they could. American labor unions were in the "business" of selling labor. As Mills (1948) sees it,

> the business unionist pursues his particular narrow interests with no thought for the interests of society or even for his own industry, much less for workers as a class. He has always been ready and willing to co-operate with some businessmen against other businessmen, other workers, and the community. (p. 117)

In Mills's view, the trade unions and their leaders were not politically radical at all. Rather, the labor leaders, as individuals and as a group, desired only to stabilize their power and position. Much to Mills's dismay, labor leaders were too conservative politically and too inhibited intellectually to seek the egalitarian, democratic society. Instead, labor leaders, bent on getting a larger cut of the economic pie, were quickly becoming absorbed into the national power system and had thus relinquished any aspirations for structural change in American society. The unions had been partly integrated into the new corporate-government complex as a junior partner due to certain structural shifts that had occurred in the economy.

Mills further believed that "bossism" and corruption within the unions had increased their tendency to engage in policies that were opportunistic. He voices concern about the growing authoritarianism and corruption in the ranks of organized labor since bossism and graft had made considerable inroads into trade union politics. Moreover, labor racketeering—in the form of embezzlement, bribery, and collusion with businesspeople—was used by labor leaders to improve their business position. These labor leaders, whom Mills (1948) calls "business unionists," were trying to make a bigger business out of the unions in the same way that the robber barons had made bigger businesses in 19th-century America. "The racketeering business unionist . . . will reward his personal friends in a personal pecuniary way, and he will punish his individual enemies in an individual way, by withholding from them the monetary fruits of business–labor co-operation" (p. 131).

To the business–labor partnership was added the influence of politics, thus forming a tripartite relationship of mutual benefit to all three sectors. At the local level, the machine politician provided legal protection in return for money from the union treasury and jobs for the political machine members provided by the labor leader. In addition, the businessman provided more money for the labor leader and for the machine politician. For Mills, the local business–labor–political cartel was the backbone of labor racketeering. In short, labor's political development as an independent force had been inhibited by both external changes that integrated it into the corporate-government complex and by internal changes that weakened its capacity for independent action. Mills holds that labor had been co-opted into a collaborationist policy with business and government, and this served to pave the way for the development of a corporate type of political economy.

Similarly, and on a scale beyond the municipality, Mills's argues that the nationwide cooperation between labor unions and business enterprises had come under governmental control. Thus, contrary to the liberal theory of the state, the government was not a neutral umpire using its impartial wisdom to effect a fair balance; instead, the federal government had become the regulator of the national labor force. Mills assumes that the federal government would outlaw strikes and compel arbitration of various kinds. Under such conditions, strikes would become more political than ever. Free collective bargaining would become less a contest between the economic powers of business and labor and more a contest between political pressures and influences.

Ultimately, the political program of the sophisticated conservatives, which treated everything as an object of profit, had global ramifications. Mills posits that the sophisticated conservatives were planning a program that amounted to the New Deal on a worldwide scale operated by big business. This "new" New Deal would be a war economy rather than a welfare economy, although the sophisticated conservative's liberal rhetoric might put the first in the guise of the second. Simply stated, the New Deal global plan for saving capitalism meant that instead of raising wages at home to give workers purchasing power, the plan was to subsidize capitalistic countries such as Japan, Germany, and Great Britain with politically guided loans paid for by the American people so that during a time of economic slump, U.S. business could control all investments. The end result would be that when confronted with the governmental encroachment upon labor–business relations, whether at the local, national, or global levels, the economic power of the unions would be drastically reduced.

Mills's Disillusionment With Labor

Mills had little confidence that the leaders of American labor would broker any opposition to the main drift. Indeed, he did not believe that they were politically alert to it. They had power but were not entirely certain what to do with it. Mills also accuses labor of lacking long-range comprehensive plans for social reconstruction. Thus, instead of being levelers for historical change, the labor leaders and their unions had become a conservative force as they take on the "the strategy of maximum adaptation," which is to say, they reacted more than they led. The labor union movement had become bureaucratized—politically and economically incorporated into the system—and there was little that ideologically distinguished the union leaders from those leaders in the political, corporate, and military spheres. What labor wanted was not an egalitarian society but an emulatory one in which it could adopt the consumption patterns of the money elite. This meant that the union leaders' chief function was to obtain higher wages and more benefits for its rank-and-file workers so that they could emulate the consumption patterns and lifestyles of the upper class. Mills attributes the labor leaders' craving for status and respect to a strong undercurrent in their personal lives. He believes that this craving stemmed from the fact that, compared with business leaders, most labor leaders had been "self-made men," were less well educated, and their incomes did not approach that of the business executive. They therefore felt socially inferior to the businessmen and less secure in their jobs. Furthermore, the labor leaders believed that, relative to the unions, business was more influential in national affairs because of the money it possessed. Thus, owing to their anxious character as well as to the tradition of the organizations they led, labor leaders initiated the standard middle-class businesslike mode of living. They thought that they could gain status only if they could securely hold power and class superiority.

The bottom line for Mills is that business unionism was not concerned with the underdogs—those who get the least of what there is to get—and he faults labor for not paying more attention to the problems of those who were poorly paid or unemployed and who were not members of unions nor eligible for their benefits. In short, labor had no utopian vision of the union community. The major tendency of the union leader, as an organization man, had been to move from the ideological program of political ideas that gave long-run answers to major political questions, to the expediency of practical politics based on short-run decisions. Similarly, the labor intellectual moved from ideas to career. Thus, as a consequence of their long-term pursuit of the short term, labor leaders and labor intellectuals had become active participants in the main drift.

As he examined more closely the inner workings of labor, Mills by the late 1940s began to lose faith in its ability to participate in a political movement and historically transform American society. He saw organized labor, in its opposition to the practical right, as being insidiously drawn into a political alliance with the sophisticated conservatives. In Mills's view, the liberal New Deal reforms were partly to blame, since they offered labor a place among the coalition of pressure groups and consequently destroyed its independent political action and radical activity. Indeed, Mills holds that of all the spokespeople, Franklin D. Roosevelt (at that time the major party politician of the 20th century) was the most expert with the liberal rhetoric. For Mills, the relation of the New Deal to labor was opportunistic. As such, it had left no durable instrument for liberal, much less radical, activity. The New Deal's effects had been to strengthen further the bossism of union leaders and to destroy labor's chances of engaging in independent political action.

By the mid-1950s, Mills's disillusionment with labor as an agent for radical change had reached fruition. He no longer saw the labor leaders as players in the higher circles of power. "[T]he current crop of labor leaders," he wrote in 1956, "is pretty well set up as a dependent variable in the main drift with no role in the power elite. Neither labor leaders nor labor unions are at the present juncture likely to be 'independent variables,' in the national context" (p. 265). Mills ends *The New Men of Power* (1948) on a pessimistic note as he acidly remarks, "Never has so much depended upon men who are so ill-prepared and so little inclined to assume the responsibility" (p. 291).

White Collar

His disenchantment with the leaders of labor unions notwithstanding, Mills remained steadfast in his search for agents of left-wing social and historical change. In the last chapter of *The New Men of Power* (1948), he begins to shift his attention from the labor movement of the working class to the white-collar professionals of the new urban middle class: "the crucial middle groups who hang in the balance and whose interests are one with the workers', but who are psychologically hard to win" (p. 277). Mills reasons that the labor intellectuals' failure to raise the workers' level of political awareness in order to fight the main drift had left middle-class leftward intellectuals—that is, college professors, journalists, and research technicians—as the last hope for American society to achieve a genuine democracy. Mills, therefore, continues his inquiry into the alliance of power and intellect, his exploration of the intellectuals' role in the stratification system that led him to investigate middle-class life in the great metropolis.

In Mills's view, the intellectual center of American culture at mid-century was New York City. It was there, he believed, that the important intellectual debates of the time, the main currents of political and cultural life, were being discussed. Mills had been an active participant in the intellectual circles of New York even before he arrived at Columbia University (indeed, since shortly after moving to Maryland in 1941). To be sure, his second major work, *White Collar,* was motivated by his desire to articulate his own experience in New York City. This book, which soon after its initial appearance in September 1951 became a huge commercial success, selling about 1,000 copies a month, exhibits a distinctive autobiographical tinge. The work clearly reveals Mills's attempt to forge a fusion, advocated through intellectual craftsmanship, between his personal and professional life. If read between the lines, *White Collar* is partly an account of how Mills's life experiences fed his sociological work; more generally, it is "the story of a Texas boy who came to New York" (Wakefield, 1971, p. 68). In the book, Mills quite obviously displays his great disdain for the all-pervasive distrust and self-alienation so characteristic of New Yorkers and other metropolitan people.

Quite beyond that, *White Collar* is a social psychological study of the new middle classes and their white-collar world: their place within the social structural context of mid-20th-century America. As such, the book covers many of the same themes previously examined by Riesman in *The Lonely Crowd* (1950), and that were later developed further by Whyte in *The Organization Man* (1956). In this, the second volume of his stratification trilogy, Mills strives to uncover how the economy's rationalization and bureaucratization affects the psychological character, the social biographies, and the social roles of the white-collar workers of the new middle class. Five years before it was published and with the manuscript still very much in progress, Mills described the book on white-collar workers as being a "book for the people":

> It is all about the new little man in the big world of the 20th century. It is about that little man and how he lives and what he suffers and what his chances are going to be; and it is also about the world he lives in, has to live [in], doesn't want to live in. It is, as I said, going to be everybody's book. For, in truth, who is not a little man? (as quoted in K. Mills & Mills, 2000, p. 101)

An Occupational Shift

Mills begins with the historical premise that the most decisive social transformation in the 20th century had been an occupational shift that began to take place in the class structure of the United States during the 19th century. Before the Civil War, business was composed of moneylenders and bankers, controlled by powerful vested interests in eastern urban centers. These early self-employed enterprisers also included merchants, speculators, shippers, and "cottage" manufacturers. Further down the occupational ladder was the worker who was apt to be a mechanic or journeyman and who looked forward to owning his own shop; or a farmer to whom manufacturing was a sideline, carried on sometimes as a cottage industry. Later, the industrialization of America, especially after the Civil War, gave rise to the captain of industry: the businessman who was an active owner of the business he had created and then managed. This was the era of classic liberalism, of laissez-faire, and of expanding capitalism. At this point in time, economic life was largely decentralized.

However, as American society became increasingly bureaucratized during the 20th century, and as corporate power became more centralized, the "old" middle classes of the small entrepreneurs that owned the property that they worked (i.e., free enterprisers such as small farmers, shopkeepers, independent professionals, and so forth) began to diminish in numbers and importance. As small business became smaller and big business became bigger, that is to say, as the United States was transformed from a nation of small proprietors to a nation of hired employees, the captains of industry (such as Andrew Carnegie, William H. Vanderbilt, J. P. Morgan, and the like) and other owner-operators gave way to different types of businessmen—what Mills refers to, in the manner of the ideal type, as the Manager, the Absentee Owner, the Corporation Executive, and the New Entrepreneur.

In addition, changes in the distribution and type of property affected the way the old middle classes lived, thus making the self-sustaining property owner increasingly rare. Liberalism's ideal for the domain of small "democratic" property that the owner worked was quickly being replaced by the "class" property that others were hired to work and manage. In the countryside, the old middle class that had consisted of small farmers became part of what Mills refers to as the "rural debacle," the polarization of the rural middle class into two factions: subsistence cultivators, wageworkers, and sharecroppers on the one hand, and big commercial farmers and rural corporations on the other. At the time that Mills was writing *White Collar,* the family-sized farm was quickly becoming a thing of the past.

In brief, the numerical decline of the old middle classes, both urban and rural—and their vanishing liberal heroes, the small businessmen and the small farmers—marked the decline of property and the emergence of occupation as the primary basis of stratification. Occupation rather than property was becoming the source of income for those who received any direct income. The possibilities of selling their services in the labor market, rather than of profitably buying and selling their property and its yields, began to determine the life-chances of most of the American middle class.

These structural and occupational changes—namely, bureaucratization and centralization as well as the consolidation of property holding—not only ended the union of property and work as a basis of people's essential freedom, it also signaled the incipient demise of the independent entrepreneur of the old middle classes. By the mid-20th century, bureaucratization and centralization had brought agribusiness to the countryside, and in the cities these structural changes made for the subsequent rise of a world of big organizations inhabited by the **new middle class,** or those propertyless white-collar workers involved primarily in sales and management and whose work situation was increasingly bureaucratized by the "command hierarchies" of business and government.

Mills notes that major shifts in occupations since the Civil War had assumed one industrial trend: As a proportion of the labor force, fewer individuals manipulated things, and more manipulated people and symbols. This shift in needed skills was another way of describing the rise of the white-collar workers, for their characteristic skills involved the handling of paper, money, and people. They were expert at dealing with people transiently and impersonally; they were masters of commercial, professional, and technical relationships. In short, the white-collar workers of the new middle class—which constituted about one-fourth of the labor force at the time Mills was writing—did not live by making things; rather, they lived off the social machineries that organized and coordinated the people who did make things. As propertyless, dependent employees, they planned, administered, recorded, distributed, and managed for others.

As a class of workers, the new middle class included corporate managers, clerical workers, and bureaucratic professionals such as salespeople and public relations specialists who were needed to manage, design, sell, and keep account of production. For them, as for wage workers, the United States had become a nation of employees for whom independent property ownership was no longer a viable option. Labor markets, not control of property, "determined their chances to receive income, exercise power, enjoy prestige, [and] learn and use skills" (Mills, 1951, p. 63). By the middle of the 20th century, the new middle class was becoming the dominant reality in American life, and the image of the big businessman as master builder and profit maker, as was previously the case with the captain of industry, no longer held. This generational shift in occupations, from free entrepreneur to dependent employee, is illustrated in *The Man in the Gray Flannel Suit* (Wilson, 1955), when the antihero, Tom Rath, informs his grandmother that he has applied for a job as a public relations expert with the United Broadcasting Company:

> "I'm thinking of going into business."
>
> "Your grandfather was very successful in business," she said. "At one time he owned a fleet of twenty-eight vessels. Are you going into shipping?"
>
> "No," Tom said. "This will be different, Grandmother." (pp. 20–21)

The rationalization, and more specifically, the bureaucratization, of Western civilization that Max Weber had foreseen, had centralized property ownership, producing a shift from independent property holding to dependent job holding. In other words, in the course of three or four generations, the United States had been transformed from a nation of free and independent small capitalists to a nation of employees hired to work in large corporations. The U.S. economy had become a bureaucratic cage in which bureaucratic types of organization men (and women) emerged.

Cheerful Robots

As previously discussed, Mills, in *Character and Social Structure* (Gerth & Mills, 1953), had explored what he regarded as one of the master trends of modern times: the psychological aspects of bureaucracy, by which he meant that white-collar workers working in large firms experienced feelings of frustration, despair, anxiety, and insecurity. Thus, much like Marx had found the proletariat, the industrial wageworkers of the mid-19th century, so Mills finds the new middle class, the white-collar professionals (e.g., salaried specialists of the clinic, junior partners in the law factory, captive engineers of the corporation) of the mid-20th century, to be powerless and alienated. They had become this way because, unlike the free entrepreneurs of the old middle classes of the 19th century, the white-collar workers of the new middle classes could not realize themselves in their work, for work had become a set of skills sold to another, rather than something mixed with their own property. For example, Mills contends that as the organization of the market becomes more formally rational, salespeople lose autonomy. They sell the goods of others and have nothing to do with the pricing. They are alienated from price fixing and product selection. Further, the last autonomous feature of selling—the art of persuasion and the accompanying sales personality—becomes expropriated from the individual salesperson.

Moreover, as the locus of power shifted from the propertied class to the hierarchies of large-scale institutions, explains Mills, the form of power concomitantly shifted from explicit authority to impersonal manipulation through management. Management took the form of subtle manipulation through an impersonalized and anonymous system of control. In this case, exploitation became less material and more psychological:

> Management is something one reports to in some office, maybe in all offices including that of the union; it is a printed instruction and a sign on a bulletin board; it is the voice coming through the loudspeakers; it is the name in the newspaper; it is the signature you can never make out, except it is printed underneath; it is a system that issues orders superior to anybody you know close-up; it blueprints, specifying in detail, your work-life and the boss-life of your foreman. Management is the centralized say-so. (Mills, 1951, p. 80)

These transformations of power stripped the white-collar workers of any control over their work. They lacked a sense of craftsmanship, of creating their own product. Just as the worker of 19th-century society did not own the machine but was controlled by it, so the middle-class person of the middle 20th century no longer owned the enterprise but was controlled by it. Indeed, the enterprise had come to seem autonomous, with a motive of its own: to manipulate everyone and everything in order to make a profit. The white-collar managers, clerks, and bookkeepers were cogs in a business machinery that had routinized greed and made aggression an impersonal principle of organization. They had become bureaucrats, professionalized occupants of specified offices and specialized tasks. Mills asserts that the white-collar salaried professionals were forced to accept the meaninglessness of their working life. In Marx's terms, they became alienated from power, work, and self.

Further, the more the middle classes experienced their life as one of powerlessness, the more apathetic and indifferent they became to politics of any kind. They were neither radical, nor liberal, nor conservative, nor reactionary. They were *inactionary,* that is to say, strangers to politics, and history was being made behind their backs. This state of affairs—which Mills believed was at the heart of the political malaise of the time—threatened the democratic and liberal spirit of the American past, which assumed that once given political rights, the individual citizen would naturally become politically alert and would act on his or her political interests. Only by breaking through the political indifference of the white-collar *salariat* (the class of workers receiving salaries) could their power be mobilized to promote the development of a peaceful industrial society. Unfortunately, this was not going to happen. Mills (1956) explains that "[t]he white collar middle classes do not form an independent base of power: economically, they are in the same situation as propertyless wage workers; politically they are in a worse condition, for they are not as organized" (p. 262).

Lacking what Marx called class consciousness—feeling that they belong together or that they can best realize their rational interests by combining— the middle classes have no awareness of their political means and ends. And because they possess no class consciousness they will not, indeed cannot, pose a significant challenge to the power structure of the economic elites. In short, says Mills, middle-class white-collar workers have become **cheerful robots**, a mass of confused and unfocused automatons adrift in a bureaucratic world not of their own making. Mills's implication is that middle-class America was drifting toward a bureaucratic age of organized irresponsibility.

The Managerial Demiurge

Mills sees the white-collar people as occupying the most ambiguous social positions in the stratification hierarchy of the United States. The images that members of the upper and lower strata had of the different occupational income levels was of big business at the top with labor at the bottom, and everyone else was thrown together into a vague "middle class." Indeed, there is no clearly identifiable middle class. These classes are diversified in social form, contradictory on material interest, dissimilar in ideological illusion, and there is no homogenous political base among them. White-collar people could not be adequately defined along any one possible dimension of stratification—skill, function, class, status, or power. Because they were generally in the middle ranges on each of these dimensions and on every descriptive attribute, their position was more definable in regard to their relative differences from other strata than in any absolute terms. Mills subdivides the new middle class into four occupational subcategories: office workers, salaried professionals, salespeople, and managers. According to him, these formed the ambiguous mass of white-collar employees.

Mills notes that as the means of administration were enlarged and centralized, there were more managers in every sphere of modern society, and the managerial type of person became more important in the total social structure. What Mills refers to as the **managerial demiurge** consists of those executives, "the new entrepreneurs," whose power is given and circumscribed by the hierarchical corporation for which they work. The new entrepreneurs are very much at home in the less tangible of the business services—commercial research and public relations, advertising agencies, labor relations, and the mass communication and entertainment industries. The new entrepreneurs are agents of the bureaucracy they serve, and they compete for the goodwill and favor of those who run the system. They do not usually stay within one corporate bureaucracy; their paths are within and between bureaucracies, in a kind of uneasy but calculated rhythm. They make a well-worn path between big business and the regulatory agencies of the federal government, especially its military establishment and political parties. The new entrepreneurs are "fixers" who use their own initiative and wile to create something where nothing was before. The power of the new entrepreneurs rests upon their personality and upon their skill in using it to manipulate the anxieties of the corporation chieftain. The new entrepreneurs' success or failure is decided by the personal anxieties and decisions of intimately known corporate chief executives.

The managerial demiurge involved not only business but also the professions, and in *White Collar* Mills maintains that in practically every profession— including the ministry, medicine, law, and the professoriate—the managerial demiurge worked to build ingenious bureaucracies of intellectual skills. Examining how the managerial demiurge operated in the academy, Mills contends that persons of brilliance, energy, and imagination were not often attracted to college teaching. He charges that the specialization required for successful operation as an academician is often deadening to the mind that would grasp for higher culture in the modern world. To make their mark, professors must specialize. Thus, a college faculty of several members is split into several departments, each autonomous, each guarded by the established or the almost-established professors who fear encroachment or consolidation of their specialty. According to Mills, academe has also produced its own new entrepreneurs. The new academic entrepreneurs further their careers in the university by securing prestige and small-scale powers outside of it. Above all, they are able to set up on the campus a respectably financed institute that brings the academic community into contact with people with a declared interest in political and social affairs, thus becoming the envy of their more cloistered colleagues and are looked to by them for leadership in university affairs.

In the chapter of *White Collar* entitled "Brains, Inc.," Mills examines that most far-flung and heterogeneous of all middle-class groups, the intellectuals. As people who specialize in symbols, the intellectuals produce, distribute, and preserve distinct forms of consciousness. They are the immediate carriers of art and of ideas. Intellectuals qua intellectuals live *for* and not *off* ideas. Mills, however, observes that after World War II, American intellectuals came to be affected with the malaise of a spiritual void. Indeed, the prosperity after the war, in which intellectuals shared, had become for them a time of moral slump. Attempts to reinstate the old pragmatic emphasis on the power of people's intelligence to control their own destiny had, by the 1950s, not been taken up by American intellectuals, racked as they were by new worries and anxieties. According to Mills, in order to understand what had been happening to American intellectual life, we have to realize the effects on intellectuals of three deep-lying, long-term trends of modern social and ideological organization. These three trends are part of the managerial demiurge.

First is the general trend that limits independence of intellect as it transforms the free-floating intellectual into a bureaucrat, a commodity of the large company. As the new bureaucracies—of state and business, of party and voluntary association—developed, they needed intellectuals to run their technical, editorial, and communication machinery. Thus, the new bureaucracies became the major employers of intellectuals and the main customers for their work. Involved in opinion molding, the communications intellectuals (idea persons, technicians, administrators) at the top of the bureaucracy blended with the managerial demiurge in more concrete businesses. This meant that the styles of work and life of intellectuals and managers, as well as their dominating interests, coincided at many points. More significantly, it meant that intellectuals, as hired employees in the information industry—namely in publishing and entertainment—were no longer free to speak their minds in dissent. As Mills puts it, the freedom of the freelance intellectuals is minimized when they go to market, and if they do go, their freedom is without public value.

Mills also sees the trends limiting independence of intellect at work in the large universities. The real restraints on the professors' academic freedom, says Mills (1951), do not involve obvious external prohibitions such as firing; instead, they are more insidious and involve "manipulative control of the insurgent by the agreements of academic gentlemen" (p. 151). As a consequence, there developed a vague general fear that led to self-intimidation and that finally turned into a kind of voluntary censorship that academic intellectuals unconsciously imposed on their own teaching and research.

Second, the recent bureaucracies had an ideological demand for the creation and diffusion of new symbolic fortifications for the new and largely private powers these bureaucracies represented. Acting as the mouthpiece for the corporation, the intellectual's job was to compose myths—that is, acceptable ideas, attractive modes of statement of interests, passions, and hatreds—that would be disseminated among the mass publics and that would serve the vested interests of the bureaucracy and those who work in it. Further, Mills posits that since the middle classes were filled with anxieties and the need for new opinions of the new world of bureaucracies making irresponsible decisions, or for diversion from it, it was the intellectuals' task to divert the middle classes and keep them oriented to an appropriate manner despite their deep fears and anxieties.

The third social development (and one that Whyte, in *The Organization Man* [1956], was to explore in greater detail some 5 years later) that Mills believed placed constraints on the intellectual's freedom has to do with the victory of the technician over the intellectual. As Mills sees it, intellectuals have become administrators, idea persons, and goodwill technicians working in big companies and joining the expanding world of those who live off, rather than for, ideas. The intellectual, remarks Mills, is becoming a technician, an idea person, rather than one who resists the environment, preserves the individual type, and defends himself or herself from death-by-adaptation. Mills (1951) says the following about the intellectual-turned-technician:

> In class, status, and self-image, he has become more solidly middle class, a man at a desk, married, with children, living in a respectable suburb, his career pivoting on the selling of ideas, his life a tight little routine, substituting middle-brow and mass culture for direct experience of his life and his world, and, above all, becoming a man with a job in a society where money is supreme. (p. 156)

These three trends of the managerial demiurge—the bureaucratic context, the ideological demand, and the rise of the technician—which lead to the constraint and rationalization of intellect, also defeat and make powerless the intellectuals. "The defeat of the free intellectuals and the rationalization of the free intellect have been at the hands of an enemy who cannot be clearly defined" (Mills, 1951, p. 160).

Character and Personality

Mills is at his sociological best when he analyzes and dissects the white-collar workers' style of life. In so doing, he identifies several character types found within the white-collar strata of the new urban culture who are involved with selling (making up "The Great Salesroom") and with the handling of people (understood in terms of the "personality market"). As the shift in the direction of business from production to sales continued to take place, and as the gap between mass production and individual consumption widened, the art of selling had become a lifestyle that turned the country into a great salesroom where its corporate executives were driven by an intense obsession with selling all sorts of commodities.

Mills states that the "new society" of the postwar era had not only transformed itself into a fabulous salesroom, but it had also become the biggest bazaar in the world. He asserts that in this new society of employees, selling was a pervasive activity where everyone had become a salesperson. In the business world, the sales hierarchy consisted of several levels. At the top are the "Prima Donna Vice-Presidents" of corporations who boast that they are merely salesmen. Next in the hierarchy are the "Distribution Executives" who design, organize, and direct the selling techniques of sales forces. Close to them are the "absentee salesmen" who create the slogans and images that spur sales from a distance by mass media. At the bottom of the sales hierarchy are the five-and-dime-store "salesgirls" who work part-time for several months before leaving their jobs for marriage.

Mills introduces the reader to a lively panorama of salesgirl social types who work in the large department stores of big cities. These types of salesgirls (actually, they were women, between 18 and 30 years of age) are "The Wolf," "The Charmer," "The Ingénue Salesgirl," "The Collegiate," "The Drifter," "The Social Pretender," and "The Old-Timer." While these typologies describe different sales personalities, most of the social types have one thing in common: They attempt to identify and borrow prestige from customers. This attempt usually fails for three reasons. First, most customers are strangers, so the contact with them is brief. Second, class differences are frequently accentuated by the sharp and depressing contrast between home and store, customer, or commodity. Third, being "at their service" and "waiting on them" is not conducive to easy and gratifying identification with the customers. The result is that the salesgirl ends up seeing the customer as her psychological enemy, rather than the store as her economic enemy. At bottom, the salesgirls experience a feeling of powerless depression and an intense hatred of their customers.

Mills next pays closer attention to the psychological aspects of white-collar work. He states that in the new society of hired employees, people first of all sell their services on the labor market. The employers of many white-collar jobs, especially sales work, not only buy the employees' services but also their social personalities, and thus they produce that most decisive effect and symptom of the great salesroom, *the personality market*.

Customers, therefore, come to know the salesclerk not as a person but as a commercial mask, a stereotyped greeting and appreciation for patronage. Kindness and friendliness become aspects of personalized service or of public relations of big firms, rationalized in order to make a sale. With anonymous insincerity, the successful salespersons make an instrument of their own appearance and personality. Loyalty to the anonymous organization requires that salespeople be friendly, helpful, and courteous at all times. The smile behind the sales counter is a commercialized lure. In *White Collar*, Mills shows great contempt for the world of the cheerful robot's painted-on smiles where everyone pretends interest in others in order to manipulate them. From *The Man in the Gray Flannel Suit* (Wilson, 1955), we learn something about this world's rationalized, artificial politeness:

"Mr. Hopkins is busy," the gray-haired woman said to Walker, and smiled. Everybody in this building smiles, Tom thought—even Ogden managed a thin little twinge of the lips whenever he spoke. It must be a company rule. (p. 40)

The imposition of a sales personality upon the employees, Mills argues, not only stifles their creativity, it also contributes to their estrangement. For example, contrary to the classic heroes of liberalism, that is, the small businessmen and small farmers, the salesgirls of the new society cannot form their character by promotional calculations and self-management. Consequently, in the normal course of her work, because her personality becomes the instrument of an alien purpose, the salesgirl becomes self-alienated.

Alienation and Status Panic

Mills (1951) further describes the white-collar workers' alienated world as **the enormous file**, an impersonal administrative hierarchy consisting of an army of clerks and a cadre of managers, divided according to specialized and standardized tasks performed in various divisions and units. The enormous file, with its extreme form of human mechanization and social rationalization, is most graphically illustrated by multiple offices with rows of identical desks within the skyscraper where "the paper webwork is spun; a thousand rules you never made and don't know about are applied to you by a thousand people you have not met and never will" (p. 189).

As a result of the alienating conditions of modern work—the bureaucratic routinization of productivity, management's subtle manipulative grip over the employee, the managerial demiurge, the rise of personality markets, and the growth of the enormous file—for the mass of employees, work had a generally unpleasant quality. And because there existed a separation between the product and the processes of work, white-collar professionals had never acquired a sense of craftsmanship—of meaning and gratification—from their jobs. Indeed, one of the most crucial psychological implications of the structural decline of the old middle classes was that the Protestant ethic, the work compulsion, of the old middle-class entrepreneurs had not deeply gripped the new middle classes. For them, work had no intrinsic meaning and provided no gratification. According to Mills, the white-collar personnel of the enormous file, that uniform mass working in a soundless office or salesroom where the day itself is regulated by an impersonal time schedule, sought instead to derive meaning and gratification from their leisure time.

In the society of employees, the Protestant work ethic had come to be replaced by a leisure ethic. Thus, the white-collar people relentlessly pursue pleasure outside work only to be bored at work and restless at play. Mills (1951) baldly describes the modern workers' dilemma: "Each day men sell little pieces of themselves in order to try to buy them back each night and week end with the coin of 'fun'" (p. 237). The cycle of work and leisure gives rise to two quite different images of self: the everyday image, based upon work, and the holiday image, based upon leisure. The leisure of the white-collar middle classes diverts them from the restless grind of their work with the absorbing grind of passive enjoyment of glamour and thrills. To the modern worker, leisure is the way to spend money; work is the way to make it. When the two compete, says Mills, leisure wins hands down.

Succinctly put, Mills's main thesis in *White Collar* is that by the middle of the 20th century, occupation, which involves the selling of services on the labor market, had come to replace property as the source of income for the white-collar worker. However, because the income of the salaried white-collar workers was not significantly higher than the wages of the lower-class blue-collar workers, in order to distinguish their social position, the former became dependent on **status**, or prestige. Mills contends that the white-collar workers, as they find themselves in their propertyless class situation and as their situation relative to that of the working class became more indistinct, were suddenly struck by a panic for status. He argues that by the 1950s, status had become even more insecure than before, and psychologically the white-collar employee was transformed into "the little individual scrambling to get to the top" (p. 309).

According to Mills, the enjoyment of prestige was often "disturbed and uneasy" because its basis, expression, and gratification were subject to strain that often took the form of a virtual "status panic." As a consequence of the status panic, the white-collar strata frantically sought to *borrow* prestige. It did so in three ways: (1) by associating with those of higher status: entrepreneurs, supervisors, and other higher-ups in the managerial cadre; (2) from the firms and the companies for which they worked (in the case of the salesclerk, the prestige source included the merchandise itself as well as the store); and most significantly, (3) by attaining a relatively high level of education. Thus, for the white-collar salariat, formal, and sometimes expensive education in high school and "business college" became the primary vehicle for upward social mobility. "For the new middle class," Mills (1951) writes, "education has replaced property as the insurance of social position" (p. 245). Whereas the object of schooling during the 19th century was to turn out "the good citizen" that could participate in a "democratic republic," in the new society of the mid-20th century, the goal of education was to produce "the successful man" in a "society of specialists with secure jobs" (p. 266).

The New Little Man

This bleak and pitiful portrait of the postwar American middle classes that Mills paints in *White Collar* is aptly depicted on the book's black-and-white dust jacket. In this photo, which was taken by Mills himself, we see toward the bottom a solitary white-collar man—representative of the new middle class—in his long overcoat and fedora, dwarfed by the big-city landscape as he hurries past the National City Bank on Wall Street. Four years later, when *The Man in the Gray Flannel Suit* made its appearance, Tom Roth muses,

> I really don't know what I was looking for when I got back from the war, but it seemed as though all I could see was a lot of bright young men in gray flannel suits rushing around New York in a frantic parade to nowhere. They seemed to be pursuing neither ideals nor happiness—they were pursuing a routine. For a long while I thought I was on the side lines watching that parade, and it was quite a shock to glance down and see that I too was wearing a gray flannel suit. (Wilson, 1955, p. 272)

Mills (1951) contends that by examining white-collar life, something can be learned about what is becoming more typically "American." We can "understand better the shape and meaning of modern society as a whole, as well as the simple hopes and complex anxieties that grip all the people who are sweating it out in the middle of the twentieth century" (p. xv). In order to comprehend the diverse, quite often Kafkaesque, white-collar worlds of the new middle class, we have seen that Mills pictures society as a great salesroom, an enormous file, an incorporated brain, a new universe of management and manipulation. The "new little man," the product of these impersonal white-collar worlds, declares Mills, "seems to have no firm roots, no sure loyalties to sustain his life and give it a center. . . . Perhaps because he does not know where he is going, he is in a frantic hurry; perhaps because he does not know what frightens him, he is paralyzed with fear" (p. xvi). Tom Roth is exemplary of the new little man who works along unnoticed in somebody's office, never talking loud, never talking back, never taking a stand:

> I'm just a man in a gray flannel suit. I must keep my suit pressed like anyone else, for I am a very respectable young man. . . . I will go to my new job, and I will be cheerful, and I will be industrious, and I will be matter-of-fact. I will keep my gray flannel suit spotless. I will have a sense of humor. I will have guts—I'm not the type to start crying now. (Wilson, 1955, p. 98)

In the final analysis, despite its phenomenal success and its rich descriptive detail concerning the American middle classes, *White Collar* is not a book of high theoretical value. As Horowitz (1983) points out, "*White Collar* is more interesting for the ways in which it reveals the ethos of the early 1950s than for its explanation of that ethos" (p. 253).

The Power Elite

In his most famous and controversial book, *The Power Elite* (1956)—a social psychological study of stratification focusing on a tripartite ruling stratum in America—Mills continues discussing the issues that he had previously raised in *The New Men of Power* and *White Collar*. The book's central theme is that, as the institutional means of decision, information, and power became more centralized and efficient, and as the public became more politically uninformed, there had arisen a national group made up of a governing triumvirate, a **power elite,** with tiers and ranges of wealth and power of which people in the rest of society knew very little.

Before entering into a detailed discussion of Mills's assessment of this ruling stratum, it is important to point out his personal prejudices against the elite of power. "Ever since I can remember," he states candidly and straightforwardly, "I have had a constitutional inability to sympathize with the upper dogs, and a temperamental distrust of all of them" (as quoted in K. Mills & Mills, 2000, p. 250).

Mills (1956) identifies these upper dogs, the power elite of U.S. society, as constituting "those political, economic, and military circles which as an intricate set of overlapping cliques share decisions having at least national consequences. In so far as national events are decided, the power elite are those who decide them" (p. 18).

Put another way, the power elite are that often inaccessible small group of individuals and families who possess more than others do of what there is to possess, which generally includes money, power, and prestige, as well as all the lifestyles—that is, the experiences, privileges, and trainings—which these resources provide. These families, as members of the upper stratum of a capitalistic society, are quite insulated from the economic jolts and lurches felt by members of the other social classes. Since Mills defines the power elite in terms of institutional position, he sees them as occupying pivotal positions in the three major hierarchies and organizations of modern society—namely, (1) the machinery of the state, (2) the big corporations, and (3) the military establishment. Accordingly, as members of the *political directorate,* the *corporate rich,* and the *high military,* the U.S. power elite are selected, trained and certified, and permitted to preside over the strategic command posts in the structure of American society. They command the dominant institutions of a dominant nation and are in a position to make decisions of enormous consequence for the underlying populations of the world and to determine the course of events. The public often does not know that these decisions are being made until well after the fact. Mills (1956) relies on a Weberian view of power when he refers to the power elite as "those who are able to realize their will, even if others resist it" (p. 9). In short, the power elite are people of power within the coordination of political, economic, and military decision.

Mills makes it clear, however, that the American power elite do not constitute a secret club of personal friends with a permanent membership and fixed and formal boundaries. Nor does he believe that they form one monolithic structure. Instead, he sees the power elite as a complex set of variously related and often antagonistic cliques: unified only on certain coinciding points and mostly during periods of crisis. For Mills, the American power elite is not a bloc of conscious and malicious conspirators most of the time, for that is unnecessary. Instead, he argues that a community of interests, a commonality of values, and control of basic social institutions enable the power elite to coordinate policy without planning and plotting in smoke-filled rooms in the wee hours of the morning. Nevertheless, despite the fact that their continued association is marked by common beliefs and social congeniality, Mills refers to the power elite as involving an "uneasy coincidence" between the big three domains of power: the political, economic, and military orders.

Their uneasy coincidence notwithstanding, the power elite does tend to form a coherent kind of grouping, with an anonymous "inner core" made up of select individuals who interchange commanding roles at the top of one dominant institutional order with those in another. For example, the military chief of staff becomes a corporate chairman of the board, and the chief executive officer of a major business corporation also functions as a member of the president's cabinet. The unity of the American power elite, therefore, consists of the ease of interchangeability of personnel within the political, economic, and military institutions. This is especially true of the movement of representatives of the corporate world into and out of top political positions. Consider, for instance, that Donald Regan of Merrill-Lynch became Ronald Reagan's Chief of Staff and Robert Rubin of Goldman Sachs became Bill Clinton's Secretary of the Treasury. Moreover, Dick Cheney, Vice President in the George W. Bush administration, had previously been Chairman of the Board and Chief Executive Officer of Halliburton, the oil-field services contractor used by the U.S. government during the Iraq conflict; and Rahm Emanuel, Barack Obama's Chief of Staff from 2008 to 2010, had previously been an investment banker with Wasserstein Perella.

Additional examples of this interchangeability in the bureaucracies of power and decision include the following secretaries of defense who served during the Nixon, Ford, Carter, Reagan, George H. W. Bush, Clinton, George W. Bush, and Obama administrations, and their influential involvement in the corporate arena subsequent to leaving political office:

- Melvin Laird led the Pentagon under President Richard Nixon and sat on the boards of Science Applications International and the IDS Mutual Fund Group.
- James Schlesinger, Nixon's second defense secretary, was a senior advisor at Lehman Brothers and a trustee of the Mitre Corporation.
- Donald Rumsfeld, Secretary of Defense under Presidents Ford and George W. Bush, was an investment banker with Forstmann, Little; an advisor to General Instrument Corp., and a director of RAND Corporation.
- Harold Brown, defense secretary during the Carter administration, after leaving office served as director of IBM and as a partner in the venture-banking firm Warburg Pincus.
- Casper Weinberger, defense secretary under Ronald Reagan, was a counsel with the law firm of Rogers and Wells, representing major corporations.
- Frank Carlucci was Secretary of Defense under Reagan and afterward served as a key executive with the Carlyle Group, a merchant-banking firm backed by the Mellon family, and sat on the board of the Kaman Corporation and Westinghouse.
- Robert Gates, Secretary of Defense under President Obama, has been a member of the board of trustees of Fidelity Investments, and on the board of directors of NACCO Industries, Inc., Brinker International, Inc., and the Parker Drilling Company.

We now look, in turn, at each of the three higher circles—the political elite, the corporate elite, and the military elite—and the social types of decision makers involved in each domain.

The Political Elite

The **political elite,** or the *political directorate,* consists of higher politicians and key officials of government but in particular the president, vice president, and the members of the cabinet. It also includes the White House staff as well as the most important appointed heads of major regulatory agencies and commissions. Indeed, the executive branch of government was far more influential at the time that Mills was writing than at any previous period in U.S. history, and there were no signs of its power diminishing. Mills attributes the political directorate's increased power to two factors: (1) the massive growth of the federal bureaucracy since the beginning of the

New Deal in 1933 and (2) the greatly enhanced role of the president in making foreign policy after 1939.

The political elite consists of politicians likely to have reached their positions through appointments rather than elections. Mills notes that the Eisenhower administration was largely made up of "political outsiders," members and agents of the corporate rich and the high military who were appointed to their political posts and who had never before held office. Indeed, in that administration, 36% of the higher politicians had been elected, 50% had been appointed, and 14% had never before held any political office. Aside from occupying the executive command posts of the political order and forming the political directorate, the political elite are also the legal, managerial, and financial members of the corporate elite.

The Corporate Elite

The second group composing the triangle of power, the **corporate elite,** or *corporation chieftains,* consists of persons who occupy the top command posts in the giant corporations. The corporate elite also includes top-level management, the major stockholders, and the corporate lawyers representing the largest financial and industrial corporations in the country. At the very top stratum of the mid-century U.S. economy were the high-ranking executives, the "corporate rich," who manage the corporate complexes and make the key economic decisions. These corporation chieftains receive fabulous salaries as well as bonuses, either in stock or in cash, and often in installments over a period of years. As such, they come to inhabit a corporate world of privilege and prerogative.

Behind this corporate wealth, there is that class of people that Mills calls "the very rich," who are the actual owners of the corporations and the recipients of the greatest monetary rewards. Among the very rich during the middle years of the 20th century were men like H. L. Hunt and Hugh Roy Cullen, both of whom were worth billions. By that time, the very rich had become deeply entrenched in the higher corporate world of the American economy and were involved in such corporation activities as promoting and managing, directing and speculating. Indeed, all of the people and families of great wealth were by the 1950s identified with large corporations in which their property was seated. The corporate rich thus includes members of the big-city rich and the national rich who possess the great American fortunes, as well as chief executives of the major corporations. Most of the money that the very rich receive comes from corporate property: from dividends, capital gains, estates, and trusts. Mills (1956) maintains that no one can become or stay rich in America without becoming involved, in one way or another, in the world of the corporate rich. Put another way, "all the rich are now corporate rich," many of whom "possess far more money than they can personally spend with any convenience" (pp. 150, 161).

What is more, Mills states that the corporate rich have translated the power of corporate property into political use. To be sure, many of them have historically served as unofficial advisors to politicians. As the corporate world became more intricately involved in the political order, these executives became intimately associated with the politicians, and especially with the key politicians who form the political directorate of the United States government. In addition, as increasing numbers of corporation chieftains enter government directly, the result is the emergence of a new political economy at the apex of which are situated those who represent the corporate rich, the political elite.

The Military Elite

Finally, Mills argues that as military men became more powerful during the wars and during the warlike interludes between, they, too, joined the power elite. Consequently, the third sector of his ruling triumvirate is the **military elite,** or the *warlords* of Washington, who oversee the largest and most expensive feature of the U.S. government, the military order. At the top of the military order's bureaucracy, just below the president and the secretary of defense, is the military board of directors, the Joint Chiefs of Staff. Immediately below the Joint Chiefs there is a circle of generals and admirals presiding over the elaborate and dispersed military forces as well as the economic and political liaisons necessary to maintain those forces. Thus, alongside the corporation chieftains and the political directorate, the generals and admirals of the Pentagon have gained and have been given increased power to make and to influence decisions of the gravest consequence.

Mills points out that since 1939, the United States had become a militarized society as it had millions of personnel continuously under arms, supporting a huge and far-flung military apparatus, and often acting aggressively as a consequence. World War II and the protracted Cold War had greatly increased the power of the military, and the militarization of American society was due to the United States' rise to international political prominence. The Joint Chiefs of Staff, along with the munitions contractors who supply them with weapons, comprised a new and potent force in making the key decisions regarding U.S. foreign policy and international relations. Indeed, the military and corporate elites became political insiders serving as the president's most influential advisors. As politics gets into the army, Mills maintains, the army gets into politics. This movement of the warlords into diplomatic and political circles is what Mills refers to as the "politicalization" of the high military.

As will be recalled, Mills in *The New Men of Power* (1948) argued that the United States was rapidly becoming a garrison state. Now, in *The Power Elite,* he again warns of a new corporatism—directed by the political, industrial, and military elites—that points to the main drift of the 20th century: the great structural shift of modern American capitalism toward a continuous war footing as a way of handling the slump–boom cycle. The merger of the corporate economy and the military bureaucracy—the economic–military alliance—first occurred during World War II as the warlords intervened in political and economic matters in a truly decisive way. Mills explains that given the nature of modern warfare, the warlords had to become politically and economically involved whether they wanted to or not, just as they had to invite the corporate chiefs into the military. For unless the military sat in on corporate decisions, they could not be sure that their programs would be carried out, and unless the chief executives knew something of the war plans, they could not plan war production. Thus, as generals advised corporate executives and as corporate executives advised generals, the economic and military hierarchies became structurally and deeply interrelated. The result is that the U.S. economy was being transformed into a permanent military economy.

Mills further contends that world reality is principally cast in the warlord's terms. This state of affairs has led to the general adoption of a military definition of political and economic reality, a **military metaphysic,** where everything in the world situation is officially defined in terms of military necessity. The military metaphysic has not only resulted in the elite shifting its focus from domestic problems to "defense" and international affairs, but it has also resulted in the elite considering problems of war and peace, more completely than ever before, as political problems. In addition, Mills posits that the enlargement of the political role of the high military in key decisions threatens the democratic process in the United States in two ways. First, the pervasiveness of the military metaphysic is so strong that it does not permit free and wide debate of military policy. Americans have come to believe that international conflicts can be resolved only by force or the threat of force and that no further discussion on the matter is necessary. Second, Mills argues that information given by the military to the secretary of defense, the president, and his advisors is withheld from the general public. Such secrecy makes it difficult to have a politically informed citizenry.

On the lower echelons, the political, economic, and military elite fade off into the middle levels of power, into the pressure groups that are not vested in the power elite itself as well as a multiplicity of regional, state, and local interests. Further, as the executive branch of government becomes more dominant, the legislative branch, Congress, as well as the judicial branch, the U.S. Supreme Court, are likewise relegated to the middle levels of national power. In fact, these middle levels—which also include the labor unions, all consumers, and all major white-collar groups—are really quite powerless. Mills considers them to be in a "semi-organized stalemate," unable to link the top with the bottom. Furthermore, the bottom level of society is politically fragmented, increasingly powerless, and in danger of becoming a mass society that subverts democratic principles.

The subtle transformation into a mass society subject to elite control and domination is being accomplished behind people's backs, declares Mills. By using the mass media, the power elite are able to persuade people into believing that, through the democratic process, they have made the key decisions, when in fact they have not. Rather, it is the power elite who determine the course of historical events. The decisions that the political directorate, the corporate chieftains, and the warlords make or fail to make carry more consequences for more people than has ever been the case in the history of humanity. This centralization of the means of power in the three interlocking and coordinated directorates—the machinery of the state, the big corporations, and the military establishment—makes for a trend toward a totalitarian state. Thus, Mills argues that political publics have every reason to hold the American power elite accountable for a decisive range of historical events that make up the history of the present. However, in the conservative mid-1950s, at the height of the Great Celebration of American society, and when Mills was writing *The Power Elite,* it was "fashionable" to suppose that there was no power elite.

The Higher Immorality

Much like he had done previously with the union leaders, Mills paints a collective, social psychological portrait of the elite of power. He posits that they constitute a similarity of personality types who hold the values and make the policies that they do because of the similarity of their origins; lifestyles; education; the bureaucratic institutions' influence on them; as well as the intersection of the four dimensions of stratification: class, status, power, and occupation.

In the big cities like Boston, New York, Philadelphia, Baltimore, and San Francisco, there flourishes a recognizable upper class of old and new wealthy families—the so-called "metropolitan 400"—from which the national power elite is derived. Chosen for their money, their family name, and their lifestyle, the members of these wealthy families are included in *The Social Register,* a listing of people who, by descent or social standing, are established in the proper society of any particular city or cities. The elite of wealth are predominantly White, Anglo-Saxon, and Protestant.

The processes of socialization and co-optation are important in understanding the power elite. According to Mills, since they are largely recruited from the upper classes, the power elite's socialization depends upon a network of upper-class wealth that supports private schools, elite universities, country clubs, and vacation resorts, which most of them experience before they are co-opted into the higher circles of power. The fashionable boarding or "prep" school becomes a training ground for the socialization of the children of the power elite. It is here that they are taught not only the proper style of conduct, but also how to acquire the upper-class character. To be sure, the prep school is the most important agency for transmitting the traditions of the upper social classes as well as for regulating the admission of new wealth and talent into the power elite. The same holds true for higher education and thus the corporation chieftains, for example, are likely to have graduated from the exclusive Ivy League colleges such as Harvard, Princeton, and Yale. Similarly, many of the generals and admirals of the Pentagon have attended one of the two most elite training schools of the armed forces, West Point and Annapolis. Education at these military academies produces a commonality of outlook and an uncritical adherence to the military metaphysic.

Because they share certain psychological (mental and ideological) and sociological (demographic) traits, the power elite is a fairly homogenous group of individuals. Its members' similarities of social origin, nativity, and education are important to their psychological and social affinities; that is to say that the individuals who occupy the top positions in the state, the corporation, and the military establishment are broadly similar in social background and outlook, and this develops in them character of a specific type. Mills further posits that not only does the power elite rest upon the social and psychological affinities of its members, but it also coalesces around their personal and official relations with one another. Thus, more important than their social and psychological affinities are their shared codes and criteria of admission, praise, honor, and promotion. In other words, through their continued association with one another, they feel responsibility to each other. What binds the American power elite together, then, are an internal discipline and a community of interests.

Perhaps Mills's most trenchant critique of the most wealthy and powerful members of the United States' political, corporate, and military echelons is his insistence that they are engaging in what he terms the **higher immorality**. The higher immorality has to do with the "crackpot realism"—the unrealistic decisions and unethical and corrupt behaviors—of the power elite. It involves the American system of organized irresponsibility that has produced a general erosion of the old middle-class values and codes of uprightness. The wealthy and powerful, says Mills, are irresponsible, predatory, and morally ruthless in their unprecedented use of power and in their pursuit of easy money and estate building. The only value that they hold is the value of money and of the things that money can buy. The power elite, according to Mills, is engaged in white-collar crime—smart rackets and shady deals—and in that which is "merely expedient." Accordingly, it fails to produce people with an inner moral sense, a conscience, and personal integrity. Mills is struck by the fact that despite this structural immorality and the widespread corruption characteristic of the power elite, the mass public is not morally indignant. In fact, the complacent mass public couldn't care less about the higher immorality.

The Power Elite is by far Mills's most controversial book. It is the book that Fidel Castro told Mills, during Mills's visit to Cuba in August 1960, that he, Castro, had studied during his guerrilla campaign in the Sierra Maestra (1957–1958). It may be said that, in sum, *The Power Elite* is principally concerned with the structure of power in the United States and the position of the power elite within it.

Diversity in the Power Elite

In 1956, Mills found a power elite that was largely, if not exclusively, WASP (White Anglo-Saxon Protestant) and male. These White, Christian men were principally recruited from "the upper third of the income and occupational pyramids" (Mills, 1956, p. 279). Half a century after Mills's *The Power Elite* made its debut, social scientists Richard L. Zweigenhaft and G. William Domhoff (2006) examined whether the 1960s social movements for equal opportunity and affirmative action policies changed the power elite in regard to gender, ethnicity, race, religion, and sexual orientation. And if so, what effects has this new diversity had on the functioning of the power elite and on its relation to the rest of society?

While it is the case that the power elite in the United States became more diversified in the late 1980s and early 1990s, Zweigenhaft and Domhoff (2006) look specifically at Jews, women, African Americans, Latinos, Asian Americans, and gay men and lesbians to see to what extent these previously excluded groups now occupy positions in the political, corporate, and military elites. Although Mills did not see Congress and the U.S. Supreme Court as belonging to the power elite proper (but rather to what he considered the "middle levels" of power), Zweigenhaft and Domhoff examine Congress and the Supreme Court for two reasons. First, and contrary to Mills, they consider Congress and the Supreme Court to be key institutions within the power elite. Second, they are keen to know if there is more diversity in the legislative and judicial systems than in the political, corporate, and military elite.

Jews

Jews in the United States have in the past few decades achieved full representation, even overrepresentation, in the power elite, Congress, and the Supreme Court. The successful assimilation of Jews into the highest circles of power is all the more noteworthy because of the widespread religious discrimination that persisted until the years following the publication of Mills's *The Power Elite* in 1956.

For example, in 2004, the percentage of Jews in the U.S. population was only 2.2%, yet they made up 11.1% of the corporate elite (Zweigenhaft & Domhoff, 2006, p. 22). Zweigenhaft and Domhoff found that Jews who were successful in the corporate world had been even more likely than other Jews to assimilate; they were less likely to see Jewishness as a salient part of their identity. For Jews at the top of the class hierarchy, class had come to supersede religious identity.

With the exception of Presidents Ronald Reagan and George H. W. Bush, who had no Jews in their cabinets, each presidential cabinet since 1956 has included at least one Jewish person. Jimmy Carter appointed four. Bill Clinton appointed five during his two terms in office. George W. Bush appointed one, to the newly created Department of Homeland Security. In 2009, Barack Obama appointed three Jews to cabinet-level positions: Secretary of the Treasury, Director of the Office of Management and Budget, and White House Chief of Staff.

At the time that Mills published *The Power Elite* in 1956, there were only two Jews in the Senate. By 2009, the 111th Congress consisted of 45, with 13 in the Senate and 32 in the House. The steady increase in the number of Jews in Congress (8.4% of all members in 2009) means that their numbers are considerably higher than the percentage of Jews in the general U.S. population (2.1% in 2009). And as for the U.S. Supreme Court, since 1916, when Louis D. Brandeis was appointed associate justice, a total of eight Jewish justices have served the Court. In 2010, there were three Jewish justices on the Court.

The clear evidence of overrepresentation of Jews in all the higher circles of power reflects a dramatic reversal of the discrimination experienced by Jews in these arenas earlier in the century. Zweigenhaft and Domhoff (2006) identify a number of variables that seem to be important in understanding the successful entry by Jews into the power elite: They are predominantly White, and those who rise the highest are likely to have been born in relatively privileged circumstances; they have excellent educational credentials; and many of them are second- or third-generation Americans and thus have had time to become fully acculturated.

Women

The power elite depicted by Mills was exclusively a male preserve. He did not consider women in the corporate elite—which for Mills constituted only the top two or three positions in the top "hundred or so" corporations—because, at the time, there were none. Four decades later, in 1995, a study of *Fortune* 1000 companies revealed that 9.5% of the corporate directors were women. By 2003, the number had jumped to 13.6%. However, of the top five earners at these companies—those holding the titles of chairman, chief executive, vice chairman, president, chief operating officer, or executive vice president—only 5.2% were women (Zweigenhaft & Domhoff, 2006, p. 52).

In looking at *Fortune* 500 companies, Zweigenhaft and Domhoff (2006) found that there was only one woman CEO in 1977, two in 1991, and eight in 2005 (p. 60). By 2010, there were 15 women CEOs of *Fortune* 500 companies (*Fortune,* 2010, para. 1). But if we restrict ourselves to Mills's rather stringent standard of the "hundred or so" corporations of the power elite, we find that, in 2008, only 5% of CEOs at *Fortune* 100 companies were women (*N*=5) (Jones, 2009, n.p.). Despite all the gains made by women in the corporate world, it is clearly the case that a glass ceiling blocking them from the highest ranks of U.S. corporations continues to exist.

When Mills's *The Power Elite* appeared, only two women had served in presidential cabinets: Frances Perkins who was Roosevelt's secretary of labor from 1933 to 1945, and Oveta Culp Hobby who was Eisenhower's secretary of health, education, and welfare from 1953 to 1955. (Mills does not mention either woman in his book.) Clearly the percentage of women in cabinet posts has increased considerably since Mills's time. When we look at posts in the "inner cabinet"—which includes the secretaries of state, defense, and treasury, and the attorney general—we find President Clinton's appointment of Janet Reno as U.S. attorney general in 1993 and of Madeline Albright as secretary of state in 1997. In 2001, George W. Bush named Condoleezza Rice to be the first woman national security advisor, and then in 2005 Rice began serving as the first Black woman secretary of state. By late 2009, a full 30% of Obama's cabinet positions were occupied by women (the highest percentage to date), which included Hillary Clinton as secretary of state.

As regards their socioeconomic status, Zweigenhaft and Domhoff (2006) found that most (14) of the 20 women who had served in cabinet posts between 1953 and 2005 "were born into economically secure families in which the fathers, or both parents, were well-educated professionals" (p. 65). Of the 20, only 4 were from middle-class backgrounds and the other 2 seemed to come from genuine working-class origins. It may perhaps correctly be assumed that a similar socioeconomic profile for female cabinet members has persisted to the present.

In 1956, there were no women among the military elite. In 1972 (the year prior to the shift from conscription to an all-volunteer military), women made up only 1.9% of the total military force on active duty. By 2003, that number had increased to about 15% (Zweigenhaft & Domhoff, 2006, p. 70). By 2008, it had dipped slightly to 14% (Swarnes, 2008, para. 8). To be sure, there have been tremendous increases in the numbers of women on active duty since 1973 and of their rise to the ranks of officer. Indeed, between 2000 and 2010, there were 11 female generals and two female admirals. However, to date, there have been no women among the highest-ranking military officers, the Joint Chiefs of Staff.

At the time Mills wrote *The Power Elite,* only one woman was serving in the U.S. Senate: Margaret Chase Smith of Maine. Prior to Smith, only a handful of women had ever been senators. Then, due in large part to the first and second waves of the women's movement, between 1960 and 2006, no less than 27 women had served or were serving in the Senate, 16 of whom were Democrats. By 2009, of the 100 senators in the 111th Congress, 18 were women, 14 of whom were Democrats (Office of History and Preservation, Office of the Clerk, 2010b, n.p.). The presence of women in the U.S. House of Representatives has also increased dramatically since Mills's day. In 1956, there were only 17 women in the House, 10 of whom were Democrats. In the November 2004 election, 65 women were elected or reelected to the House, 42 Democrats and 23 Republicans (Zweigenhaft & Domhoff, 2006, p. 76). Then, in 2007, Nancy Pelosi was elected the first female Speaker of the House, and by 2009, there were 78 women serving in the House of Representatives of the 111th Congress (18%) (Office of History and Preservation, Office of the Clerk, 2010b, n.p.).

Only four Supreme Court justices have been women: Sandra Day O'Connor, Ruth Bader Ginsburg, Sonia Sotomayor, and Elena Kagan. All of them graduated from prestigious law schools: Stanford, Columbia, Yale, and Harvard, respectively. In 2010, one-third of the Court was female.

Zweigenhaft and Domhoff (2006) conclude their chapter on women in the power elite by stating, "A close look at the class backgrounds of those women who have made it to the top . . . demonstrates that the upper classes are overrepresented by a factor of ten or fifteen to one" (p. 80).

African Americans

The entrance of African Americans into the corporate elite came only after the civil rights movement of the 1960s, and in particular in the wake of the enactment of the Civil Rights Act of 1964—the federal legislation that outlawed racial discrimination and ended racial segregation. By mid-1971, there were about a dozen Blacks on *Fortune 500* boards, all with similar backgrounds that characterize them as a group: "[T]hey were highly educated, many were from families that were economically comfortable or even quite wealthy, and some had developed valuable political connections" (Zweigenhaft & Domhoff, 2006, p. 93). Indeed, the early 1970s saw the doors of corporate boardrooms open up more and more to African Americans. Thus, in 1973, there were 67 Black men and 5 Black women on the board of directors of slightly more than one hundred major U.S. companies. In 1981, there were 73 African Americans who held directorships in 112 companies (p. 99). In 1994, there were 34 Black men and women sitting on three or more corporate boards (called interlocking directors or "interlockers"). About 40% of those interlockers came from families that were economically comfortable, 25% were from solidly working-class backgrounds, and the remaining 35% came from poverty. What is more, they were all very well educated, as all but two were college graduates, and 31 of the 34 held postgraduate degrees (Zweigenhaft & Domhoff, 2006, p. 103). These advancements notwithstanding, Blacks continue to remain underrepresented on corporate boards. And when it comes to the very highest levels of corporate positions—chairman of the board, president, or vice president—one study found that Blacks were almost entirely absent (only 0.2%) during the fiscal year 1983–1984 (p. 100). However, by June 2005, there were 13 African American CEOs in *Fortune* 1000 companies (p. 109).

In *The Power Elite,* Mills (1956) contends that as a result of "the great cultural shift of modern American capitalism toward a permanent war economy," there was "increased personnel traffic . . . between the military and the corporate realms" (p. 215). At the time that Mills wrote this, the armed forces had largely desegregated its troops; still, most African Americans served in support units and there were relatively few officers among them. Then, in 1989, the first African American—the retired four-star Army General Colin L. Powell—was named to the top of the military elite, the chairman of the Joint Chiefs of Staff. To date, General Powell has been the only Black solider to serve in that capacity. Despite having a Black general numbered among the warlords, in 2004 a mere 5.2% of men with general officer rank (the equivalent of one-star general or higher) were African American (p. 119).

Between 1964, the year of the passage of the Civil Rights Act, and 1993, with the election of President Bill Clinton, only five Blacks had served in presidential cabinets. Clinton was the first president to appoint more than one African American to his cabinet. During his 8 years in office, he appointed a total of five. When first elected in 2001, George W. Bush appointed four African Americans to his initial cabinet. Of the total of 14 African American appointments made by presidents from Lyndon B. Johnson to George W. Bush, 9 came from relative privilege. All 14 went to college, 4 to prestigious "White" schools and 4 to prestigious "Black" schools. A total of 8 of the 14 went to law school, 1 went to medical school, and 3 completed doctoral work (Zweigenhaft & Domhoff, 2006, p. 118).

The first Black U.S. President, Barack Obama, made an initial appointment of four African Americans, the highest number so far, to fill the following cabinet posts: U.S. attorney general, head of the Environmental Protection Agency, U.S. trade representative, and U.S. ambassador to the United Nations. Of these only one was from a working class background; the others came from comfortable middle class backgrounds. All but one attended prestigious universities (Princeton, Columbia, Oxford) where they earned advanced degrees. One had an MA degree, one a PhD, and two had law degrees.

Since the 1940s, only four African Americans have served in the U.S. Senate, three of whom were Democrats. Blacks have fared much better in the U.S. House of Representatives. Indeed, in 2009, there were 41 African Americans in the House of the 111th Congress (9.4%) (Office of History and Preservation, Office of the Clerk, 2010a).

In looking at the Black men and women who were elected to the House between 1990 and 2005, Zweigenhaft and Domhoff (2006) concluded that they had come from less privileged backgrounds than those that had been appointed to *Fortune*-level boards of directors or presidential cabinets, that about 20% of them had grown up in economically comfortable backgrounds, that half were from stable working-class families, and that about one-third had come from real poverty (pp. 127–128). It may be safe to conclude that a very similar socioeconomic pattern held for African Americans in Congress in 2009.

Only two African Americans have served on the Supreme Court: Thurgood Marshall and Clarence Thomas.

Latinos

While Mills did not identify the "very rich" as exactly the same people who occupied positions in the political, corporate, and military elite, he did find considerable overlap between the very rich and the corporate elite (whom he called the "corporate rich"). However, notwithstanding the fact that there are several "very rich" Latinos, very few members of this ethnic group have become part of the corporate elite. Only 11 of the 75 wealthiest Latinos for 1995 sat on a *Fortune* 1000 board. In 2005, only 12 Latinos had been CEOs in *Fortune* 1000 companies (Zweigenhaft & Domhoff, 2006, pp. 152–153). By 2010, Latinos had made some small gains, as they represented 3.28% of corporate board members and 2.90% of members of executive teams in *Fortune* 500 companies. Still, these individuals comprised only about one-fifth of the 15% Latinos represented in the U.S. population (Menendez, 2010, p. 4). Thus, while it is clear that some Hispanics are in the corporate elite, and that their numbers as directors and CEOs have increased in the last 50 years, they nonetheless remain very much underrepresented in the higher levels of the corporate world—this despite the fact that Latinos constitute a percentage of the total U.S. population that is increasing substantially.

When Zweigenhaft and Domhoff (2006) analyzed the social, educational, and career backgrounds of Latinos who sat on corporate boards, they found that, like Jews, women, and African Americans, the majority of Latino corporate directors seemed to have been raised in at least middle-class circumstances. Many of them had had elite educations at the undergraduate and graduate levels and very few of them "could be considered genuine bootstrappers, making their way to the top of corporations without the benefit of family backing or an elite education" (p. 148). These background advantages were particularly prevalent with Latinos in the corporate elite who were of Cuban American background. Moreover, Zweigenhaft and Domhoff found that, as in the case of the African American corporate elite, the majority of the Latinos in the corporate elite tended to be light-skinned.

The first Hispanic to be appointed to a cabinet-level position was Lauro Cavazos, secretary of education in the Reagan administration in 1988. In addition to keeping Cavazos, George H. W. Bush appointed another Hispanic, Manuel Lujan, to his presidential cabinet. Bill Clinton appointed three Hispanics to his cabinet, as did George W. Bush. Obama's Latino appointments numbered two in 2010 (one of whom was the first Latina, Hilda Solis). In all, there have been 10 Latinos in presidential cabinets, five Democrats and five Republicans.

Few Hispanics have made it to the rank of general officer in the U.S. armed forces. In 2007, Latinos constituted about 12% of the total military population. Yet, they represented only 1.3% of all flag and general officers. For several years, Lieutenant-General Ricardo Sanchez, who commanded coalition troops in Iraq for a year beginning in June 2003, had been the highest-ranking Latino in the military. He had been 1 of just 8 Latinos ever to rise to the rank of General of the Army by 2003. With Sanchez's retirement in 2006, only three Latino generals were left on active duty (Schmal, 2009, para. 6).

When Mills wrote *The Power Elite,* there had only been one Hispanic elected to the U.S. Senate: Dennis Chavez, a Democrat from New Mexico. In 1964, Joseph Montoya, also a Democrat from New Mexico, was elected. There were no Latinos in the Senate until 2005 when Ken Salazar, Democrat from Colorado, and Mel Martinez, Republican from Florida, were elected. Then, in 2006, Bob Menendez, Democrat from New Jersey, became a senator.

Between 1956 and 2010, no less than 39 Latinos were elected to the House, only 5 of whom were Republicans. According to Zweigenhaft and Domhoff (2006), typically the Democrats have been Mexican Americans from Texas or California and Puerto Ricans from New York. Until 1996, none of the Mexican Americans had been from a well-to-do background. The five Latino Republicans (three of whom have been Cuban Americans from Florida) have tended to come from solidly middle-class or higher backgrounds (p. 163).

There had never been a Hispanic person on the U.S. Supreme Court until 2009 when Sonia Sotomayor was named the Court's first Hispanic justice and its third female justice. Sotomayor, who was nominated for the nation's highest court by President Barack Obama, is a Puerto Rican who grew up in poverty. When *The Power Elite* appeared in 1956, Sotomayor, then 2 years old, was living with her family in a housing project in the South Bronx, less than 10 miles from Mills's office at Columbia University.

Asian Americans

Asian American immigrants tend to be very highly educated, either in their country of origin, in the case of immigrants since 1965, or else in the United States. In 2004, a total of 96 Asian American men and women held 127 board seats in S&P (Standard and Poor's Composite Index) 1500 companies. This represented less than 1% of all directors. Fifteen of the 96 Asian American directors were of East Indian background. Of the remaining 81 directors, 54% were Chinese Americans, 25% were Japanese Americans, and 9% were Korean Americans; the other 12% were distributed among men and women born in Singapore, the Philippines, and Vietnam (Zweigenhaft & Domhoff, 2006, p. 176). The most frequent path for Asians to take to become directors of *Fortune*-level companies is that of the immigrant entrepreneur, that is, to have started their own businesses or worked in businesses started by their parents or grandparents (p. 189).

There were no Asian Americans in a presidential cabinet until 2000 when President Clinton nominated Norman Y. Mineta, a Japanese American, to be secretary of commerce. George W. Bush named Mineta as secretary of transportation and Elaine Chao, a Chinese American, to be his secretary of labor (Zweigenhaft & Domhoff, 2006, p. 190). When Barack Obama took office in 2009, he appointed three Asian Americans (two of Chinese and one of Japanese ancestry) to his cabinet-level positions, making his cabinet 13% Asian American. These are Gary Locke, secretary of commerce; Steven Chu, secretary of energy; and Eric K. Shinseki, secretary of veterans affairs.

Prior to becoming secretary of veterans affairs, Eric K. Shinseki had retired as a four-star general and was Army Chief of Staff and thus a member of the Joint Chiefs of Staff. As of 2004, there were six generals of Asian background in active service, five of them in the army and one in the air force. Among them were two Filipino immigrants (Zweigenhaft & Domhoff, 2006, p. 192).

In 2010, there were nine Asian Pacific Americans in the House of Representatives (two of Filipino background, three Chinese Americans, three Japanese Americans, and one Vietnamese American) and two in the Senate (one of Japanese and one of Chinese ancestry). Almost all are Democrats.

According to Zweigenhaft and Domhoff (2006), the wealthier and better-educated Asian immigrants, in this case Chinese Americans, tend to be corporate directors and appointees in Republican administrations. Asian immigrants coming to the United States from less privileged socioeconomic backgrounds, in this case Japanese Americans, are more likely to be elected officials (p. 196).

Gay Men and Lesbians

When it comes to gays and lesbians in the power elite, the picture becomes quite murky. As Zweigenhaft and Domhoff (2006) point out, "Presumably, there have always been homosexuals in the power elite, but there is no way to know how many or who they are" (pp. 203–204). Indeed, very little can be said, by way of hard data, about gay men and lesbians in any of the higher circles of power. Based on the evidence that is available, Zweigenhaft and Domhoff believe that gay men and lesbians continue to encounter prejudice and discrimination in the corporate world. Moreover, there is reason to believe that the higher one moves in the executive ranks, the less likely it is for homosexuality to be acceptable. In addition, several studies indicate that the higher one rises in the corporate hierarchy, the more being open about one's homosexuality serves as an impediment to one's career. Zweigenhaft and Domhoff believe that those gay men and lesbians who start at large corporations and do manage to rise through the ranks are likely to go off on their own at some point to begin companies or to work in more comfortable environments. Zweigenhaft and Domhoff assume that there are, and have always been, homosexuals in the power elite, but to stay there, they have to "manage" their image by not appearing too effeminate (in the case of gays) or too "masculine" in the case of lesbians.

The Ironies of Diversity

Zweigenhaft and Domhoff's (2006) findings reveal that, compared to the 1950s when Mills was writing,

1. The power elite is now more diverse in regard to women and minorities. However, its core group continues to be composed of wealthy, White, heterosexual, Christian males.

2. With some exceptions in Congress, in general, it still takes at least three generations to rise from the bottom socioeconomic stratum to the top in the United States.

3. Class backgrounds, current roles, and future aspirations are more powerful in shaping behavior in the power elite than gender, ethnicity, race, or sexual orientation.

4. Women, African Americans, Latinos, Asian Americans, and openly homosexual men and women are all underrepresented in the power elite, but to varying degrees and with different rates of increasing representation.

5. There is greater diversity in Congress than in the power elite, and a large percentage of minority elected officials are Democrats.

6. Although the corporate, political, and military elites have diversified, in general, the presence of more diverse members at the top has given the WASP power elite a way to feel legitimate by tokenizing minorities.

As an important and significant update to Zweigenhaft and Domhoff's (2006) findings, we may add the following two characterizations. First, of the three top levels of national power that Mills identified, since the Obama administration, there has been much greater race/ethnic/gender diversity in the political elite—which includes the president, members of the cabinet, and appointed heads of major regulatory agencies—than in either the corporate or the military elite. Not only was Barack Obama the first African American to become U.S. president, only 43% of his cabinet in 2010 consisted of White men—almost all of whom were not WASPs.

Second, although Mills relegated both Congress and the U.S. Supreme Court to the "middle levels" of power, Zweigenhaft and Domhoff (2006) regard both of these institutions as integral to the higher circles of power. And while it is true that women and people of color have served in Congress in increasing numbers since the 1990s—and that very significantly, Nancy Pelosi was elected the first female Speaker of the House—they still constitute a minority in the legislative branch of government. The most diverse institution, however, is now the U.S. Supreme Court. In 2010, the Court's composition consisted of three women, one of whom was Latina, and one African American man. In addition, the religious background of the justices reveals that six are Roman Catholic and three are Jewish. For the first time in its 221-year history, there are no WASP males on the Court.

However all this may be, Zweigenhaft and Domhoff (2006) conclude that the men and women of previously excluded groups who have risen to the top of the power elite share the prevailing perspectives and values of those already in power. As a consequence, the diversification of the power elite actually reinforces the unchanging nature of the class structure, increases the tendency to ignore class inequalities, and therefore has had no effect on the way the power elite functions.

Conclusion

It is against the backdrop of the stratification trilogy, with its unflinching critique of the class structure and power system in the United States, that the following questions suggest themselves:

- How accurate is Mills's description of power relations in U.S. society given that he sees power strictly in zero-sum terms and does not consider pluralistic democracy?
- To what extent is Mills's understanding of the power elite based on the notion of conspiracy?
- How realistic is it for contemporary radical sociologists to look for agents of social change in various populations?
- Who really runs America today?

By the mid-1950s, Mills had achieved international acclaim for his radical or "critical" sociology largely on the weight of his immensely popular books on power and social stratification. The next chapter considers four works of his that have been largely ignored by the sociological community: his writings on Latinos and on Latin America.

5

On Latinos and
Latin America*

lthough C. Wright Mills did not conduct a systematic study of Latinos
or Latin America as such, his various writings on these topics are
nonetheless important because, like his more popular ones, they address his
continuing concerns with power relations, issues of character structure
(symbols, self-image, personality), status, pragmatism, history, and social
structure.

The corpus of Mills's writings on Latinos and Latin Americans consists of
four items: (1) "The Sailor, Sex Market, and Mexican" (1943b), a magazine
article on Mexican Americans and the Zoot Suit Riots in Los Angeles written during World War II; (2) *The Puerto Rican Journey: New York's Newest
Migrants* (Mills et al., 1950), a research study on the Puerto Rican migration
to New York City during the 1940s; (3) *Listen, Yankee: The Revolution in
Cuba* (1960d), a paperback explaining what the 1960 Cuban Revolution
meant to the Cuban revolutionary; and (4) a 1960 interview (published in
1961) with Mexican leftist intellectuals published under the title "On Latin
America, the Left, and the U.S." Again, it must be pointed out that Mills
never undertook a self-conscious, methodical examination of Latino as an
ethnicity and these four pieces, singly or collectively, cannot be regarded as

*An earlier version of this chapter appeared in *The American Sociologist* (vol. 28, no. 3, 1997,
pp. 29–56). *The Hispanic Writings of C. Wright Mills* by A. Javier Treviño. With kind permission from Springer Science+Business Media B.V.

such. However, these writings do provide us with an opportunity to examine Mills's social psychological analysis of Latino populations. Accordingly, this chapter sets forth three objectives: (1) to understand how Mills's personal experiences and convictions influenced his associations with and views toward Latinos from 1943 to 1960; (2) to analyze the social structural conditions that four specific Latino populations—namely, Mexican American youth, Puerto Rican migrants, Cuban revolutionaries, and Latin American intellectuals—experienced as their personal troubles in their day-to-day struggles during that period in history; and (3) to study the character structure—the motives and self-images, personality traits and conduct patterns, moods and wishes, aspirations and discontents—of these four Latino populations. The chapter concludes with a synopsis and appraisal of Mills's personal perceptions of Latinos, the social structural factors that impacted on the four Latino groups, and the personality traits of Latinos as Mills saw them.

Because the social psychological approach that Mills most clearly articulates in *Character and Social Structure* (hereafter *CSS*) informs all of his work, including the four pieces considered here, its basic concepts, as already discussed in Chapter 3, will be employed in better understanding Mills's views on Latinos, their motives, moods, and self-images.

Mexican American Zoot Suiters

Mills wrote "The Sailor, Sex Market, and Mexican" at the height of World War II and while he was working on *CSS*. This article is a social psychological assessment of the Zoot Suit Riots, the confrontation between Mexican American youth and "Anglo" servicemen that took place in downtown Los Angeles during June of 1943. This piece, written for the political and cultural magazine *The New Leader,* was published less than 2 weeks after the riots had ended. In a letter accompanying the article, Mills informed the magazine's editors,

> I would like to point out that nobody has explained the occasion of the riots. . . . I haven't explained [the riots] in the enclosed but I do offer a rationally understandable pattern, based on 3 or 4 years experience with the night life of Mexicans and soldiers in San Antonio, Texas. (p. 5)

Implied in this letter is the idea that, through his previous acquaintance with these two groups, Mills is able to make some systematic observations about the character structures of Mexican Americans and servicemen. As concerns the soldiers, Horowitz (1983) intimates that "The Sailor, Sex Market, and Mexican" is marred by two powerful sentiments and experiences of Mills:

his deep antipathy toward regimentation and his ambivalence about having done everything he could to escape military duty. It would appear that these sentiments and experiences stem from two specific sources: (1) from Mills's experience as an undergraduate student at the military-oriented Texas A&M University where he found the regimentation to be "childish" (Gillam, 1966) and (2) from his refusal to be drafted during World War II.

The riots, in brief, involved an attack on Mexican American "zoot suiters" by servicemen on leave. During the 10-day confrontations, some 5,000 civilians joined the servicemen in chasing, stripping, and occasionally beating zoot suiters and non–zoot suit wearing Mexican and African Americans (Mazón, 1984). The main outward symbol, or emblem, giving the zoot suiters their identity was their distinctive attire. This "uniform" consisted of a long suit coat with trousers pegged at the cuff, draped around the knees with deep pleats at the waist, and a low-hanging watch chain. In addition, the zoot suiter distinguished himself from other youths by keeping his hair well greased and duck-tailed (Scott, 1970). Indeed, during the 1940s, the zoot suit was the dominant symbol and style by which tough Chicano youth—the *pachucos*—sought status. The zoot suit provided them with a unique self-image and, concomitantly, a certain level of self-esteem.

Mills eschews the explanations that had recently been advanced in understanding the Zoot Suit Riots in Los Angeles: crowded slum conditions, "war emotions," the segregated military, various forms of ethnic oppression, and so forth. He admits that while these features may contribute to, sanction, or permit riots, they are not sufficient to "let them loose." Instead, he finds a partial explanation for the riots in social structure (the war condition of the "sex market") and in character structure (the inner lives of the sailors and zoot suiters).

For Mills, the sex market, or "the opportunities of one sex to offer favors and attentions which the other sex will take up," is not the cause, but a precipitating factor, one "immediate irritant," of the riots. To begin with, Mills contends that war affects the sex market by distributing the sex ratio in two ways: In some places, war makes available more women than men; in other places (like metropolitan Los Angeles with its large military population), it concentrates single men (young sailors on leave) without increasing the supply of the young, sex-able women. The latter situation makes for an increased competition among men for the favors of the women available. Thus, the condition of the sex market during wartime is that, as a social structure of the city, it acts as a "tension-center." Indeed, "if the 'tension-centers' of the original troubles were plotted on a map of Los Angeles," explains Mills (1943b), "they would be clustered where men meet women at night: the dance halls, the bars, the streets of the districts where a girl is too poor to be too choosy" (p. 7). What is more, this tense competition for women has the potential to become a dangerous conflict between Anglo soldiers and Hispanic civilians, particularly if the women involved are also ethnically mixed.

In addition to the war condition of the sex market, Mills advances another explanation for the riots: the social psychology—that is, the moods, wishes, and motives—of the Mexican American boys and the sailors on leave. The young sailor on leave for a night in Los Angeles is "on the make," searching for sexually available women. He believes that his uniform (which he perhaps sees as a visible symbol of the "generalized other" that was dominant in wartime America: the military order) exempts him from the moral restraints of civilian life and, in the anonymity of the large city, he can make the most of his freedom during his leaves. Moreover, the soldier has been trained to realize his will in groups with violence and wants to test himself against the zoot suiters, a less formidable group than the Japanese and German enemy. Under these conditions, existing within the context of a military esprit de corps, the sailors may riot.

The sailor's moods and wishes center around women: Those "little tornadoes of sexual stimuli swishing and flouncing down the streets of our cities hit him straight in the groin" (Mills, 1943b, p. 5). The Mexican girl is attractive to the sailor, and the impersonal competition for her quickly becomes a personalized conflict that turns into a fight. Group lines are drawn between the sailors and zoot suiters, and the situation becomes a riot.

Looking next at the motives of the Mexican boy, Mills notes that built into his character are many frustrations stemming from racial segregation, job disappointments, and class antagonisms that he experiences as an underprivileged minority. Out of these frustrations comes his desire to wear the zoot suit as a badge that calls others to notice him. Mills says the Mexican youth will not soon forget the humiliation he received during the riots, as his suit—the tangible symbol designating his underprivileged minority status—was torn off him in public. He received an even greater humiliation when the soldiers proceeded to "unpants" him in front of "his girls." For it is before his women that the zoot suiter's underprivileged social status is most painfully obvious. Next time, warns Mills, the Mexican boy will carry a knife.

In CSS, Gerth and Mills (1953) propose that status, in its psychological effects and meanings, is "close up" to the person because the level of self-esteem is a direct function of status position. Moreover, the type of self-image, as well as styles of conduct defining types of persons, is most readily understood in terms of the status sphere. According to Gerth and Mills, racial and ethnic minorities are status phenomena; more than that, they are status phenomena of an extreme enough nature to help illustrate how the status sphere affects character structure:

The status of any minority is revealed by their exclusion from specific occupations, educational opportunities, social clubs, preferred residential areas, as well as resistance to their intermarriage with members of the majority society. It is in this situation that the minority child comes to awareness of his status. In time, he also comes to experience its conflict with majority groups as his conflict—as others significant to him reveal hostile stereotypes based on it. Finally, he attempts to come to terms with the status situation in which he finds himself; and in the process he is organized into one of several types of personality. Whatever traits he has as a mature person of minority status will be a product of his status situation and of his cumulative reactions to it and interactions with it. (p. 326)

Gerth and Mills (1953) contend that there are two points in terms of which "minority types" of personality may be constructed: (1) the groups in terms of which the minority group members seek status—be it their own minority group or the majority society—and (2) the status symbols used by minority group members to claim status—again, those of their minority group or those of the majority society. In reference to these two points, Gerth and Mills produce four personality types (see Figure 5.1).

Figure 5.1

The Symbols and Styles by Which Status Is Sought	The Groups in Which Status Is Sought	
	IN HIS OWN MINORITY	IN THE MAJORITY SOCIETY
Of His Own Minority	I	II
Of the Majority Society	III	IV

Source: *Character and Social Structure* by Hans Gerth and C. Wright Mills. © 1953 Houghton Mifflin.

Gerth and Mills (1953) make it known that many possible varieties and types of men and women exist within each of these four situations. Applying this scheme in *CSS* to the Mexican American zoot suiters, they best fit into status situation II. This situation illustrates the minority personality types that have been formed by identification with the zoot suit lifestyle as a whole and who seek status from this identification, but from Anglos. These personality types may also include those resentful militant *pachucos* who ascribe all Mexican American ills to Anglos.

Returning to "The Sailor, Sex Market, and Mexican" and Mills's analysis of the social structure of the sex market, he maintains that when the sex problem is not handled either as a commercial proposition (as in professional prostitution) or as a thoroughly personalized arrangement (as in the middle class "date"), contentious competition for the few women available can incite a riot. Mills closes the essay by suggesting one practical solution to the problem of the unregulated sex market: the establishment of properly licensed and medically supervised houses of prostitution segregated for sailors and soldiers on leave. Such houses, Mills acknowledges, would not solve racial and class contradictions, nor remedy local conflicts between civil and military authorities; they would, however, lessen both of these tensions by minimizing and regulating a major irritant of them both.

Horowitz (1983) maintains that race and ethnic problems did not occupy Mills's attention either before or after the war. (As we will see in the next sections, this assertion is only partially correct since Mills, if only superficially, did study the racial composition of Puerto Rican migrants.) Why, then, did he write "The Sailor, Sex Market, and Mexican"? Horowitz finds a partial answer in Mills's biography. He states that Mills's apparent concern for ethnic tensions in this article was part of his ever-deepening alienation from the American mainstream. The article enabled Mills to address the sociological problem of deviance, detached from the much larger political and global considerations he was already exhorting others to take into account. Despite Mills's deeply sexist commentary, "The Sailor, Sex Market, and Mexican" is his "most forward-looking comment on the period" (Horowitz, 1983, p. 67).

Puerto Rican Migrants

According to Eldridge (1983), Mills's two most well-known writings on Latin Americans, *The Puerto Rican Journey* and *Listen, Yankee,* "have in common a sense of the interdependency which exists between the USA and Latin America. . . . Both studies remind us of the asymmetrical economic and political linkages which the United States has had with Latin American client cultures" (p. 90). To be sure, given his great contempt for American expansionism, Mills, when discussing the peoples of these two cultures—Puerto Ricans and Cubans—always explains their conduct and motivations, their hopes, dreams, frustrations, and discontents, in relation to the political, economic, and cultural influences of "the colossus of the north." In these two books, Mills makes a serious attempt at understanding the social world from the viewpoint of both the Puerto Rican migrant and the Cuban revolutionary. This and the following sections examine *The Puerto Rican Journey,* followed by *Listen, Yankee,* within the social psychological framework provided in *CSS.*

The Puerto Rican Journey (1950) is a study on the Puerto Rican migration to New York City. The book, with Mills as senior author, was written in collaboration with Clarence Senior and Rose K. Goldsen. All three worked for the Bureau of Applied Social Research (BASR) at Columbia University. Horowitz (1963) recounts how Mills suggested to Paul F. Lazarsfeld, who at that time was the BASR's overall supervisor, that he take the Puerto Rican study off Lazarsfeld's hands as a way of compensating the BASR for major expenses that Mills had frivolously incurred. If this is the case, then, at least initially, Mills had no personal interest in the project; his involvement was motivated not by intellectual curiosity, but by expediency and indemnity. In any event, Mills ultimately designed the study and was in charge of its execution.

Mills's somewhat estranged, if not disinterested, attitude toward Puerto Ricans during the time he was working on this study may be gleaned from three sources. First, in a letter to the novelist Dan Wakefield, Mills writes candidly about his efforts at data collecting in San Juan:

> [M]y own experience with them [the Puerto Ricans] was disappointing, especially in PR itself. They've little Spanish stuff and they've only the most blatant U.S. stuff. A sort of culture-less people. Hollow and really hysterical. But I don't really know them. My stuff was at a great distance and necessarily statistical in nature. (as quoted in Wakefield, 1971, p. 68)

Second, as concerns Mills's research in New York City, his coauthor Rose Goldsen (1964) describes Mills's Olympian detachment during the study's data-gathering phase:

> In the days when we worked together on *Puerto Rican Journey*, I found much pleasure and excitement in wandering around Harlem and the East Bronx, chatting, drinking coffee with Puerto Ricans, questioning, arguing, wondering, commiserating, checking. Mills rode around Harlem and the East Bronx in his impossible open Jeep. He did not interview migrants or try to share their views. He interviewed English-speaking officials and intellectuals. (p. 90)

Finally, in a thinly disguised statement of self-reference, Mills, in *The Puerto Rican Journey*, expresses bafflement at Puerto Rican folkways: "To the New Yorker fresh from Texas, for example, behavior on the lower East Side is every bit as strange as that in Spanish Harlem" (as quoted in Mills et al., 1950, p. 126). In short, Mills's posture vis-à-vis Puerto Ricans, both islanders and migrants, was elitist at best and racist at the worst.

An Ambiguous and Ambivalent Identity

In *The Puerto Rican Journey*, Mills, Senior, and Goldsen undertake a comparative analysis of those Puerto Ricans who migrated to New York

City and those who stayed on the island. Focusing first on Puerto Rico, they maintain that the growing infiltration of United States influences on the island had produced a Puerto Rican identity characterized by ambiguity and ambivalence. On the one hand, island Puerto Ricans proudly identified with their Spanish heritage, a heritage strikingly different from mainland culture. To take but one example, on the island, kinship was organized in the Latin tradition with the despotic father-husband being the dominant pattern, and family structure extending beyond the primary family group to include aunts, uncles, cousins, grandparents, nieces, nephews, *compadres,* and *comadres.* On the other hand, in addition to possessing a distinctly Latin tradition, the islanders strongly identified with the culture of the continental United States. For example, largely as a result of mainland advertising, their Spanish language was full of English words and phrases.

Mills, Senior, and Goldsen note that the status of island Puerto Ricans was ambiguous in yet another way: They occupied a marginal position between the United States and Latin America. Politically, economically, and culturally, islanders felt neither wholly American nor wholly Latin American. Focusing on economics, Mills et al. assert that when judged by North American standards of life, most Puerto Ricans were frightfully poor, but by Latin American standards, they were quite well off.

In light of the island's various social problems—high illegitimacy rate, low educational level, political uncertainty, poverty, a population explosion, and so forth—Puerto Ricans of the postwar generation found themselves caught in a situation that strongly impelled them to leave the island. While it might be expected that their Spanish cultural ties might have drawn them to Latin American countries, Mills maintains that, strictly speaking, the Puerto Ricans were not Latin American. So influenced were they by United States culture that they had become "Puerto Rican American." If they left the island, their standard of living, way of life, mannerisms, and values made the pull of the States especially strong. These general cultural and specific economic pulls, along with the unrestricted migration that Puerto Ricans enjoyed as U.S. citizens, operated so that migration from Puerto Rico meant, by and large, migration to the United States mainland, and principally to New York City.

In articulating the islanders' reasons for migrating to New York City, Mills and his associates couch them in terms of a series of push–pull motivations. First was the push from the homeland because of the population pressure, manifested in the objective facts of low living standards and lack of jobs. Indeed, Puerto Rico's population had doubled during the previous half-century.

Second, the various island sources of information about New York City were generally favorable. These information sources took the form of informal face-to-face contact as well as conversations with and letters from friends who were living in or had visited the city. In addition, compared with New York, which had the greatest concentration of Puerto Ricans, other scattered settlements of Puerto Ricans in the States had only very weak pulling power. This supports the finding that most of the people who considered leaving the island thought specifically of migrating to New York City and never seriously considered any other place. Thus, when Puerto Ricans were ready to leave the island, they were already "psychologically prepared" to move into one of the Puerto Rican enclaves of New York City.

Third, and the most crucial motivating force of Puerto Rican migration, was New York's economic pull; the islander was beckoned by the city's reputation for economic opportunity. Indeed, the majority of respondents expressed their motivations to migrate in terms of the pull of New York City rather than the push of the island. Mills, Senior, and Goldsen also point out the sex differences in the Puerto Rican's motivation to migrate: The men tended to migrate for economic reasons; the women migrated for family reasons. That is, the women were either responding to the pull of relatives already settled in New York, or they wanted to escape or avoid difficult family situations on the island. Subjectively, however, economic reasons were more often experienced as a push from the island, while family reasons were associated with the experience of a pull to New York. Mills and his colleagues state that, all things considered, the immigrants' motive for transit was primarily an economic one.

Since the Puerto Rican journey to New York was primarily an economic transit, it required occupational aspirations. In point of fact, only a few of the migrants eventually rose occupationally, the majority remaining at island levels, with more than a few sinking lower, ending up concentrated in, and restricted to, semi- and unskilled wage work. This pattern created in the migrant community a "poverty of aspiration," meaning that those who aspired to a different type of job were as likely to wish for a low- as for a high-skilled job. Of all the migrants interviewed, only 18% of the men and 10% of the women articulated a job aspiration of any kind. These lowered occupational aspirations of the Puerto Ricans departed from the classic pattern of assimilation of other migrants to the United States who, upon learning the language and customs of their new residence, began to aspire to jobs requiring a little more skill.

Mills et al. attribute the Puerto Rican migrants' leveled aspirations to the lack of a Protestant work ethic, or the willful feeling that the individual can command the future to serve his or her ends. Mills, to be sure, always maintained a fierce devotion to the Protestant work ethic, what he called, "the gospel and character of work" (as quoted in K. Mills & Mills, 2000, p. 41), the idea of working hard for work's own sake, a notion that he claimed he learned from his father. This character structure of the Puerto Rican migrant contrasts sharply with the character structure of the 17th-century English Puritan that Mills describes in CSS. The English Puritan sought to "master the world" through all the traits that Mills personally admired: hard work, self-discipline, and control over external circumstances. In CSS, Gerth and Mills (1953) write approvingly about the classic Puritan's character type:

> The heroic Puritan of seventeenth-century England could methodically pursue his quest for salvation by disciplining himself for hard work and thriftiness, and thus by his success assure his religious worth and his salvation in the hereafter. He could, in short, relieve his anxieties by hard work, by work for work's sake, and, under the appropriate premiums, take great pains to develop a new "contract morality" in business relationships. Thus perfectionism and moral rigor, punctiliousness, and pleasure-denying work, along with humility and the craving for his neighbor's love all combined to shape the character structure of the classical Puritan who sought to master the world rather than adjust to it. (p. 188)

Mills, Senior, and Goldsen explain that Latin American conditions of life had not encouraged this kind of ambitious focusing on one's future and deliberate searching for the means of achieving it. The migrant Puerto Ricans, in the quality and connections of their dream life, were caught between two conflicting cultures; some few had begun methodically to strive, but most retained the Latin (read: Catholic) heritage of their island background that was bereft of the Puritan notion of worldly work as duty. The future, as Mills and the others saw it, was not a hopeful one for the Puerto Rican migrants of New York City.

Given that the racial makeup of the Puerto Rican enclaves in New York City was Spanish, Caribbean Indian, and Black, Mills instructed his interviewers to record the respondents' physical type according to a three-category distinction: (1) "White," of Spanish ancestry; (2) "intermediate," which included the *indio* who had copper-colored skin and prominent cheekbones, and the *grifo*, who might be quite light complexioned, with blue or gray eyes, but had kinky hair (*pelo malo*), or had some other combination of racial features; and (3) the "Negro," which included Blacks and mulattoes. In general, the interviewers were expected to classify the respondents with respect to skin color (white, tan, brown, black), hair (kinky, wavy, straight), lips (thick, medium, thin), and nose (narrow-thin, medium, broad-fleshy).

Upon arriving in New York, the Puerto Rican migrants were either plunged into one of two worlds, or they had to exist between them. If they were White, they had to adjust themselves to the dominant White culture of New York; if they were not White, they had no choice but to blend into the

African American community. Whereas the White migrants had to take on the behavior and values of White America, the "colored" migrants found that they had to adapt themselves to Black America. Although no other community would accept them, the intermediately colored Puerto Ricans were frequently unwilling to identify themselves with the African American community.

Mills and his colleagues found that in New York, the Puerto Rican migrants became products, producers, and victims of ethnic, social, and cultural conflict. They had been products of cultural and racial conflicts on the island where, even though discrimination was subtle, they nevertheless had created racial classifications on the basis of skin color and physical appearance. The Puerto Rican migrants were producers of further ethnic antagonisms in New York City where they became acutely aware of other minorities. However, the migrants did not absorb ethnic group prejudice to any great extent, as indicated by their willingness to work with other ethnic and racial groups. All of the Puerto Ricans, but especially those in the intermediate racial classification—the *grifos* and *indios*—believed that they were victims of racial prejudice in the metropolis. Mills and his colleagues found strong indications that, among the intermediate group, problems of adjustment were more acute.

Difficult Adaptation

Mills and his associates point out that in order for the Puerto Rican migrants to find even minimal comfort, they had to cross an enormous cultural and social gulf to a world that contrasted sharply with the community they knew back on the island. Indeed, in the metropolis, and even in the clusters of Puerto Rican settlement, the migrants had no community in the sense of a shared life in a familiar area. In New York, instead of "communities in the sun" like those realized in the Puerto Rican plaza, there was only congregation in the crowded, often cold and dirty, always hurried streets. The streets of New York offered a poor substitute for the community interaction that existed in the slower-paced and more ample life of Puerto Rico.

The Puerto Ricans' legal status as U.S. citizens notwithstanding, Mills, Senior, and Goldsen contend that psychologically and culturally they were foreigners in New York City because of the dramatic contrast between their largely rural island with its Spanish heritage and the American metropolis. It is easy to see how Mills himself may have personally understood the migrant's difficulty with the process of assimilation through adaptation. Try as he might, Mills was never able to escape his outlander status. In effect, Mills lived on the cultural margins of provincial Texas, on the one hand, and of metropolitan New York, on the other, while never completely belonging to either.

For the Puerto Rican migrants arriving in New York, adaptation to their new environment was particularly difficult. This was so primarily because New York City, being multicultural, did not offer the migrants a consistent set of available norms to which to adapt. The only constants in this heterogeneous world were the representatives of society at large, that is, the official authorities. Moreover, the usual and most obvious way a person becomes conspicuous to the society as a whole is by coming to the attention of these authorities and their agencies, which occurs when he or she causes them trouble. In the United States in particular, economic trouble is viewed as considerable, both for the individual and for the officials. In fact, "trouble" for the official agencies is likely to be anything that costs them money, directly or as time and effort. The degree to which money trouble made the Puerto Rican community conspicuous was illustrated by the publicity given to Puerto Ricans on welfare.

Mills et al. posit that there are objective as well as subjective meanings of *adaptation.* Objectively, and from the standpoint of society, adaptation can have only a formal meaning: to stay alive by not coming to the attention of the authorities. This means that the migrant must "function inconspicuously." Subjectively, and from the psychological point of view of the migrant, satisfactory adaptation must include some kind of psychic contentment. Combining its objective and subjective meanings, Mills et al. (1950) define adaptation as "inconspicuous functioning with psychic contentment" (p. 141). The opposite of this state is conspicuous lack of functioning accompanied by psychic discontent. According to Mills et al., low fluency in English and coming into trouble with the official authorities and agencies were the factors that contributed the most to the migrants' psychic discontent. Lack of language proficiency was a threat to the migrants' ego, and this created in them feelings of suspicion, anger, dejection, and hostility toward that in which they could not participate. This caused them to further withdraw from the wider New York scene. In addition, if the migrants needed help with family problems or money troubles, to the extent that they came to the attention of official agencies or even thought of going to them, that entailed an insecurity, which is to say, a certain amount of psychic discontent.

Mills and his researchers found that language proficiency was the most important factor in adaptation, having money troubles was next in importance, and coming in contact with official agencies was the least important. In addition, Mills, Senior, and Goldsen isolated several major variables influencing the adaptation of Puerto Ricans in the New York milieu. They found that the Puerto Rican migrants with the highest predisposition for adaptation—that is, for functioning inconspicuously and having a high degree of psychic contentment—were White males under the age of 35 who were employed and had at least some high school education. In contrast, the migrants with the lowest predisposition for adaptation were older women of intermediate color who had little or only grammar school education and were unemployed.

Puerto Ricans who planned to leave or thought about leaving New York were about evenly divided between those who felt pulled back to the island and those who felt pushed from New York City. Those who felt pulled toward the island intended to return to Puerto Rico because of a job or family expecting them. The other half—those who felt pushed from New York—indicated the limitations on real aspirations in the city, the difficulties of properly rearing children, and the impossibility of finding peace of mind in New York.

In New York, the family—or more precisely, the household (since the Puerto Rican "family" was defined by residence rather than blood)—formed the migrants' basic set of relations. Their center of social organization was, therefore, the household—which itself tended toward fragmentation into homeless and anxiety-ridden individualism. Any attempts by the migrants to enlarge their world beyond the household and street were frequently beset with great difficulties and frustrations.

Outside of the household, the migrants' social world usually became impersonal, casual, distant, and confusing. The lack of community and the subsequent isolation of the individual, generally characteristic of modern metropolitan society, became all the more acute for the migrant, a man or woman on the cultural margins of two worlds. There is, however, a positive side, according to Mills and his associates. The migrants' personal freedom had increased in the city; they were freer to pursue new ideas and ambitions and were also able to escape from the island's rigid moral standards. Yet, in many cases, their freedom did not compensate for the loss of psychic security and comfort previously provided by the tight social control of small communities in Puerto Rico.

Furthermore, according to Mills and his coauthors, the Puerto Rican migrant's circumscribed worlds of Spanish Harlem and Morrisania were not unified, and they did not produce strong feelings of solidarity beyond the general slogans of national pride. However, the researchers discovered that the migrants exhibited growing feelings of solidarity with other Spanish-speaking peoples in New York City. There seemed to be emerging a Spanish consciousness and a Latino type. In its less formal aspects, the Latin solidarity was suggested by conversations among recently arrived Puerto Ricans who called themselves "Latinos" and referred to East Harlem as "El Barrio Latino." Indeed, when dealing with Latinos, Puerto Ricans considered them as "belonging to our race." This feeling of identity and the creation of a Latino type are based on several factors. First, there was the common language, Spanish, implying a preexisting connection with Latinos of all nationalities. Second, there existed a kind of abstract community feeling maintained by a pervasive "anti-Yankee" sentiment. For some Puerto Ricans, the Latino type of solidarity served as a core of resistance to assimilation and to the hard travail attending it. It led Puerto Ricans toward both a non–Puerto Rican and non-American type of adjustment, a type that was easier than and more congenial to their previous orientation. Mills and his colleagues note that this Latino pattern of conduct and feeling was a somewhat "Americanized" variety of the general pattern of Spanish culture. At the very least, there were parallels within it that were closer to American than to Puerto Rican cultural habits. Finally, Mills et al. explain that the Latino identity allowed Puerto Ricans to rise in their status as minority group members. Their self-image was better served as Latinos than as *Puertoriqueños*. In their struggle to escape their minority position, they could reach out and borrow prestige from some larger and more favored minority group. To the extent that there were romantic elements in this Latino image Puerto Ricans had of themselves, these elements were a thing of pride and necessary for enduring their difficult life.

Whereas "The Sailor, Sex Market, and Mexican" ignited Mills's interest in Hispanics as minority populations, *The Puerto Rican Journey* served as an intellectual transit obliging him to undertake an intense investigation of the Latin American question: the problem of how the Latin American countries are positioned with respect to the United States' hegemonic control of hemispheric affairs. In his intellectual biography on Mills, Horowitz (1983) states that "[s]ince the mid-1940s, when he had written essays on Mexican barrios in Los Angeles (which were followed, later, with research on the Puerto Rican communities of New York), Mills had had a special at-a-distance love affair with Latin peoples" (p. 299).

Clearly, by 1960, Mills's familiarity with Latinos had been transformed into a near-obsessive desire not only to understand their world thoroughly, but also to educate others, particularly North Americans, on the Latin American struggle for self-determination in the face of U.S. imperialism. Mills inveighed against U.S. intervention in Latin America and began to see the significance of the newly achieved Cuban Revolution as an opportunity for the United States to rethink its foreign policy in relation to the third world Cold War strategy and Latin American containment.

Cuban Revolutionaries

"In Mexico, in Cuba, in Brazil," writes the Mexican novelist Carlos Fuentes (1970), "Wright [Mills] discovered a world that was worth fighting for"

(p. 104). By 1960, Latin America had become for Mills the object of intense fascination. It was also during this period that his pamphleteering and evangelical fervor reached a fevered pitch. With this in mind, we now turn to a discussion of Mills's book about the revolution in Cuba, the highly controversial and much maligned *Listen, Yankee* (1960d).

Largely as a result of his meetings and discussions with Fuentes and other Latin American intellectuals during the early part of 1960, Mills became captivated by the recent triumph of the revolution in Cuba. Mills (1960d) frankly admits that,

> [u]ntil the summer of 1960, I had never been to Cuba, nor even thought about it much. In fact, the previous fall, when I was in Brazil, and in the spring of 1960, when I was in Mexico for several months, I was embarrassed not to have any firm attitudes towards the Cuban revolution. (p. 9)

While in Mexico, Mills decided "to look into Cuba," and upon completing his lecturing tour, returned to the States with tentative plans to write about Cuba's 3-month-old indigenous insurrection, which had been created and successfully completed by intellectuals and pragmatists: Fidel Castro, Ernesto "Che" Guevara, Camilo Cienfuegos, and the *Fidelistas*. Castro and his rebel army had supposedly studied *The Power Elite* during their guerrilla campaign in the mountains of the Sierra Maestra, from 1957–1958 (K. Mills & Mills, 2000). Readily accepting Castro's personal invitation to visit a Cuba in revolutionary transition, Mills traveled to that country in August of 1960. On his trek through the island, he observed the common people building new schools, poultry houses, and fisheries. He saw the *campesino* rebel soldiers planting thousands of eucalyptus trees, and raising peanuts, cotton, and tomatoes. In short, Mills witnessed the innovative ways in which Cubans were beginning to build, at breakneck speed, an entirely new society. He regarded the Cuban Revolution as a humanist revolution because it did not deprive people of their essence, but found its justification in caring for their needs (Mills, 1960d).

Armed with a tape recorder, Mills spent three 18-hour days and an additional half-day with Castro. Having been given complete access to information, Mills interviewed many of the principal government officials, including Oswaldo Dorticós Torrado, the Cuban president, and Che Guevara, president of the National Bank of Cuba and Castro's right-hand man. Evidently, Mills held Guevara in high regard, as 2 years later he included an excerpt from Guevara's "Notes for the Study of the Ideology of the Cuban Revolution" in *The Marxists* (1962).

Mills also greatly admired the pragmatism of the young intellectuals and students from the University of Havana who, seemingly devoid of political dogmatism, were leading the revolution. He refers to the young intellectuals as the "new men" and sees them as being original, spontaneous, and unafraid of what had to be done in Cuba. He describes their pragmatic organization as a "do-it-yourself outfit," not oriented to any particular ideological blueprint. The plan for the new Cuba, Mills tells his readers, is not informed by capitalism or Stalinism, but by "socialism of a sort." He fully expected other Latin American countries to follow the spontaneity and pragmatism of the Cuban model in overcoming their own abject poverty and miserable conditions.

Mills also spoke to hundreds of Cubans while traveling the length of the island; in particular, he interviewed those close to events of the revolution and who, once trust was established, Mills maintains, were eager to express everything they felt. Mills (1960c) contends that trust was given to him, not because of any particular viewpoint he held toward the Cubans or their revolution, but simply because of their acquaintance with his books. Mills's interviewing strategy was straightforward (and presumably in accordance with his rules for interviewers listed in chapter 2): He asked a few fruitful questions and then sought out and listened closely to as wide a variety of answers as he could find. The object was to apprehend the Cubans' revolutionary mood, to understand their agonies, hopes, and aspirations. No doubt Mills was deeply moved by what he heard, for by the time he completed his intensive study of the small Caribbean nation, he had already personalized—and internalized—its revolution as a symbol of the properly developing society.

After a few weeks in Cuba, Mills returned to the United States and immediately began work on *Listen, Yankee*, which he completed in just 6 weeks' time. The book was published within a few months, as a paperback, and sold nearly half a million copies. "My major aim in this book," comments Mills (1960d), "is to present the voice of the Cuban revolutionary, as clearly and as emphatically as I can, and I have taken up this aim because of its absurd absence from the news of Cuba available in the United States" (p. 8).

Cuba Speaks

Listen, Yankee consists of a brief introduction followed by eight "letters" in which Mills uses direct speech to convey a composite viewpoint of how the Cuban revolutionaries see their revolution as well as how they define their aspirations and their relationship with the United States. As a point of startling fact, it is instructive to note Mills's social psychological use of three literary devices in *Listen, Yankee*. First, there is the ostensibly depersonalized "we," which he employs as part of his ongoing effort to reach the masses, and which is really a generalized "I" (Horowitz, 1983). Mills's (1960d) disclaimer notwithstanding—"insofar as I have been able, I have refrained from expressing a personal opinion" (p. 12)—he is clearly speaking for his partisan self; that is to say, he is writing as a propagandist who has internalized and converted to the idea of Cuba's revolution. According to Gerth and Mills (1953), "[a]bsolute belief justifies and motivates the actions of the propagandist who would convert others and thus spread his faith" (p. 292).

Second, speaking specifically to North Americans, Mills throughout the book doggedly, almost mercilessly, addresses them by the moniker used by Latin Americans in referring to citizens of the United States: "Yankee." This appellation presents Americans with the idea that *others* hold views of *them*. Thus, in employing this politically charged epithet, Mills intends to dislodge Americans from their provincialism and political indifference and make them conscious and self-aware of the fact that a hatred had been building up of what the U.S. government and American corporations were doing in the third world:

> What is done and what is not done In Your Name about Cuba, is being watched by people all over the world. In it, these peoples see "the Yankee" revealing himself; when they read about Cuba and about the United States, they are reading about what "Yankee" means today. . . . Nobody ever sees himself as others see him, and we've tried to explain in our very first letter why you and we have not really known each other. (Mills, 1960d, pp. 151–152)

In letter eight, Mills tells Americans that "Yankee" has principally meant one thing to Cubans: insane hurtfulness. The appellation, being synonymous with arrogant imperialism, is not a favorable one, and Mills presses its dubious significance to great advantage by peppering the book with the revolutionary cry of defiance, *Cuba sí, Yanqui no!* Furthermore, the designation "Yankee"—as a symbol—confronts North Americans with an image of their national character, an image dramatically different from that which they hold of Latin Americans. Accordingly, Mills not only makes it clear that Yankees are not Cubans and Cubans are not Yankees, but that there are "two Americas," a rich northern half and an impoverished southern half. Speaking in the voice of the Cuban revolutionary, Mills exhorts that "perhaps we Latin Americans had better realize that the people of whom we are a part is not part of whatever civilization you North Americans belong to. Once and for all, let us get it straight: we belong to the peoples of the hungry nations" (p. 30).

The third, and perhaps most effective, rhetorical technique that Mills adroitly employs is that of speaking in the voice of the Cuban revolutionary. This "voice" is presumably a synthesis of the various sentiments Mills heard articulated while in Cuba. However, in order to give legitimacy to this collective voice, in the book Mills appears not as an observer, but as an actor in the revolutionary process. In effect, he takes on, that is, internalizes, the role of the Cuban revolutionary. The end result is that Mills introduces North Americans to the voice—the vocabulary of motive—of the generalized other that was emerging in revolutionary Cuba. There is, however, a great irony in the fact that Mills, being severely monolingual, presents the Cuban voice to the American public in English, the language of imperialism. "Of all our social acquisitions, perhaps our vocabulary is most directly geared to our perceptions. Our perception is organized in terms of symbols, and our vocabularies influence the perceptions to which we are sensitive" (Gerth & Mills, 1953, p. 71).

To be sure, Mills considers Cuba's voice as the voice of the hungry-nation bloc (that is, Asia, Africa, and Latin America), and the Cuban revolutionary, he believes, was speaking (mainly through Mills's book) in the name of many people in that bloc. For Mills, it was imperative that Cuba's voice be heard in the United States because this country was too powerful, its responsibilities to the world and to itself too great, for North Americans not to listen to every voice in the hungry world. Up to that point, the American public had virtually ignored Cuba, and Mills pleads with them to hear well the message of the Cuban Revolution. For only by dealing with the perils of ignorance could the perils of disastrous mistakes be avoided.

Indeed, Mills maintains that mistakes with calamitous global consequences had already been made by the U.S. government through its clandestine plan to train an exiled paramilitary Cuban force for the purpose of overthrowing Castro. Ironically, at the time that Mills was interviewing Cubans in order to present the truth about the revolution to the American public, President Dwight D. Eisenhower was approving a budget of $13 million for the covert operation, which had by that time become somewhat of an open secret.

Aftermath

After the publication of *Listen, Yankee*, Mills came under scrutiny by the investigative agencies of the U.S. government. He also received threatening phone calls from the "Tigres" and other counterrevolutionary organizations of Cuban exiles in the United States. In one such anonymous call, Mills was told that if he continued to defend Cuba, he had better take care to prevent his little daughter from having an accident (Fuentes, 1970). What is more, a Cuban exile, who claimed he had been libeled in the book, filed a lawsuit against Mills. About these Cuban exiles—"The Batistas" and "The Defectors"—Mills

(1960d), in the voice of the Cuban revolutionary speaking to North Americans, writes,

> The Batistas who got away and The Defectors who ran off—they will, of course, try to make the counterrevolution. Most of them certainly don't have the courage to become military men themselves. But they are conspiring against us and we believe that Yankee interests and your Yankee Government is helping them do this. . . . Your Government is protecting in the U.S.A. war criminals from the old Batista regime. Probably your CIA is recruiting some of them while they plot to harass our work and quite possibly to invade us. (p. 64)

Mills wrote these lines just one year prior to the abortive Bay of Pigs invasion of Cuba planned by the CIA in conjunction with the Cuban exiles in the United States. In *CSS*, Gerth and Mills (1953) outline the steps leading to counterrevolutionary formation:

> New leaders of a counterrevolution are appraised as past experience is rationalized. New theories are developed which dispute the legitimacy of the revolutionary regime and debunk, psychologically, theoretically, and politically, its new measures and styles of life. So after the first revolutionary shocks have been overcome, fatalism and defeatism tend to wane and give way to political plotting, inspired by the observation of incipient cracks and points of strain in the new structure. Out of informal gatherings grow nuclei of political and perhaps eventually military organizations. Their leaders play on the sentiments of the disappointed, woo the good will of foreign governments who may hesitate to grant recognition to the revolutionary regime. (pp. 444–445)

Despite his internalization of the Cuban Revolution, Mills cautions its supporters against being caught up in a state of ecstasy, being beyond themselves, against being taken by the revolutionary euphoria of the moment. Careful not to become infected by the revolution's ebullient spirit, Mills (1960d) worries that the charismatic figure of Fidel Castro could potentially subvert freedom and democracy in Cuba. "I do not like such dependence upon one man as exists in Cuba today, nor the virtually absolute power that this one man possesses" (p. 182). In *CSS*, Gerth and Mills identify three psychological aspects experienced by the charismatic leader and his or her followers immediately following a revolution: (1) Charismatic leaders experience time as a crisis, a turning point. They see their time as the beginning of all time. (2) Charismatics and their followers experience social life as a new reality, one that is optimistic and seemingly infinite. "With eyes fixed on the distant yet foreshortened goal, they move ahead with the certainty of the sleepwalker, often immunized against the costs of blood, self-sacrifice and terror which the deliberate destruction of the old entails" (p. 447). (3) The charismatic leader and followers feel that freedom has increased for all. This newfound liberation produces an expanded generalized other, which inspires the charismatic group's sense of mission. These three aspects of revolutionary mentality are seldom experienced self-consciously; if left unbridled, they could potentially subvert the revolution.

Castro had personally promised Mills that he would never embrace communism. By 1961, Mills's faith in Castro had peaked. But it was not long before Castro, with his identification with the Soviet Union, had seemingly broken his promise, and Mills could not help but feel betrayed. "In his last months Mills was torn between defending *Listen, Yankee,* as a good and honest book, and acknowledging publicly for the first time in his life that he had been terribly wrong" (Swados, 1963, p. 42). In a larger context, however, for Mills, Latin America seemed to represent the ideal typical oppressed region, whether in Spanish Harlem or Playa Girón, Cuba (Horowitz, 1983). His intention, at the time of his death in 1962, was to write a book on Latin America (Landau, 1965).

Whereas the North American public either dismissed or condemned Mills's message in *Listen, Yankee,* Latin American intellectuals praised him. Indeed, the affection seemed to be mutual as Mills increasingly turned his attention away from the English-speaking first world and toward the Spanish-speaking third world. As Horowitz (1983) explains, Mills "became lionized by everyone from Fidel Castro to Carlos Fuentes, receiving the sort of flattery his colleagues in American sociology, especially at Columbia, had entirely denied him" (p. 296).

Latin American Intellectuals

In March of 1960 and just prior to his Cuban sojourn, Mills was interviewed in Mexico City by four writers and intellectuals—Víctor Flores Olea, Enrique Gonzáles Pedrero, Carlos Fuentes, and Jaime García Torres—about his thoughts on Latin America, the Left, and the United States. Judging from the tang and feel of the interview questions, these cultural figures of the noncommunist or independent Left were apparently expecting Mills not only to condemn U.S. imperialism in Latin America, but also to identify that imperialism as the main factor contributing to the region's underdevelopment. If this was indeed their expectation, Mills disappointed them, for he exhorted Latin American intellectuals not to consider the major source of Latin America's abject poverty to be the imperialist power of the United States (although Mills makes it clear that he is not an apologist for U.S.

policies), but rather the power elite in their own countries. Mills (1961) goads the intellectuals to take a pragmatic approach in understanding and rectifying the Latin American countries' political and economic plight:

> Another point I want to make, you probably won't like. It is this: one of the chief obstacles to the development—the modernization and the industrialization—of many Latin American countries does not lie *outside* those countries at all. Nor does it lie in the "ignorance," "laziness," "apathy," and so on of the populations of these countries. It lies with the ruling groups of those countries. . . .
>
> What I am trying to say is this: were I a Latin American in any given country I would first of all try to explain why my country was not further developed, or not developing faster, by exhausting all the internal factors that I possibly could. Only then would I search for the external mechanics. I think that this is not only good methodology, but it is also, if I may say so, politically more effective, for the simple reason that the Chilean intellectual, for example, can do very little *directly* about United States policies. But he can declare political and economic war on his own ruling groups in so far as they are deterring real development. (pp. 117–118, emphasis original)

Mills proceeds to admonish the Latin American intellectuals for their tendency to excuse their own political inactivity by reference to what the United States will or will not do. He chides them to get on with the business of conducting a serious sociological study of every Latin American country that would (1) render a penetrating account of the ruling structures in each country and (2) give a measurement of the extent to which these ruling structures, and the entire lack of development of these countries, could be conscientiously imputed to the economic, political, and military policies of the United States. When the answers to these two questions are obtained, Mills informs his interviewers, they will have no more excuses for their political inactivity and will stop imputing Latin America's misfortune to relations with the United States.

One main inference can be made from Mills's comments: that the national character of Latin Americans in general, and Latin American intellectuals in particular, is centered around blaming the United States for their countries' economic misery, abysmal backwardness, and various social injustices. By the early 1960s, Mills quite consciously rejects the negative stereotypical traits typically attributed to the Latin American personality—ignorance, laziness, apathy—and holds Latin Americans responsible for their own fate. Mills is well aware of the fact that true freedom of action, that is to say, engaging in free initiative for self-determination and accepting responsibility for choices made, can occur only after negative stereotypes—selected images of the symbol sphere that highlight a group's liabilities of conduct—are dispelled.

Individuation of the self results from the variety and scope of voluntary actions which we undertake. It involves the reality of individual decision and being held responsible for personal choices.

Personal or joint "responsibility" exists socially when the individual, as an individual or as a member of a group, is held accountable for his activities, in short, when his acts are ascribed to his self or his group. In a society where roles are quite stereotyped, this reality of alternatives, and such conceptions as personal responsibility, may not exist. (Gerth & Mills, 1953, p. 100)

Latin American Identity and Latino Personality

In sum, it may be said that Mills's 20-year fascination with, first, Latinos, and later, Latin American affairs was significantly informed by the social psychological theoretical framework proffered in CSS. Mills's view of Latinos, their traits and motives, yielded a character structure that was initially (and during a time when he had little knowledge of these populations and was in the process of formulating the social psychological paradigm) based on gross stereotypes of them as minority members within the context of United States culture. Thus, in 1943, Mexican American zoot suiters were seen by Mills as frustrated young men who were afflicted with low self-esteem and continuously seeking the attention and respect of the Anglo majority. In 1950, he considered Puerto Rican islanders to be "culture-less," hollow, and hysterical. In New York City, Puerto Rican migrants were, according to Mills, motivated by economic forces, but had low economic and educational aspirations, and suffered from a considerable amount of psychic discontent. As a provincial Texan, he found the behavior of Puerto Ricans living in the Lower East Side of New York and in Spanish Harlem to be "strange."

However, by 1960, after he had traveled through Latin America and years after completing his social psychological conceptualization, Mills came to understand the Latin American personality within the context of United States imperialism. Cuban revolutionaries were viewed favorably as innovative, original, and pragmatic, and Latin American intellectuals as capable of helping their countries achieve self-determination.

Biographical Experiences

An examination of Mills's biography, including his view of individuals and society, helps to assess the personal experiences and convictions, the associations and views, that he had regarding Latinos during the most active and productive period of his career, 1943 to 1960. Mills, who had moved from the relative calm of the Maryland suburb of Greenbelt directly to the frantic environment of the metropolis in order to become a "New York intellectual," hopelessly remained a product of his parochial Texas heritage. To be sure, Mills throughout his life was culturally and psychologically an "outlander," caught between two worlds, isolated and never quite belonging anywhere. He did not feel accepted by, nor was he accepting of, academic sociology, his colleagues at Columbia University, or the New York Jewish intellectuals. Mills's marginal status and identity doubtless instilled in him a dialectical disposition toward other marginal peoples. For example, while on the one hand, he maintained his distance from the Puerto Rican migrants (whom he obviously did not wish to interview since he interviewed only English-speaking officials and intellectuals), he on the other hand was deeply curious about "the full human meaning of the journey from Puerto Rico to New York City and of the splendors and miseries of the people who make it" (Mills et al., 1950, p. lvi). His compelling interest in statuses and identities and which of the two, *Puertoriqueño* or Latino, was most advantageous for the Puerto Rican migrant to adopt, seems to express his own unresolved dilemma of self-image in New York City: whether to, psychologically and culturally, identify and conduct himself as a southwestern cowboy or as an East Coast intellectual.

Mills's romanticized recollections of his maternal grandfather, Braxton Bragg Wright, also involved an odd admixture of views about Mexicans. In Mills's mind at least, his grandfather had had amorous affairs with (or at least was attracted to) Mexican women and had a deadly encounter with a Mexican man. According to Mills, Bragg Wright was shot in the back with a 30-30 rifle for one of two reasons: It may have been because he "liked the girls—married and unmarried, Mexican and white. This one was Mexican and married, a bad combination for him" (as quoted in K. Mills & Mills, 2000, p. 25). Or else Bragg Wright was killed "over somebody's waterhole," from a bullet fired by a Mexican as an act of vengeance. Regardless of which colorful version of the story he did or did not believe, Mills's image of his rugged ancestor prominently involved Mexicans, rifles, and death (see Gillam, 1966, p. 9 ff.). Indeed, in Freudian fashion, sex and violence are the two lenses through which Mills viewed the Mexican American zoot suiters and their *pachuquitas* in understanding their sentiments and motives.

While his mother's Roman Catholicism made no particularly strong impression on Mills, his Protestant father's emphasis on "the gospel of work" remained for him a significant influence throughout his life. This may explain Mills's contempt for the Catholic Puerto Rican migrants' low aspirations toward work and getting ahead.

Pragmatism, as an early intellectual influence upon Mills, taught him to forge a fusion between theory and practice. In this regard, he admired the Cuban intellectuals for their attempts to make a "do-it-yourself" revolution.

Further, borrowing from Mannheim's notion concerning the social influence of free intellectuals, Mills saw them as capable of constructing reality for others. This idea of the union of power and intellect, which he first articulated in *The New Men of Power,* may shed some light on Mills's peculiar combination of admiration and fear, respect and suspicion that he had for the charismatic authority of Fidel Castro.

As we saw in Chapter 2, Mills viewed individuals as possessing a nature that is volitional and active and that endows them with the potential to be free. In his view, the good society—the properly developing society—was a democracy in which social issues were debated openly before a community of free and knowledgeable publics. Thus, while Mills was much inspired by the ability of the Cuban intellectuals to make history, he was also concerned about the revolution imposing limits on their political freedom. In addition, he appears to have had great faith in the ability of Latin American intellectuals to make their own history, to be responsible for their own fate, despite U.S. interference in their countries' political and economic affairs.

Historically Located Social Structures

Mills's analytical approach, which maintains that in order to understand the inner lives of individuals, they must be placed within the context of historically located social structures, provides several insights into the epochal events and institutional setup that the four Latino groups experienced as part of their private troubles in their daily lives.

Mills intimates that during World War II, Mexican Americans in general, and zoot suiters in particular, were subjected to several onerous influences of a racist society: crowded slum conditions; the segregated military; and various forms of ethnic oppression including racial segregation, job discrimination, and class antagonisms. However, he specifically attributed the 1943 Zoot Suit Riots to one major structural factor: the war condition of the sex market. In this case, the sex market involved a place (Los Angeles) where there were large numbers of single men (young sailors on leave) versus a much smaller number of sex-able women (the *pachuquitas*). This sex ratio created tension-centers throughout the city which turned riotous when the sailors and zoot suiters competed for the Mexican girls.

Mills also explained the personality types of people in Puerto Rico and Cuba with reference to social structural and cultural factors—in particular, the political, economic, and cultural dominance that the United States exerted over these tiny Caribbean islands. As concerns Puerto Rican islanders, Mills suggested that mainland culture—through advertising, language, patterns of race consciousness, and the like—had distorted their Spanish lifestyle, mannerisms, and values, and thus transformed the islanders from "Latin Americans" to "Puerto Rican Americans." Mills also recognized that a series of economic, familial, and other structural forces operated as push-pull mechanisms impelling some Puerto Ricans to migrate to New York City.

In Cuba, the social structural—that is, imperialist—forces of the United States affecting the island in the early 1960s were politically and economically coercive. Owing to the rabid anticommunism of the Cold War era, the U.S. government was overtly and covertly, politically and economically preparing Cubans, both islanders and exiles, to overthrow Fidel Castro and counter the revolution that he had started. By contrast, Mills saw the economic and political orders as well as the symbols, status, technology, and education spheres that the rebel soldiers and intellectuals were constructing in Cuba in largely positive terms: as pragmatic and humanistic.

Again, as concerns his analysis of social structural factors, Mills found that the Puerto Rican migrants, as members of an ethnic and racial minority group, were generally uninvolved with social agencies and organizations in New York. Instead, the migrants' household became almost their entire social world, as they found the metropolis to be an environment inhospitable to making friends and rearing children.

Character Structures

Perhaps most significant to the four writings considered here are Mills's observations regarding the character structures of Mexican American zoot suiters, Puerto Rican islanders and migrants, Cubans in revolutionary transition, and Latin American writers and social scientists. These observations are highly informative as he renders a poignant psychological inquiry into the Latino experience in various social milieus. Mills's early stereotypical commentary notwithstanding, he accurately describes the Mexican American zoot suiters in Los Angeles as requiring a unique image of themselves that called others', but in particular the majority group's, attention to them and, through the status sphere, provided the zoot suiters with a degree of self-esteem. Thus, Mills undoubtedly understood why, in this particular social context, the zoot suiters needed to adopt a certain personality type: the personality type formed by identification with the symbol sphere of the minority group (i.e., the *pachuco* lifestyle and its emblematic zoot suit), and that seeks status from this identification. When his main status symbol, the zoot suit, was literally torn off his "person," and he was subsequently degraded further in front of his girlfriend, by the very people from whom he craved deference, the Mexican American youth, Mills predicted, will vent his rage through lethal violence.

As noted above, Mills saw the Puerto Rican islander's identity as being driven by an ambivalence that stemmed from the competing Latin and continental United States cultural influences and ways of thinking that barraged the island population. The predicament for the islanders was whether to identify with the Latin culture, the American, neither, or both. Elements of the two cultures invariably prevailed (the mainland culture infiltrating the island primarily through commercial advertisements), and the islanders adopted an ambiguous identity: that of Puerto Rican Americans. Thus, politically, economically, and culturally the islanders occupied an indeterminate position, being neither Latin American nor full cultural participants in the dominant U.S. culture.

The migrants in New York, as minority group members, were doubly and even trebly endowed with an ambiguous and ambivalent identity. If the New York migrants were White, they had to adjust to the majority culture of White America; if Black, the Puerto Rican migrants had to try to insinuate themselves into the African American community. The intermediate *indios* and *grifos,* however, were often unwilling to identify themselves with the African American community. Thus, the intermediates had the most ambiguous, even confusing, image of themselves. On the island they were, strictly speaking, neither Latin Americans nor North Americans. As "foreigners" in New York City, they were neither purely New Yorkers nor *Puertoriqueños.* As members of an intermediate racial group, they were neither Black nor White. Thus, due largely to their conflicted self-identity, Mills found that the intermediate group's problems of adjustment were especially acute. As concerns their psychic life, Mills found the Puerto Rican migrants to have a high degree of discontent because of their lack of fluency in English and their conspicuous contact with official authorities.

Mills states that his purpose in tape-interviewing the Cuban people was to understand their revolutionary mood, their agonies, hopes, and aspirations. It is difficult to assess to what extent he was able to truly capture the Cubans' sentiments. However, judging from the words of praise Mills received in personal letters sent to him by Mexico City publisher Arnaldo Orfila Reynal and a young Cuban scholar, Armando Betancourt, he was at least successful in understanding the revolutionary mood as Latin American leftist intellectuals would have wanted him to. Orfila Reynal wrote,

> In reading aloud your *Listen, Yankee!* with my wife, we were deeply touched with the greatness you show in your sheer understanding of the root of the problems of our Continent. It is the exact essence of the Cuban Revolution. I want to express to you the profound satisfaction I feel to be able to diffuse your beautiful message to the Spanish-speaking world. (as quoted in Horowitz, 1983, p. 297)

Betancourt wrote in similar effusive terms:

> Your name is already popular in all Cuba, to say Wright Mills sounds to say a friend [sic]. We thank you very deeply from the bottom of our hearts for having done that task, of telling our neighbors to the north the truth about this little island, little in size, but great in hopes, and spirit, and courage. (as quoted in Horowitz, 1983, p. 297)

Finally, the prime example of Mills's pragmatic use of the social psychological approach is found in *Listen, Yankee* where he tries to proselytize to his readers and open their eyes to the "message" of the Cuban Revolution. Mills concretely utilizes his social psychology—and more specifically his sociolingual theory of mind (Mills, 1939) first formulated by G. H. Mead—by organizing his tract into eight letters, "epistles" of a sort, in which he sermonizes to North Americans by employing the collective "we," the appellation "Yankee," and the Cuban revolutionary's "voice." Indeed, Press (1978) attests that "Mills, the Preacher" endeavors "through language to change peoples' minds" (pp. 20–21). In so doing, Mills, speaking in the voice of the Cuban revolutionary applied Weber's concept of Verstehen (interpretive understanding) and, at the end of his life, came to interpretively understand, not only the Cuban revolutionary mood, but also the Latin American identity and the Latino personality.

Conclusion

The foregoing discussion of Mills's writings on Latinos and Latin Americans reveals that the more involved he became in their lives, Mills, in both his personal sentiments as well as in his social psychological theorizing about these populations, seemed to shift his perceptions about them. In the earlier writings, where he considers gang members and immigrants, Mills explains their motives, moods, and self-images in reference to the dominant society exemplified either by the "Anglo" world or by "mainland culture." Thus, in the context of the internal United States—where we can more clearly discern an in-group and an out-group in reference to ethnicity—he characterizes these two minority populations largely in negative terms: as frustrated, discontent, disrespected, hollow, ambiguous, and ambivalent.

It has been suggested that the sociologist Erving Goffman first made use of the term "identity politics" in his classic book, *Stigma*. Here, Goffman (1963) talks about the politics of identity in terms that appear eerily similar to Mills's social psychological apperception of Hispanics as members of a minority group:

The in-group and the out-group, then, both present an ego identity for the stigmatized individual, the first largely in political phrasings, the second in psychiatric ones. The individual is told that if he adopts the right line (which line depending on who is talking), he will have come to terms with himself and be a whole man; he will be an adult with dignity and self-respect.

And in truth he will have accepted a self for himself; but this self is, as it necessarily must be, a resident alien, a voice of the group that speaks for and through him.

But all of us, sociology sometimes claims, speak from the point of view of a group. The special situation of the stigmatized is that society tells him he is a member of the wider group, which means he is a normal human being, but that he is also "different" in some degree, and that it would be foolish to deny this difference. . . .

In brief, he is told that he is like anyone else and that he isn't. . . . This contradiction and joke is his fate and his destiny. (pp. 123–124)

We can only wonder about what Mills's social psychology would have made of a politics of identity had he possessed the conviction to carry it out in this direction.

In contrast to Latino minority populations in the United States, after having traveled and lectured throughout Latin America and having considered those countries' geopolitical situation relative to "the colossus of the north," Mills depicted Latin Americans, but particularly intellectuals and revolutionaries, in more hopeful terms: as masters of their destiny, responsible for their self-determination. In the end, it may have been mere elitism on Mills's part that influenced his humanist concern about these populations: Latin American intellectuals and revolutionaries are volitional and active; Latino gang members and immigrants are complacent and inactionary.

One small but interesting comment may help disclose further Mills's divergent feelings about Latinos, on the one hand, and Latin Americans on the other. In a letter he wrote to his parents 6 days after the Bay of Pigs invasion, Mills contrasted his mother's experiences of Mexican Americans—by whom she was raised in Texas, for whose culture she had the utmost respect, and who formed for her the ideal images of the human being—with the revolutionary Cubans. "The Cubans," Mills explains to his mother, "are my Mexicans" (as quoted in K. Mills & Mills, 2000, p. 331).

Several questions for thought suggest themselves:

- Despite his four writings on Latinos, why is it that Mills never earnestly took up the subject of ethnic discrimination in his more general sociology?
- How accurate are Mills's mid–20th-century perceptions of Latinos in regard to those same populations today?
- How have U.S.–Latin America relations changed, or not changed, since Mills's time?
- Is there a Latino/a sociology that can be derived from Mills's four writings?

6

Mass Society and
Media Markets

Throughout his major works, and in some of his minor ones as well, C. Wright Mills makes repeated reference to the mass media in the context of mass society. Scholars have certainly acknowledged his commentaries on the latter, though few have discussed his thoughts on the former. This chapter constitutes a systematic analysis of Mills's writings on the mass media. While it is true that some of his views about the mass media have been outrun by events since he articulated them, this does not mean that they are outdated. Indeed, readers will find that many of Mills's keen observations about the American media, which he made between the late 1940s and the early 1960s, remain surprisingly fresh and relevant today. Despite his penetrating foresight, however, neither Mills nor his contemporaries could have anticipated the Internet, for example, or, for that matter, the degree to which corporate ownership of the media and entertainment industry has today become concentrated in only a very few conglomerates: the Walt Disney Company, Time Warner, News Corp, and Viacom.

In considering Mills's statements on the mass media, this chapter focuses on what he says about the power elite's monopolization and manipulation of media symbols, the media markets in mass society, the community of publics and the democratic ideal, the public of public opinion, and the media's effects on five distinct populations.

The Monopolization of
Mass Communication and
the Manipulation of Symbols

One of the most intriguing assertions that Mills makes in *The Power Elite* (1956) is that the mass media, as organized and operated during the mid-20th century, was among the most important means of power at the disposal of the political, industrial, and military elites. Using the mass media, the power elites were able to persuade individuals into believing that, through the democratic process, they, as citizens, were making the key decisions affecting the country, when in fact they were not. The reality was that the elites of wealth and power were the ones who truly determined the course of historical events.

In Mills's view, some of the higher agents of the mass media—namely, the image makers involved in opinion molding and in the art of persuasion—were themselves either among the elites or very important among their servants. His point is that the positional relation between the elites and the more influential media agents was not only a close one, but one that, through the manipulation of public opinion, maintained the ideological status quo and thus protected the material and social interests of the former. "Alongside or just below the elites," Mills (1956) explains, "there is the propagandist, the publicity expert, the public-relations man, who would control the very formulation of public opinion in order to be able to include it as one more pacified item in calculations of effective power, increased prestige, more secure wealth" (p. 315).

Indeed, in *Character and Social Structure* (Gerth & Mills, 1953), Mills had previously warned that as the public came to rely less on primary experience and more on such secondary means of communication as the printed page, radio, and motion pictures, the power elite controlling the media were given greater opportunity to select, associate, manipulate, and diffuse symbols that would justify their structural position of power. (As we saw in Chapter 3, Mills describes **symbols** as visual or acoustic signs, signals, emblems, formulas, vocabularies, types of conversation, music, or other arts used in understanding the conduct of human actors.) In addition, Mills maintains that monopoly ownership of the means of communication by the power elite, along with the forceful prohibiting of all counter-symbols, tended to result in a unified symbol sphere dominated by certain images of "legitimation," or master symbols. But master symbols that are forcefully imposed, Mills reminds us, are not likely to be deeply and unquestioningly internalized by the public. In this case, these symbols will not only lack justification, but they will also be devoid of meaningful relevance to the roles, institutions, and feelings characteristic of a given public.

What is more, as the power elite seek to legitimate their power, that is to say, as they endeavor to have the public voluntarily, and out of a sense of duty, comply with their authority, they begin to "grasp all the more compulsively for the channels of mass communication, but their monopolization of these media does not necessarily mean that the symbols they diffuse will be master symbols" (Gerth & Mills, 1953, p. 297). Mills's point, and one that he presses several times in his works, is that, in the United States at least, the means of mass communication possess a measured degree of autonomy. Thus, while the system of mass communication indeed mirrors society, it does so with discrimination and largely independent of the various institutional arrangements. This is not to say, however, that the power elite's monopolization of the media does not have a persuasive, even manipulative, psychological influence on the public's motives and self-images, personality traits, and conduct patterns. On the contrary, Gerth and Mills are well aware that, in a society like the United States where the dominant institutional orders are the political, economic, and military, the legitimating symbols of the whole social structure—prevailing images that are reinforced by the mass media—will likely be related to those orders. In such a society, a type of false consciousness and alienation may be created:

> A person may incorporate, believe in, and use a symbol which motivates a role which he does not enact, or legitimate an institution to which he does not belong. . . . [For example, w]age workers in modern capitalist states may repeat the formulae of laissez-faire, although these symbols may be against the economists' imputation of the workers' rational interest, that is, his interests as "adequate" to his economic and political position within the whole system were he to act "rationally" as an "economic man." Such "mislocated" adherences are increased by modern techniques of mass communication which are, on the one hand, monopolized in favor of some one type of institution, system, or authority, and on the other, used to satisfy irrational fantasies and distract from both art and reality. (p. 302)

But why, we may ask, does the power elite's manipulation of the means of mass communication (subtle though it may be) fail to arouse a clamor of protest, some feeling of outrage, among the public? Broadly speaking, Mills gives two explanations for the public's passivity. First, no general outcry is forthcoming because the American citizenry has been told repeatedly, by commentators and analysts, that the U.S. political system operates on the principle of checks and balances. This rhetorical formula, this ideology of fairness, which has been extensively disseminated through the media, asserts that no centralization of the means of power is possible because there exists a plurality of independent, relatively equal, and conflicting groups—from a multiplicity of regional, state, and local interests to numerous associations and lobbying groups, from labor unions and consumers' groups to Congress and the Supreme Court—all of which are engaged in the political process of balance and compromise. Regrettably, however, this 18th-century doctrine of the equilibrium of powers masquerades as a description of political fact in the realm of "crackpot realism." It obfuscates what Mills regarded as one of the master trends characterizing mid-20th-century America: the bureaucratization of modern society and the power relations it produces through the coordination of the political, economic, and military orders. The concentration of power at the very top echelons of U.S. society has realized a coherent ruling group that now commanded the three dominant interlocking and coordinated directorates (the machinery of the state, the big corporations, and the military establishment), made decisions of enormous consequence for the underlying populations, and determined the course of historical events. In *The Causes of World War Three*, Mills (1958) writes,

> The balance and the compromise in American society—the "countervailing powers" and the numerous associations, the "veto groups" and the "vested interests"—must now be seen as having mainly to do with the middle levels of power. It is about these *middle* levels that political journalists and scholars of politics are most likely to write if only because, being mainly middle-class themselves, they are closer to them. These levels provide the noisy content of most political news and gossip; images of these levels are more or less in accord with the folklore of how democracy works; and, if the master image of balance is accepted, many intellectuals, in their current patrioteering, are readily able to satisfy such political optimism as they wish to feel. Accordingly, such liberal interpretations of what is happening in the United States are now virtually the only interpretations that are widely distributed. (pp. 25–26, emphasis original)

Second, Mills contends that the rank-and-file citizens cannot realistically broker any opposition to the power elite's monopolization of the means of communication and their manipulation of media images because the majority of Americans are afflicted by civic apathy and political indifference. Mills, to be sure, was deeply concerned that the United States was fast becoming a nation of "cheerful robots," apathetic automatons who see their lives as determined by fate. Indeed, in the quiescent mid-1950s it was "fashionable" to pretend that no power elite existed. Owing to this conservative mood of complacency and denial (a mood that, incidentally, found its articulation in the "end of ideology" thesis espoused by Mills's Columbia colleagues Seymour Martin Lipset and Daniel Bell), Mills asserts that the vast numbers of people who composed the bottom level of society were politically fragmented, increasingly powerless, and in danger of becoming a mass-mediated culture—or, in Mills's terms, a mass society of media markets.

The Mass Society of Media Markets

In *White Collar,* Mills (1951) begins his commentary on the mass media with a correction, an extension and elaboration, of Marx's well-known notion that material existence is not determined by consciousness, but consciousness by material existence:

> To believe that "the ideology wherein men become conscious of class conflict and fight it out" is determined solely by "material contradictions" is to overlook the positive role of the mass media of communications. If the consciousness of men does not determine their existence, neither does their material existence determine their consciousness. Between consciousness and existence stand communications, which influence such consciousness as men have of their existence. Men do "enter into definite, necessary relations which are independent of their will," but communications enter to slant the meanings of these relations for those variously involved in them. The forms of political consciousness may, in the end, be relative to the means of production, but, in the beginning, they are relative to the contents of the communication media. (p. 333)

That Marx could make an observation concerning people's consciousness—their ideas, views, and conceptions—without due regard to the persuasive influence of the mass media is understandable given that instantaneous and prepackaged broadcasts of electronic communications did not yet exist in his day. However, in the particular time and place in which Mills was writing, postwar America, there began to emerge the "Fourth Epoch," which exhibited the beginnings of a "mass society." The mass society, which arose out of World War II, produced in popular culture a deadening sameness and vapidity that made possible the general population's commercial and political manipulation. Thus, in contradistinction to the middle decades of the 19th century when Marx was writing, the communication media of Mills's time—particularly radio, television, and motion pictures—most certainly did influence the consciousness of people's existence.

According to Mills (1951), the mass media of postwar mass society evoked in people, but in particular the urban middle classes, mass emotions suitable to their mass behavior. Consider, as does Mills, that

[c]ommerical jazz, soap opera, pulp fiction, comic strips, the movies set the images, mannerisms, standards, and aims of the urban masses. In one way or another, everyone is equal before these cultural machines; like technology itself, the mass media are nearly universal in their incidence and appeal. They are a kind of common denominator, a kind of scheme for pre-scheduled, mass emotions. (p. 333)

Moreover,

[t]he statistically calculated coverage of leisure-time hours by mass media of communication and other machinery of amusement—radio's soap opera for housewives weekday afternoons, Metropolitan Opera Saturday afternoons, NBC symphony concerts Sunday afternoons—contributes to rigidly disciplined, routinized, and therefore predictable patterns of customary mass behavior. (Gerth & Mills, 1953, p. 257)

For Mills, the dominant mass emotion, or psychological character, produced by the mass communication system among the American middle classes was powerlessness; the dominant mass behavior, or social role, was political apathy.

In Mills's view, the mass society, through the mass media's manipulation of images, created *media markets* with people as consumers receiving this propaganda delivered in the guise of "entertainment." Consumers were constantly bombarded with propagandistic messages, which, through marketing techniques were smartly packaged as clichés, shorthand slogans, and pictures, endlessly presented to the targeted audience at the ideal time: when they were "most relaxed of mind and tired of body" (1951, p. 336). In this way, Mills points out, is politics likewise squeezed into formulas which are repeated and repeated and sold to the consumers through the short news flash, the headlined column or snippet, and the editorial. Due to these compressed presentational forms and the fact that citizens have limited time— only about 15 or 20 minutes a day—to devote to the news, the mass media do not offer much in the way of critical analysis, nor does it present opposing political viewpoints, or counter-symbols. In short, the world created by the media contains very little discussion of political meanings. Small wonder that Mills regarded the American public as uninformed and devoid of political consciousness. For Mills (1951), the vested interests of the agencies of mass communication were not only engaged in sanitizing and trivializing political life by replacing form with formula and spinning "records of political emptiness," they were also involved in distracting the media markets from the larger political issues that lay beyond their immediate personal experience:

Events outside the narrow scene of the weekly routine have little meaning and in fact are mostly not known except as they are omitted, refracted, or reported in the mass media. The mass-communication system of the United States is not autonomous: it reflects society, but selectively; it reinforces certain features by generalizing them, and out of its selections and reinforcements creates a world. In so far as people live beyond their immediate range of contacts, it is in this world they must live.

The forms and contents of political consciousness, or their absence, cannot be understood without reference to the world created and sustained by these media. The deprivations and insecurities arising from structural positions and historic changes are not likely to be politically symbolized if these media do not take them up in appropriate contexts, and thus lend generalized, communicable meaning to them. Class-consciousness or its absence, for example, involves not merely the individual's experience in and of some objective class-situation, but the communications to which he is exposed. What he comes to believe about the whole range of issues is in some way a function of his experienced situation, plus first-hand contact with other people, plus his exposure to mass media. And it is often the latter which gives him his standard of reality, his standard of experience. (p. 334)

For Mills, the media's manipulation of one master symbol—the image of individual success—served as a most effective diversion from politics. Gerth and Mills (1953) note that, in the 19th-century United States, the image of individual success clearly dominated the mass media of the time: "Mass literature, from juveniles to human interest stories and novels, succeeded in publicizing the lore of success and the romance of those who had made it: the titans, the tycoons, the robber barons, the founding fathers, the pioneers, the technical heroes" (p. 467). The goals of this effort were first, to uphold the political philosophy of liberalism, the dominant ethos of capitalist societies whose tenets emphasized individual freedom, egalitarianism, liberty, private property, fair competition, a laissez-faire economy, and unlimited opportunities, and second, to celebrate its efficient, successful heroes. A century later, the mass media continued to promote and legitimate this master symbol of private success. As an example, consider, as does Mills, Christopher Morley's rags-to-riches novel, *Kitty Foyle*, which became an instant bestseller when it was published in 1939. (The motion picture based on the book was released the following year.) It is the story of "a modernized Horatio Alger heroine" who aspires to live in affluent suburban Philadelphia. Kitty is an Irish immigrant who turns white-collar career girl. Though she spends her formative years in small-town Illinois, she ultimately ends up pursuing the American Dream in the cosmetics industry in New York City. As Mills (1951) points out, the book ends on a most positive note, with Kitty becoming a successful career woman "in a depression year, with Kitty earning $3,000 a year, about to buy stock in her firm" (p. xi).

By the middle of the 20th century, the master symbol of individual success was no longer used only for the purpose of advancing the tenets of liberalism (for Mills believed that this ideology was in rapid decline), but also with the insidious intent of distracting people's attention from all *structural* political issues. According to Mills (1951),

> The image of success and its individuated psychology are the most lively aspects of popular culture and the greatest diversion from politics. Virtually all the images of popular culture are concerned with individuals, and more, with particular kinds of individuals succeeding by individual ways to individual goals. Fiction and non-fiction, movies and radio—indeed almost every aspect of contemporary mass communication—accentuate *individual* success. Whatever is done is done by individual effort, and if a group is involved, it strings along after the extraordinary leader. There is displayed no upward climb of and by collective action to political goals, but individuals succeeding, by strictly personal efforts in a hostile environment, to personal economic and erotic goals. (pp. 336–337, emphasis added)

In Mills's view, it is the individual exception rather than the facts of collective success and tragedies that is seized upon, diffused, and generalized by the media as a model criterion. Popular culture's romanticizing of mythical figures—stereotyped successful individuals—and the concomitant glamorizing of their private lives divert the public's attention away from social problems such as those resulting from economic inequality. This effort by the entertainment media, this "divertissement" as Mills calls it, serves to forestall, for example, a popular insurrection aimed at distributing wealth and power more equally. Thus, it is not issues, but ideological stereotypes that determine political orientation and conduct. And the ideological stereotypical symbols that legitimate a political order, write Gerth and Mills (1953),

> may be so deeply embedded in mass media and popular mentality that counter-symbols are avoided—even if they stand for programs or policies which people actually want. Thus a majority of certain groups may be in favor of specific policies for which "socialism" stands, but reject the "socialist party" or socialist terminology. (p. 284)

Psychological Illiteracy

Mills (1956) was convinced that the mass media had transformed the American public into a set of media markets in mass-like society. As a result of this transformation, there had developed "a sort of psychological illiteracy," an idiocy in the Greek's definition of the term, among the U.S. citizenry that was facilitated by the media in four ways (p. 311).

To begin with, Mills posits that very little of what people think they know about the social world have they discovered through firsthand experience of raw events. Most of the pictures that people have in their heads about specific social problems, for instance, have been acquired from the media—even to the point where they often do not really believe what they see before them until they read about it in the paper, hear about it on the radio, or see it on TV. In other words, individuals do not trust their own experiences, their own *interpretations* of those experiences, until they are confirmed and deciphered by the newspapers, radio, or television. The media, then, serve as a guide, or more accurately, a substitute, for people's experiences. The upshot is that individuals' standards of what is true and real tend to be set, first and foremost, by these media of mass communication. Consequently, even if the individual has direct personal experience of events, it is not really direct and primary, says Mills: It is mediated by and organized in ideological stereotypes (the theory of balance and the master symbol of individual success being two such examples) that create a pseudo reality. These ideological stereotypes, or "stereotypes of loyalty," act as lenses through which people see their social world and form their specific opinions and views of events. Mills apprises that it takes extended and skillful training to eradicate such stereotypes and see the world anew, in an unstereotyped, unbiased manner. In this regard, Mills (1953), from his mid-20th-century vantage point, was clearly pessimistic about the future, proclaiming that "'the common sense' of our children is going to be less the result of any firm social tradition than of the stereotypes carried by the mass media to which they are now so fully exposed. They are the first generation to be so exposed" (p. 13).

A second way in which the media promote psychological illiteracy among the public is by the lack of genuine competition in the form of informational diversity among the different news sources. Because of the near-absence of this type of competition, the individuals constituting the audience of media markets cannot usually play one medium's content off against another by comparing reports on public events or policies and, in this way, resist the information that any one of those media puts out. Even if the media were not entirely monopolized, whatever competition may exist between the several media takes the form of variations on a few standardized themes, and not the presentation of clashing issues of substantive importance. In addition, comparison of news reports is severely limited because most people tend to strongly select only those radio programs, editorials, and magazine articles that present opinions that resonate with and reinforce their own prior convictions. Very few search out such counter-statements as may be found in alternative media offerings. It therefore comes as no surprise to Mills (1956) that "[t]he freedom to raise issues effectively seems more and more to be confined to those few interests that have ready and continual access to these media" (pp. 313–314).

Next, Mills points out that not only have the media infiltrated people's experience of the external social world, but they have also entered into people's personal experience of their own selves. The media of mass communication have furnished individuals with new identities and new aspirations of what individuals should like to be, and what they should like to *appear* to be. Magazines, radio, and television have provided in the models of conduct they present to people a new, larger, and more flexible set of appraisals of their very selves. In regard to the social psychological notion that people seek out those others who appraise and confirm their prized or aspired-to self-image, Mills maintains that the modern media present the reader, listener, and viewer with many highly influential reference groups. These reference groups—real or imagined, up-close or vicarious, personally known or distractedly glimpsed—that are created by mass media personalities and happenings are character-forming influences. They confirm and appraise people's desired self-image but do so through a psychological formula that has no basis in the real world and is therefore incongruent to the development of the human being. In addition, the media inform individuals in the mass society of four things: (1) The media tell people who they are by giving them identity; (2) they tell people what they want to be by giving them aspirations; (3) the media tell them how to get that way by giving them technique; and (4), they tell people how to feel and that they are feeling a certain way even when they are not, by giving them escape.

Finally, Mills blames the mass media, but especially television, for frequently encroaching upon the small-scale discussion and destroying the chance for any reasonable, leisurely, and human interchange of opinion. Moreover, the media fail to articulate for the viewers and listeners the broader social structural sources of their private tensions and anxieties, their inarticulate resentments and half-formed hopes. The media of mass communication neither enable individuals to transcend their narrow milieu nor clarify its private meaning. Although they provide much information and news about what is happening in the world, the media actually hinder their audiences from truly connecting their daily lives with these larger realities. In this sense, news sources stifle the sociological imagination because they do not associate the information they provide on public issues with the private troubles experienced by the viewing and listening public. The media also fail as an educational force because they do not increase rational insight into either psychological tensions or social tensions that are reflected in the individual's psychology. On the contrary, "the machinery of amusement" or "the mass of media distraction," as Mills sometimes derisively calls the entertainment media, not only amuse, they bemuse, and therefore obscure people's chance to understand themselves or their world. The entertainment media fasten people's attention upon the artificial frenzies of the radio or television program—highly dramatized situations that are resolved (at least for the *characters* in these programs) by sex, violence, or comedy. For the viewer, on the other hand, these stirred-up passions and animated commotions are not resolved; rather, they are exacerbated by the continuous broadcasting of enticing and seductive images that remain forever elusive. Indeed, Mills maintains that the chief distracting tension of the media is between the wanting and the not having of commodities or of sex symbols.

The Public of Mass Society

Mills (1963b) believed that the United States had moved a considerable distance toward the mass society, and, according to him, there are at least four conditions which, when taken together, characterize the ideal type "public" in a mass society. First, the role of mass media is increased and that of discussion circles is decreased. The result is that mass communications do not link and inform discussion circles; instead, it converts them into mere media markets. In the extreme, the mass communication industry, pumping opinions to media markets, displaces the face-to-face communication systems composed of a multiplicity of primary publics. What is more, the mass media do not truly communicate; they trivialize and they distract. Thus, to the extent that citizens take part in various public activities, they do so only formally and passively. Behaving like spectators rather than actors, the public of mass society acts, or better yet, *reacts*, only by acclamation, by plebiscite, and not through the interactive process of participatory democracy, the process in which the citizenry publicly engages in critical communications to and about the government and its policy decisions. The mass public's activity, then, does not spring from its autonomous decision and initiative; it is an implanted reaction to a controlled stimulus presented by centralized management.

Second, there was, as a consequence, a definitive concentration of the opinion process: Discussion circles were necessarily small and fragmented; media markets, by contrast, were huge and centralized. The rise of the mass media, especially radio and motion pictures, was accompanied by an immense enlargement of the scale of economic and political institutions that were not only highly coordinated, but also highly autocratic. As Mills saw it, there was in the United States a movement from widely scattered little powers and laissez-faire, to consolidated powers and attempts at monopoly control from powerful centers. And in both centers—economic and opinion—power was partially hidden, being that it was exercised, not through advice and command, but through the secret, quieter ways of manipulation.

Consequently, third, the way opinions *change* in a mass society is more manipulative. There is little or no self-regulation on the part of the public. The people in this media market are propagandized: They cannot answer back to the print in the column, the voice on the radio; they cannot even answer back to the media in their immediate circle of co-listeners with ease and without fear. One reason for this unilateral process is that in a mass society, far fewer people express opinions than receive them. Technical conditions of the means of communication make a selection of speakers necessary and, by determining the low ratio of speakers to hearers, limit the chances to respond. In this case, one spokesperson talks impersonally through a network of communications to millions of listeners and viewers. Thus, in a world before fiber optic cables and cheap satellite dishes, flash drives and digital video conferencing; before e-mail and social networking websites, talk shows and talk radio; before webcams and the Internet, the process of answering back was systematically unavailable in the mass society of media markets. Communication in the 1950s was not interactive; it was a one-way flow of opinion, occurring as it did between the manipulators with their mass media on the one hand, and the public, as a captive audience, passively receiving their communications on the other.

Fourth and lastly, the use of physical and institutional sanctions as well as internal and external reprisals obviates the possibility of freely replying with an opinion. In a mass society with an authoritarian political order, in a police state with one single mass party that seeks to establish totalitarian control, free and informal discussion is quickly squelched by the infiltration, into every private discussion group, of agents of the centralized authority who "fix" opinion. Another, more coercive way in which informal opinion is controlled in a mass society with an absolute monopoly on communication is by the systems of "blackmail" carried on by mutually fearful informers under a shroud of secrecy and universal suspicion. Totalitarian party-states, Mills asserts, go beyond the bureaucratization of democracies by subjecting all organized channels of communication, including radio, print, and film, to their control. This requires that various skill groups—journalists, camera operators, film directors, artists, radio announcers—be organized into quasi-bureaucracies, that is, transformed into "officials" who have all the responsibilities of regular state officials but not their decision-making functions, their rights of tenure, their pensions, or their anonymity. Such skill groups must then define and promulgate official images of the social world and what is happening in it. They create the official "definitions of the situation," which give people their standards of reality and experience.

At bottom, Mills's major concern was that the monopolization of the media industry, the manipulation of public opinion, and the propagandization of the media markets threatened the democratic ideal of the American past that assumed that once given political rights, individual citizens, as a community of publics, would naturally become politically alert and act on their own political interests.

The Community of Publics and the Democratic Ideal

At the opposite extreme of a mass society, Mills identifies the **community of publics,** those scattered little circles of face-to-face citizens discussing their public business in the spirit of direct, participatory democracy. According to Mills (1956), a true community of free and knowledgeable publics can exist only when four dimensions are present. First, there must be the same ratio of people giving their opinions as those receiving them. The forums in which this reciprocal communication can occur in a democracy include assemblages, political rallies, and open discussion groups. Second, there must exist the opportunity for listeners to reply to an opinion without having to fear political reprisal. Third, there must exist the opportunity for public opinion to be realized in social action. In other words, publics must be given the freedom to collectively put their beliefs into practice. Fourth, and perhaps most importantly, the community of publics must be autonomous, free from the infiltration of governmental authority.

The public and the mass society, says Mills, may be most readily distinguished by their dominant modes of communication: In a community of publics, discussion is the ascendant means of communication and the mass media, if they exist, simply enlarge and animate discussion, linking one primary public with the discussions of another. By contrast, we have already seen that in a mass society, the dominant type of communication is the formal media, and the publics are transformed into media markets as all are exposed to the contents of given mass media.

Mills notes, however, that the idea of a society composed of a community of publics is not a matter of fact; rather, in the United States it is the proclamation of an ideal—*the democratic ideal*—and, as well, the assertion of a legitimation masquerading as fact. By the democratic ideal, Mills (1958) has in mind "a system of power in which those who are vitally affected by such decisions as are made—and as could be made but are not—have an effective voice in these decisions and defaults" (p. 118). In the community of publics inspired by the democratic ideal (that is, the democratic ideal in its classic 18th-century liberalist form), critical dialogue binds discussion circles together. In these groups, citizens are presented with problems and issues that they deliberate and decide on. They subsequently formulate various viewpoints—opinions and ideas—that support their special interests and reasoning. These viewpoints are organized, they compete, and one viewpoint ultimately wins out. The citizens then act on this viewpoint, or their elected representatives are instructed to act it out, and do so promptly (Mills, 1963b). Thus, out of the little circles of people talking with one another, the big forces of social movements and political parties develop, and the discussion of opinion is one crucial phase in a total act by which public affairs are conducted.

If there was any socially organized intelligence that was free to answer back and give support to others who might answer back, Mills (1963b) believed it was the primary public. For him, the **primary public**—the face-to-face groups of articulate individuals who have a shared interest in a public event or issue and express their opinions freely and publicly—has the ability to resist those engaged in manipulating public opinion and manufacturing consent.

The Public of Public Opinion

Mills (1956) maintained that as U.S. politics came to be understood within the context of the myth of democratic decision making, and as the means of mass persuasion became more pervasive, *the public of public opinion* had become the object of intensive efforts to control, manage, manipulate, and increasingly intimidate. However, in a paper written in 1950 and published posthumously, "The Sociology of Mass Media and Public Opinion" (1963b), he makes it clear that such coercive efforts had not been entirely successful in their outcome. Indeed, Gerth and Mills (1953) acknowledged that the "U.S. mass media, under corporate business control, often fail to 'represent' public opinion, as is evidenced by the frequent disparity between the stand taken by 'the organs of public opinion' and the electorate during presidential elections since 1936" (p. 460). That year, the *Literary Digest* predicted that Alfred M. Landon would capture the presidency from Franklin D. Roosevelt, when, in fact, Landon carried only two states, thus losing to Roosevelt in a historic landslide.

The tension and contradiction between public opinion and mass media was most poignantly demonstrated during the 1948 presidential election when the *Chicago Daily Tribune* went to press, before the election results were announced, with the banner headline DEWEY DEFEATS TRUMAN. As history now shows, Truman easily won the election over the Republican candidate Thomas E. Dewey. Clearly, both the *Digest* and the *Tribune* were wrong and biased in their predications of public opinion and voter behavior. Thus, for Mills, these and similar instances revealed two things. First, they showed that American politics had consistently displayed the fact of an overwhelmingly Republican press and a Democratic party in power. Mills points out that while most news sources during the 1930s and 1940s were for the Republican Party, most voters had for some time voted for the Democratic Party. Second, the discrepancy between what the news media announced and what public opinion actualized in the Roosevelt and Truman elections—the fact that American elections were often won against the pressure of the newspapers—revealed that a realistic depiction of American public life could not assume that public opinion was wholly controlled and entirely manipulated by the mass media. There were forces at work among the public that were independent of these media of communication that could and did at times go directly against the opinions promulgated by them. The U.S. public, to be sure, possessed a measure of what Mills describes as an "autonomy of judgment," as it made up its own mind on a variety of issues without direction from any center and without any authority but its own sovereignty.

Thus, in the United States of the early 1950s, Mills believed that two broad sets of influences were at work in changing public opinion: (1) the media of mass communication and (2) person-to-person discussion. It was a question, then, of which was the more important in different areas of opinion, at different times, and of just how the two, as forces causing opinion change, sometimes worked together and sometimes clashed. Mills (1963b) explains,

> The American public is neither a sandheap of individuals each making up his own mind, nor a regimented mass manipulated by monopolized media of mass communication. The American public is a complex, informal network of persons and small groups interchanging on all occupational and class levels, opinions and information, and variously exposed to the different types of mass media and their varying contents. There are many influences at work upon these publics and masses and within them, and there are many resistances and counter-forces to these various influences. (p. 586)

Persons Talking With Persons

In a study of Decatur, Illinois, Mills and his associates endeavored to find out how opinions changed, how the citizens of Decatur, as members of the public, actually made up their minds (Katz & Lazarsfeld, 1955). Now Mills was well aware that, in general, people of one or another opinion tend to select those mass media sources with which they ordinarily agree. Thus, insofar as they can, Democratic Party members listen to Democratic radio commentators and Republican Party members read Republican newspaper editorials. This self-selection of audiences means that the chief influence of the mass media is not really to *form* or to *change* opinion but to *reinforce* a line of opinion already held, or at least already well-known. Consider, for example, whether the conservative cable and satellite news channel Fox News, with 52% of its viewers (in 2004) describing themselves as politically conservative, really changes its audience's minds or simply reinforces (and exacerbates) their opinions on immigration, health care, the economy, or the environment (Pew Research Center, 2004).

But Mills's sample of Decatur included people who *did* change their opinions about various topics. Mills reasoned, therefore, that there must be other influences aside from the mass media at work in these changes. There must, in fact, be some way of resisting, rejecting, or reinterpreting the contents of the mass media. He discovered that it was *people talking informally with people,* more than people listening to, or reading, or looking at the mass media that really caused opinions to change. This is not to say that the formal media lacked persuasive capabilities; in fact, Mills and his researchers were able to measure the relative influences of mass media versus talking to other people in changes of opinion. They found, however, that in every topical area of opinion they studied, the personal conversations weighed a great deal heavier and was more effective than the mass media in the opinion change. Thus, for Mills, the most effective and immediate way for individuals to resist media persuasions on public opinion is by the comparison of experience and of opinions among the individuals themselves. These discussions of the primary public are at once the spearhead and the master context against which resistances to the media may develop. The undercover network of informal, person-to-person communication in the primary public may select and reflect, debunk or sanction what is said in the formal media. And everybody who talks with anybody is part of this network, this public of public opinion.

Mills was cognizant of the fact that among the public of public opinion were "opinion leaders"—people who influenced others more than others influenced them. One thing Mills and his colleagues discovered, which they thought was important to understanding how American public opinion changes, is that opinion leaders were more exposed to a variety of the mass media of communication than were the opinion followers. They listened more to various radio programs, read more magazines, and so on. What seemed to happen was that these opinion leaders picked up opinions from the mass media and passed them on to other people in face-to-face conversation.

But just as people tend to select the radio programs and editorials and magazine articles with which they already generally agree—which, as we already know, means that the media reinforce existing opinions more than they cause opinions to change—so were the opinion leaders no different from other members of the media's audience in this respect. However, listening or reading differs from conversing with others in two important respects. First, there is less self-selection according to already agreed-to lines of opinion in personal conversation than there is in media exposure. Second, the formal media also differ from causerie (informal conversation) in that it is more difficult for individuals to answer back to the media than it is for them to answer back other persons with whom they are talking: There was a reciprocity about private conversation that, at least in the 1950s, did not exist in mass media communication. These two differences mean that even though opinion leaders are more exposed to media and try to transmit these opinions to others, these others are in contact with other opinion leaders who in turn are exposed to other selected programs and articles. So it is in the give-and-take of persons talking with persons, brought about by counter-influences, that differences and clashes of opinion occur. And it is through such tête-à-tête, more than in any other way, that opinions are actually changed. Mills's conclusion is that the media are influential directly, but also indirectly through opinion leaders; there is a clash of opinion occurring in conversations between different opinion leaders and between all the people who are in contact with different opinion leaders and different media offerings. For in these conversations, these informal and unofficial relationships of persons talking with persons, public opinion is most effectively formed and changed.

Mills posits that these circles with their opinion leaders can and do reject, refract, and pass on media content. This is why American public opinion could not be understood merely in terms of what the radio, newspapers, magazines, and movies contained. They were only one force, and although they sometimes did "express" public opinion, they did not in every instance do so. Moreover, what they communicated was always subject to rejection and interpretation at the hands of the opinion circles and unofficial opinion leaders with their many shades of opinion. It was because of this fact that public opinion, at the time that Mills was writing, was still a reality to be reckoned with on the American scene. It was also because of this fact that Mills believed that if the mass media lie and distort, especially about matters that were within the experience of the public, these media would come to be distrusted and subjected to popular editorial treatment and, at times, to plain rejection. States Mills (1963b),

It is well to remember that no matter whose interests the press and radio try to serve—monopolists, or one party or another, or what not; no matter what "public opinion" the mass media may try to fabricate—their *effect* upon the opinions of various people is not dependent upon the interests it would serve or upon the content of the "opinions" it would fabricate. In the final analysis, the effective strength of any press or radio lies in its acceptability to informal opinion circles and their unofficial opinion leaders. (p. 598, emphasis original)

In addition to the power elite, the cheerful robots, the community of publics, the informal discussion groups, and the opinion lenders, Mills considers the media's effects on five major groups: labor unions, the community of intellectuals, television Christians, Cubans in revolutionary transition, and Puerto Ricans in New York City. In the case of these groups' members and their publics, Mills describes how the media of mass communication influenced their inner lives and external experiences, their personality traits and conduct patterns.

The Media's Effects on Five Populations

In *The New Men of Power* (1948), Mills makes it plain that, during the 1940s, the mass media were not kind to the labor unions or labor leaders. As a general rule, the media ignored the peaceful and stable features of the union world and instead tended to report in detail those labor actions— deadlocks, strikes, and seizures—which seemingly indicated great and irresponsible power on the part of the unions and their officials. Thus, rather than report on any constructive work the unions may be involved in, the media regarded labor violence as "the meat and gravy of labor news" (p. 32). Labor peace, on the other hand, was seldom part of that news. By Mills's estimation, the media made 5 times as many unfavorable comments about labor as they did favorable comments. In essence, then, the American press of the postwar period held such an entrenched and insidious antilabor point of view that Mills equates it with the prejudice of anti-Semitism in everyday life.

According to him, there were two generalities that characterized almost all daily newspapers. First, they did not cover labor news in the continuous and detailed way in which most of them covered business news. There were, to be sure, occasional labor columns, but there were no "labor pages" in any way comparable to the business pages. Second, although the policies of the big dailies ranged from conservative right to vaguely liberal, their view of labor was decidedly suspicious and cynical. Thus, the typical news item would communicate that the union as an institution might not be such a bad thing, or it is a good thing in principle: but certain unions and a good many labor leaders have gained too much power which they are using recklessly and selfishly, without proper regard for the effects of their actions upon our general welfare. (Mills, 1948, p. 33)

At the same time that labor was being disparaged by the newspapers, it was being ignored by that chief purveyor of popular culture, the entertainment media. Thus, in radio soap operas, in the comic strips, movies, and pulp fiction, labor unions and labor leaders were almost never mentioned. Even the factory worker was virtually unknown in the popular dramas of the time. Mass culture heroes either had no stated occupation or they were professional, business, or white-collar people. Mills was convinced that by their omissions and their whole manner of dramatizing the American scene, particularly their emphasis upon individual effort and individual goals, the mass media were biased against organized labor, and thus made it appear strange and sinister.

The Intellectual Community

As we saw in Chapter 4, Mills's central thesis in *The New Men of Power* is that only the powerful force of labor unions as agencies of protest could stop the United States from the "main drift" toward a permanent war economy that required spending large sums on munitions. The leaders of American labor—the new men of power—along with the labor intellectuals could form an alliance of power and intellect to arrest the master trend that was establishing the United States as a war economy. But, as he examined more closely the inner workings of labor, Mills, by the late 1940s, began to lose faith in its ability to participate in a political movement and historically transform the country into a democratic society "in which everyone vitally affected by a social decision, regardless of its sphere, would have a voice in that decision and a hand in its administration" (Mills, 1948, p. 252). By the mid-1950s, Mills had become completely disillusioned with labor as an agent of social change.

By the time he published *The Causes of World War Three* in 1958, he had come to believe that the intellectuals—academics, scientists, and clergy—were to be the new agents of democratic change. And since a modern democracy necessitated an end to civic apathy and political indifference, it therefore required "a media of genuine communication" open to the intellectual community. Mills believed that with the aid of this type of mass media, the intellectuals could translate the private troubles of individuals into public issues, and public issues and events into their meanings for the private life. But until such time as a genuine media became a reality, Mills instructs the intellectual community to act as follows:

> What we, as intellectuals, ought to do with the [existing] formal means of communication—in which so many now commit their cultural default—is to use them as we think they ought to be used, or not to use them at all. We should assume that these means are among *our* means of production and work; that they have been arbitrarily expropriated from us, privately and illegitimately incorporated; and that they are now being used for stupid and corrupting purposes, which disgrace us before the world and before ourselves. We should claim these means as important parts of our means of cultural endeavor, and we should attack those among us who prostitute their talents and disgrace us as an intellectual community. We should write and speak for the mass media on our own terms or not at all. We should attack those who allow themselves to be used by them merely for money or merely for prestige. We should make the mass media the means of liberal—which is to say, liberating—education. (p. 141, emphasis original)

In his unfinished manuscript, *The Cultural Apparatus* (1959/2008a), Mills instructs intellectuals on how to reclaim the mass media and shape the images and ideas that define the human condition, and in this way bring about cultural change.

Television Christians

Mills's comments about the "television Christians" revolve around religion's most obvious competitor: the entertainment industry. In their attempt to compete with these mass means of distraction, some churches had transformed themselves into minor institutions among the mass media of communication. These churches imitated and borrowed the commercial techniques of the insistent publicity machines, and in the terms of the sales pitch (with both the hard and the soft sell), they made banal the teachings, indeed the very image, of Christ.

Mills did not believe that anything recognizably Christian could be conveyed through these media-based ministries. In an age before the spectacular rise of the electronic church and the emergence of the televangelists, the "prime-time preachers" of the 1980s and 1990s (i.e., Robert Schuller's "Crystal Cathedral," Pat Robertson's The 700 Club, Jim Bakker's The PTL Club, and Jimmy Swaggart Ministries), Mills maintained that this "religious malarkey," as he calls mass-mediated religious entertainment, "diseducates" the congregations exposed to it and thus kills off any real influence religious leaders might have. Indeed, as a mass medium, religion had become a religiously ineffective part of the show that filled up certain time slots in the weekly routine of cheerful robots. Even if the crowds come, states Mills, they come only for the show, and if it is the nature of crowds to come, it is also their nature soon to go away. Mills (1958) warns about a religious illiteracy and a moral emptiness developing as a result of television Christianity:

> And in all truth, are not the television Christians in reality armchair atheists? In value and in reality they live without the God they profess; despite ten million Bibles sold each year in the United States, they are religiously illiterate. Neither their lives nor their thoughts are informed by the creeds they say they believe to be the revealed word. . . . To ministers of God we must now say: If you accept the entertainment terms of success, you cannot succeed. The very means of your "success" make for your failure as witnesses, for you must appeal to such diverse moral appetites that your message will necessarily be generalized to the point of moral emptiness. (p. 151)

Cubans in Revolutionary Transition

At the prompting of Latin American intellectuals in Mexico and Brazil, Mills, during the summer of 1960 (as noted in the previous chapter), visited Cuba in order to observe firsthand the accomplishments of Castro's revolution. After a few weeks in the small Caribbean nation, he returned to the States and immediately began writing *Listen, Yankee,* with the aim of presenting "the voice of the Cuban revolutionary, as clearly and as emphatically as I can, and I have taken up this aim because of its absurd absence from the news of Cuba available in the United States today" (Mills, 1960d, p. 8). Through the book, he tells the American people that much of what they were reading about Cuba in the U.S. press was far removed from the realities and the meaning of what was really going on in that country. Mills admits that he is not altogether clear as to how to explain this disparity between what the American press said about Cuba and the truth about the island nation. Contrary to many Cubans, however, he did not believe that it was entirely due to a deliberate campaign of vilification. On the other hand, Mills recognized that if U.S. businesses adversely affected by the Cuban Revolution did not coordinate news of Cuba, business as a system of interests (which includes the media of mass communication) could nonetheless be a controlling factor in what the American public was able to know about Cuba. Moreover, it was also true that the news editors' demand for violent headlines restricted and shaped the copy that journalists produced. Editors and journalists believed that the American people would rather read about executions, for example, than about new lands put into cultivation. In short, they printed the news they thought would sell.

Mills further suggests that people's ignorance of Cuba was due, in part, to the fact that its revolutionary government did not, in 1960, have a serviceable information agency for foreign journalists. He admits that it was not easy to get firm facts, and it was impossible to understand what was going on without skilled help from the people who were themselves in the middle of their revolution. In many cases, such people were quite unable to help, if only because they were so busy carrying out the revolution. But they were also increasingly *unwilling* to help, for they felt that their trust has been betrayed. Due to what they considered sad experiences, the Cuban revolutionaries had come to feel that North American journalists would not recognize or would distort the truth, even when they saw it before them.

Another source of trouble for Mills was that many North American journalists simply did not know how to understand and report a revolution. Reporting about a real revolution involved much more than ordinary journalists' routine. It required that they abandon many of the clichés and habits that made up their craft. It certainly required that they know something in detail about the great variety of left-wing thought and action in the Cold War world of the early 1960s. And most North American journalists knew very little of that variety. To most of them, judging from U.S. newspapers, it all appeared as just so much "communism." Even those with the best will to understand were, by their very training as well as the restraints upon their work, unable to report fully enough and accurately enough the necessary contexts, and so the meanings, of revolutionary events. Mills was not convinced that anyone had all the necessary capacities. It was, to be sure, an extraordinarily difficult task for any member of an overdeveloped society to report accurately on what was going on in the hungry world. But Mills (1960d) is clear on one point:

> We are not getting in the United States sound information about [the Cuban revolution]. Perhaps the truth is this: The mass media of information are often less coordinated by advertising pressures, official hand-outs, and off-the-record talks than by the ignorance and confusion in the minds of those who are running them. In brief: it is probable that some newspapers are often coordinated; it is certain that many newsmen—like all men—are often self-deceiving. (pp. 10–11)

Puerto Ricans in New York

In *The Puerto Rican Journey,* as discussed in Chapter 5, Mills and his associates devote a significant portion of their research to analyzing mass media influences on the Puerto Rican population of New York City. They note that the outermost reaches of the Puerto Rican world were filled with the sights and sounds of magazines and newspapers, radio and movies. Like the rest of their world, these formal media were partly Spanish and partly American. And just as among other low-income groups, the media to which the Puerto Ricans were exposed frequently distorted, rather than clarified, what was happening in their world, and failed to orient them to their place in it. Mills, Senior, and Goldsen (1950) assert that, relative to those who grew up in the United States, the Puerto Rican migrants to New York were more susceptible to, that is, less able to resist, the persuasions of the formal media:

> It may be that since the Puerto Rican does not possess the full context of American life, as do those who grow up on the continent, he accepts the content and implicit values of the mass media less critically than the continental, and is more open to the suggestions of feelings and conduct which it offers. In striving to be at home in a new environment, he may all the more easily develop a false base of security. At any rate, these formal media enable the stranger to acquire a common apperceptive mass with continentals similarly exposed, and thus share with other Americans the same standardized inner life. (p. 117)

Mills and his researchers further report that the Puerto Ricans in New York used the radio and newspaper more than they went to movies or read magazines. One reason for selecting these particular media sources, they contend, is directly related to the Puerto Ricans' typically low educational and income level. Once the migrant made the initial investment, radio listening was cheap. Another reason for their reliance on the radio had to do with island culture. In Puerto Rico, the radio was often the focus of the neighborhood, and migrants carried their radio habit with them. Indeed, Mills et al. (1950) found that in New York City as a whole, including all income ranges, 98% of all migrant families owned radios. What is more, their research revealed that 77% of the Puerto Ricans in the core areas listened to the radio after 6:00 PM, only 8% listened to early morning programs, and 6% tuned in during the day. In general, this pattern followed the listening pattern of the U.S. population as a whole.

Mills, Senior, and Goldsen (1950) found that 71% of their subjects preferred Spanish radio programs, 18% chose to listen to American programs, and 11% expressed no preference. While there were several Spanish-language programs after 6:00 PM and a new evening program at 9:00 PM, there were few such programs during the day. Owing to the fact that Puerto Rican housewives were unlikely to know English, only 7% of them listened to the radio during the day, in marked contrast to the listening habits of the American housewife in general.

Newspapers were read at least once a week by 84% of the sample. Thirty-four percent of all the migrants read New York English-language daily papers, 22% read Spanish-language papers, and 28% read both. Following the pattern of most low-income and low-education groups in their newspaper habits, the Puerto Ricans read the cheaper and more sensational papers: 67% read the tabloid the *Daily News*. The other English-language papers had only scattered readers: 13% read the *Journal-American* and 10% the *Daily Mirror*. Of the Spanish-language papers available in New York, *La Prensa* was read by 48% of the 930 readers of newspapers in the sample; although not owned by Puerto Ricans, it devoted considerable space to activities on the island and to the social life of Puerto Ricans in New York. *El Mundo* and *Imparcial,* both published in Puerto Rico, were read by 5% and 11%, respectively. There were several other smaller Spanish papers published by Puerto Ricans in New York, but altogether these were read by only 6% of the respondents.

Fifty-two percent of the respondents went to movies once a week or more, 11% attended less often than that, and 37% almost never went to the movies or not at all. For those 52%, Mills and his researchers learned that movies offered escape from the cold and from hard work. For a few hours, the realities of their life in New York could be left outside the box office; they could participate in adventure, glamour, and stories with happy endings. Mills et al. (1950) point out that many of the Puerto Ricans knew the names of all the current movie stars of the time. Some of them, for example, reported that they went for treatment to the Bette Davis Hospital (the Beth-David)!

Whether or not they attended movies frequently, 46% of all the migrants in the sample preferred Spanish films, 35% the American, and 19% expressed no preference. The Spanish-speaking core areas of New York had several movie houses where only Latin American films were shown, but the preference for the Spanish-language movies was not as marked as the level of comprehension of the English language might indicate. Mills, Senior, and Goldsen (1950) found that incomplete understanding of the films' dialogue was no great barrier to the understanding of many American movies.

Of the various mass media sources available to the Puerto Ricans, Mills discovered they were exposed to magazines the least. This was to be expected considering that magazines typically were more expensive and generally required an educational level that was higher than tabloid newspapers, and perhaps most importantly, because few magazines in Spanish were available in New York at the time. Forty-three percent of all migrants said they read magazines somewhat frequently, 29% read English magazines,

9% read Spanish, and 5% read both. Fifty-seven percent did not usually read any magazines.

Mills and his colleagues constructed an index of exposure to mass media based on the responses to the questions on the four mass media mentioned. By means of this index, they found that only 25% of the migrants had been "highly exposed" to mass media—reading at least one magazine somewhat frequently, going to the movies about once a week, reading at least one newspaper at least once a week, and listening to the radio somewhat regularly. Very few migrants (3%) were at the other extreme of never being exposed to any of these four media, but following a scale of exposure, 35% of the migrants ranked intermediate and 40% ranked lowest.

Mills and his fellow researchers discovered that education was a decisive factor in the Puerto Ricans' exposure to mass media: 47% of those who had attended school to the sixth grade or beyond were highly exposed as against only 18% of those who attended up to the fifth grade or less. There were no differences according to sex. As the migrants lived in the city longer, they become more exposed, or they developed wider habits of attention to mass media, but this was true only among the more highly educated. Among the less educated, practically the same proportions, men or women, recently arrived or not, were highly exposed to mass media. Among the higher educated, however, time of arrival made a more noticeable difference, with those who had been in New York longer raising the proportions of highly exposed from 27% or 29% to 40%. The chances, therefore, that a poorly educated migrant would become exposed to the mass media were only about 1 in 10. Mills saw this as both good and bad for the migrants. On the one hand, the migrants' lack of education kept them away from the somewhat dubious cultural level of mass media. On the other hand, this lack of education also kept them from whatever benefits they could derive from the mass media: personal enjoyment, general informational awareness of their new world, contact in any world wider than their immediate household, and whatever chance of assimilation mass media provided.

Mills et al. (1950) conclude that the Puerto Ricans' total exposure to the newspapers, movies, radio, and magazines was rather superficial. It was as if they permitted themselves to be touched in a brief and casual way by one or another of these media as the only means available to secure news or entertainment—and not because the tendency to turn to these media of mass communication was an intrinsic part of their behavior patterns. These media offered to the several types of masses in New York the lowest common denominator of participation in American culture, or at least American *mass* culture. Mills explains that when they entered the city, the Puerto Ricans also entered America's mass culture, but even on this most external level they did not participate much in it.

Conclusion

Five general observations may be drawn from C. Wright Mills's commentary on the role of the mass media in postwar America. To begin with, it is clear that he understood the media's influence from an *instrumentalist* perspective. That is to say, he regarded the mass media as a tool utilized by coordinated entities for the explicit purpose of legitimating their authority before the mass of people. While Mills is not always consistent or specific in his identification and description of these coordinated entities—variously referring to them as "the power elite," "powerful centers," "centralized authority," and "business as a system of interests"—he nonetheless believed that they monopolized, through ownership and/or influence, the means of mass communication in an effort to manipulate public opinion.

Second, Mills's approach to understanding the media's pervasive influence is *subjectivist*. This means that he paid close attention to the symbolic imagery produced by the means of mass communication; the meaning, interpretation, and definition that individuals give to these media images; and the effect that these images have on the individuals' inner lives and external experiences. In this sense, the mass media tend to distract and distort, thus producing a psychological illiteracy. By providing appealing and seductive types of image information—the lore of success and romance, the myth of sex and violence, the stereotypes of artificial men and women, the ideology of fairness and balance—the media *distract* individuals from the reality of their everyday lives. This distraction, through the use of the popular media of entertainment, becomes a diversion: a fantastic drama or animated cartoon that clouds the individual's awareness of his or her place in history and society, "diseducates" and fosters a cultural illiteracy, and inhibits the development of a political and civic consciousness through a dumbing down of the national character. Similarly, the formal media *distort*—lie and slant—people's interpretations and experiences of fact and reality by creating their own official definitions of what is true and real. Through biased reporting and the presentation of refracted images, the press creates a pseudo reality that endows people with an identity informing them of what they are and instructing them on what they should be. The standards that determine what is objective truth and what constitutes real experience are set by the media. The electronic media create reality, and they do so in their own virtual image.

Third, while Mills acknowledged a power behind the media, he also saw the media as a *power in and of itself*. Thus, while certain media agents—publishers, editors, and journalists—may be part of or closely aligned with the power elite, they, as members of mass society, were often ignorant of and confused by political events, especially events that departed from the agents' understanding of democracy. This ignorance and confusion stemmed from the media agents' own self-deception. Since they understood only what their mediated stereotypes and professionalized routines allowed them to understand, journalists and editors biased their reporting by eschewing political events and favoring sensationalism. In this case, the mass media *as a system* and journalism *as a profession* managed and manipulated what editors and journalists, the masses and the publics, could and could not know.

Fourth, Mills's solution to the problems of psychological illiteracy and personal self-deception was *liberalism*. While he acknowledged that classic liberalism was no longer viable in the political and economic spheres, he seemed to believe that, with some effort, it could still be realized in the mass media. A liberal media could offer a liberal education that would awaken the masses from their civic apathy and political indifference. As such, a liberal media would serve to inform the citizenry of a democratic society, transforming them into a community of publics. For Mills, a true participatory democracy was impossible without a liberal media to increase political discussion.

Fifth and finally, Mills believed that despite the immensely persuasive influence of the mass media, all was not lost in postwar America. Individuals could still successfully resist media persuasions. They could still freely and intelligently proclaim their opinions without fearing that these opinions were subject to governmental control and media manipulation. For Mills, the United States was at that point not quite yet a mass society of media markets.

The following questions are posed for discussion:

- Who are the main "manipulators" of mass media images and messages today?
- Is there one master symbol—one main image—that the contemporary mass media seek to promote? If so, how is it used?
- What are some of the major social and technological changes that have occurred in the media of mass communication since Mills's time, and what impact have these changes had on society?
- How might the Internet be transforming the American people into a community of publics or into a mass society?

7

Disillusioned Radical

Perhaps more than any other public intellectual of his time, C. Wright Mills epitomized the intense "angry young man" of American sociology during the middle decades of the 20th century. His passionate manner, explosive style, and the fact that he was "taking it big"—and in a hurry—no doubt contributed to his premature death. In his insightful critique of contemporary U.S. society, Mills had no equal. In the era of the Cold War, McCarthyism, and what Mills called the **Great Celebration**—the self-congratulatory trend that viewed the United States as the ideal contemporary manifestation of democracy—he, virtually in isolation, had the temerity to critique the power structure, the military-corporate nexus, and the conservative mood of the time. And like other angry, or at least restless, young men who left their indelible impression on the quiescent 1950s—Jack Kerouac, Charlie Parker, Dwight MacDonald, Allen Ginsberg—Mills also found himself at center stage. Indeed, his books and pamphlets, which were translated into several languages (German, Spanish, Japanese, Russian, Polish, Italian, French), sold in the hundreds of thousands during his time, but generally outside of professional sociology.

This last chapter considers three of Mills's final published works. First, there is the mass-market paperback that solidified his image as a public intellectual, *The Causes of World War Three* (1958). This angry little book, which sold 100,000 copies upon its release, had a significant impact in jump-starting the antinuclear peace movement. Then there is the now-canonical work of anti-professional sociology, *The Sociological Imagination* (1959b) that, ironically enough, put Mills, the academic outlander, squarely at the front and center of academic sociology. With this book, Mills entered the pantheon of "great social thinkers"—along with such notable contemporaries as Talcott Parsons, Erving Goffman, and George C. Homans, with whom he presumably had little, if anything, in common. But more than a great social thinker, Mills, unlike the aforementioned sociologists, was a radical—one who, through his hard-hitting critiques of mass society, advocated social change.

The chapter concludes with a brief discussion of Mills's famous "Letter to the New Left" (1960b), a document that had a marked influence on the student movements of the 1960s in the United States and abroad.

A Politics of Responsibility

While clearly not one of Mills's main academic writings, the small "pamphlet" on the Cold War and the urgency of political efforts to foster peace—*The Causes of World War Three*—may be seen as an embellishment on the themes of war and peace previously raised in *The Power Elite*. Published in the autumn of 1958 by Simon & Schuster, *The Causes* (which incorporated material from the Sidney Hillman lectures Mills had delivered to a standing-room crowd at Howard University earlier that year as well as from two popular articles that had appeared in *The Nation*) is nothing less than a shrill call for action—a call for a politics of responsibility. In this softcover, which originally sold for 50 cents, Mills argues that the power elites in the United States and the USSR were leading the two nations to a total and absurd war. He urgently informs his readers that the United States and the Soviet Union shared too closely the **military metaphysic,** a view through which all global issues are seen in terms of national security and defense. As such, he calls upon the clergy, scientists, and the intellectual community to take a responsible and moral stand on the issue of peace and nuclear disarmament. He also calls for a rational response and a commitment to the task of overcoming widespread public apathy, indifference, and elite irresponsibility concerning the great issue of the age, namely, the annihilation of the human species through thermonuclear war. Using the paperback as a bully pulpit of sorts, Mills endeavors to persuade American and Soviet intellectuals to prevail over the higher immorality and crackpot realism of their respective countries' power elites and to, by their own efforts, sue for a separate peace. Only in this way, Mills felt, could the present drift and thrust toward World War III and mass destruction be reversed.

In a larger sense, the publication of *The Causes* may exemplify that rare case in which a public intellectual—particularly one that had been harshly marginalized by the academic establishment—made an indirect but powerful impression on the political thinking of the time. Or perhaps it was an "elective affinity" (Weber, 1978) of contemporaneous thinking, or maybe it was nothing more than mere coincidence. In any event, shortly after the *The Causes* appeared, President Dwight D. Eisenhower, himself a member of the power elite, cautioned the American people against that which Mills had been decrying for years: the insidious power of the economic–military alliance, the power–profit relationship between the U.S. munitions makers and the Pentagon. Eisenhower, in his January 17, 1961, farewell presidential address to the nation, warns against the burgeoning "military-industrial complex":

> Our military organization today bears little relation to that known by any of my predecessors in peacetime, or indeed by the fighting men of World War II or Korea. . . .
>
> In the councils of government, we must guard against the acquisition of unwarranted influence, whether sought or unsought, by the military-industrial complex. The potential for the disastrous rise of misplaced power exists and will persist.
>
> We must never let the weight of this combination endanger our liberties or democratic processes. We should take nothing for granted. Only an alert and knowledgeable citizenry can compel the proper meshing of the huge industrial and military machinery of defense with our peaceful methods and goals, so that security and liberty may prosper together. (as quoted in Pursell, 1972, pp. 206–207)

Today, some 50 years later, the Soviet Union is no longer in existence and the dangers of a thermonuclear war, with its mutually assured destruction of the two superpowers (and most of the planet), have significantly diminished. The current war, the War on Terror—the military, political, legal, and ideological global campaign initiated by the U.S. government against organizations designated as terrorist and regimes accused of having a connection to those organizations—has, with the formation of the U.S. Department of Homeland Security, now expanded the economic–military alliance well beyond anything that Mills would have known in his day. The War on Terror has also given rise to a different military metaphysic from the one Mills was referring to in the early 1960s. Noam Chomsky (2003) has described this new military metaphysic as the use of military force to eliminate an "imagined or invented" terrorist threat (p. 12). As part of the War on Terror, the 2003 U.S. invasion of Iraq was initiated with the intent to disarm that country of weapons of mass destruction and end Saddam Hussein's alleged support of terrorism. In order to legitimate the invasion, Chomsky maintains, the administration of George W. Bush deliberately depicted the Iraq regime as the "ultimate evil and an imminent threat" to the survival of the United States (p. 17). This was a new metaphysic, a new extreme policy that aimed at permanent global dominance by relying on force when necessary and justifying its use through artifice.

Though quite successful in making a persuasive argument about the power inequities endemic in U.S. society, the fact of the matter is that Mills's trilogy—*The New Men of Power, White Collar,* and *The Power Elite*—along with *The Causes of World War Three,* gives readers little hope for a brighter future. The main thrust of these works is that the centralization of production, administration, and violence, within the hierarchies of large-scale bureaucracies, denies individuals freedom and rationality in their work and their lives. Mills therefore leaves his readers feeling that in this, the Fourth Epoch, the cheerful robots, or those persons not willing or not able to exert themselves to acquire the reason that freedom requires, are fast becoming the pervasive character type in mass society.

The Sociological Imagination

Whereas in *The Causes of World War Three,* Mills puts forth a pessimistic, perhaps even apocalyptic, view of society, in *The Sociological Imagination,* he does, to be sure, present a somewhat more hopeful picture of humanity's future. Written in 1957 (though published in 1959), the year that he served as a Fulbright scholar at the University of Copenhagen, Mills describes *The Sociological Imagination* as being "something *about* my own kind of sociology and against the current dominant 'schools'" (as quoted in K. Mills & Mills, 2000, p. 228, emphasis original) in academic sociology as he saw them—namely, Parsonian grand theory and Lazarfeldian abstracted empiricism. In this quite technical and polemical book, which came to be known to millions of undergraduate students of sociology the world over, Mills proposes a new way of thinking; one that will not only help people better understand the meaning of their epoch for their own lives, but will also help them to become active participants in history making.

What the cheerful robots of the Fourth Epoch need, and what they feel they need, says Mills (1959b), is the **sociological imagination:** a quality of mind "that will help them to use information and to develop reason in order to achieve lucid summations of what is going on in the world and of what may be happening within themselves" (p. 5). For only by using the sociological imagination can individuals cope with their personal troubles in such ways as to control the structural transformations that usually lie behind them. This way of thinking, this form of self-consciousness, allows individuals to transcend their immediate milieus and understand the major developments of their time.

The Intellectual Promise of Social Science

Mills locates the sociological imagination within the *classic tradition* in sociological theory, that is to say, within the works of Spencer, Marx, Mannheim, Durkheim, and Weber. Its objective, says Mills (1959b), is to provide people with the insight into the social conditions of their existence and an understanding of the causes of their feeling trapped and uneasy, alienated and powerless. Its practical task and its intellectual promise are to enable individuals "to grasp history and biography and the relations between the two within society" (p. 6). For only by seeing the interconnection of *biography,* or the intensive study of personality in its social setting, and *history* can people begin to understand their own experience, gauge their own fate by locating themselves within their period, and know their own life-chances by becoming aware of all individuals in similar circumstances. Consequently, in employing the sociological imagination people must ask three basic questions: (1) What is the structure of this particular society as a whole? (2) Where does this society stand in human history? (3) What varieties of men and women now prevail in this society and in this period? The sociological imagination, therefore, enables people to understand themselves fully—to "know where they stand, where they may be going, and what—if anything—they can do about the present as history and the future as responsibility" (p. 165).

Mills does not offer the sociological imagination as a panacea, nor does he present it as a religion or a philosophy that provides "answers" to life's problems. When properly used, Mills explains, the sociological imagination can free individuals to be involved in the rational making of history. But in order to be free, in order to have the chance to formulate choices and then choose among them, individuals have to make the connection between their "personal troubles" of the immediate milieu and those "public issues" at the level of historically located social structure. It is the task of those who employ the sociological imagination to continually translate troubles into issues and issues into the terms of human meaning for them. Individuals must be aware that the malaise and frustrations they experience in their inner lives are linked to the big picture of society, to those problems residing at the level of social structure.

Mills contends that the indifferent cheerful robots of the mass society are gripped by personal troubles, but, regrettably, they are unaware of the true meaning and source of these troubles. By contrast, the informed citizens within a community of publics are not only able to confront public issues, but they are also aware of the issues' meaning and source. It is for this reason that Mills believes that persons within the community of free and knowledgeable publics can transform their personal troubles into public issues and see these issues' relevance for their community and their community's relevance for them. These knowledgeable persons understand that what they see and feel as personal troubles are usually public issues shared by many others and not soluble by any one individual but by large-scale modifications of the entire social structure.

In these terms, let us consider marriage, or better yet, the dissolution of marriage—divorce. For many couples contemplating a divorce or undergoing a divorce, the event may be experienced as traumatic, painful, stressful, and uncertain. They may feel that their life, or a major part of their life, is crumbling and coming to an agonizing end. They perceive the event as their personal trouble, one that afflicts them and those in their immediate milieu—perhaps their children, their relatives, their friends. But when the couple arrives at the courthouse where they are to file for divorce, they notice that many other couples are there for the same reason. It is not only they who are undergoing this personal trouble but, if they consider the situation nationwide, hundreds of thousands of other couples as well.

In the late 1950s, when Mills wrote *The Sociological Imagination,* the divorce rate during the first 4 years of marriage was 25%. Half a century later, the divorce rate had nearly doubled. What led to the increase to 50%? Whatever the factors, we can be sure that, as Mills says, they are indications of the *structural issues* having to do, not with the individuals' personal psychology, but with the institutions of marriage and the family and other institutions that bear upon them. In thinking sociologically, we may surmise that some structural issues that have changed since 1959 and that may have been influential in increasing the divorce rate are the following: women's greater financial independence, changes in moral attitudes toward divorce, changes in the divorce laws. Whatever the factors (and these factors would have to be determined through research), the point is that structural issues affect the personal troubles of individuals. When people connect their private troubles with the larger issues of social structure, they are using the sociological imagination.

Grand Theory and Abstracted Empiricism

As we saw in Chapter 2, Mills excoriated the two tendencies prevalent in American sociology during the 1950s: grand theory and abstracted empiricism. His extended and trenchant critique of these two "schools" is the subject of the second, third, fourth, and fifth chapters of *The Sociological Imagination*.

In the chapter titled "Grand Theory," Mills launches a blistering attack on Parsons's highly abstract conceptual scheme for analyzing social systems. As previously discussed, he charges Parsons's grand style of theorizing with being an overly general, unintelligible, static, ahistorical, and ideologically conservative sociological analysis. Subjecting to careful and critical scrutiny *The Social System* (1951), the book where Parsons presents his basic outline of a general theory of society, Mills (1959b) pronounces it to be 50% verbiage and 40% well-known textbook sociology. "The other 10%," he sardonically tells the reader, "I am willing to leave open for your own personal investigations. My own investigations suggest that the remaining 10% is of possible—although rather vague—ideological use" (p. 49).

In "Abstracted Empiricism," Mills next turns his attention to sociologists like Lazarsfeld, who see themselves, first and foremost, as technicians endeavoring to emulate the scientific method of research. He charges them with being so obsessed with narrow and trifling technical matters of research that they are incapable of seeing the "big picture" and of grappling with the major problems afflicting contemporary society. Like the grand theorists, the sociological efforts of the abstracted empiricists are also ahistorical and non-comparative. Furthermore, the abstracted empiricists are apt to lapse into **psychologism**—which is to say that they explain social phenomena in terms of the personal characteristics of individuals. Mills (1959b) explicates that the psychologism of the abstracted empiricists "rests upon the idea that if [they] study a series of individuals and their milieux, the results of [their] studies in some way can be added up to knowledge of social structure" (p. 67). One major drawback to this building-block notion of social scientific progress—with its series of scattered microscopic studies—is that it never actually gets to the problems of structural significance.

Bureaucracy and Ideology

In the book's middle chapters, entitled "Types of Practicality" and "The Bureaucratic Ethos," Mills maintains that regardless of the type of social science undertaken—whether grand theory or abstracted empiricism—values are always involved in the selection of the problems studied, in the key conceptions used in the formulation of these problems, and in the course of their solution. But neither the grand theorists nor the abstracted empiricists make explicit the values that inform their work. Mills contends that in both of these styles of work, the moral and political values that underlie their assumptions and implications are inherently conservative. In the case of abstracted empiricism, this conservatism is fostered by the illiberal practicality of the "new" social science whose practitioners are installed in bureaucracies—e.g., industrial relations centers, research bureaus of universities; new research branches of corporations, the armed forces, and government—and whose technical work is intended to serve the purposes of those organizations. The result is a "bureaucratic social science" carried out by specialized technicians who have ceded their moral and political autonomy to the nondemocratic organizations for which they work. As such, they are generally accepting of the status quo.

Given the inherent conservative bias in the two sociological styles of work, Mills (1959b) proffers a particularly virulent and capacious assessment of them:

> Abstracted empiricism is used bureaucratically, although it has of course clear ideological meanings, which are sometimes used as such. Grand theory, as I have indicated, has no direct bureaucratic utility; its political meaning is ideological, and such use as it may have lies there. Should these two styles of work—abstracted empiricism and grand theory—come to enjoy an intellectual "duopoly," or even become the predominant styles of work, they would constitute a grievous threat to the intellectual promise of social science as well as to the political promise of the role of reason in human affairs—as that role has been conceived in the civilization of the Western societies. (pp. 117–118)

The Classic Tradition

In the chapter "Philosophies of Science," Mills contrasts the epistemologies of grand theory, abstracted empiricism, and the classic social science tradition. To begin with, the two main features of the classic tradition are its concern with historical social structures and with problems that are directly relevant to urgent public issues and insistent personal troubles. In other words, it utilizes the sociological imagination. The classic social analysts—which include Herbert Spencer, E. A. Ross, Auguste Comte, Durkheim, Mannheim, Marx, Veblen, and others—always sought to develop and use in their work the sociological imagination.

Eschewing grand theory's "fetishism of the concept" and avoiding being bogged down by abstracted empiricism's obsession with the minutiae of microscopic facts, classic social analysis forges a middle path and formulates its problems in terms of specific social and historical structures. As such, classic social science

> neither "builds up" from microscopic study nor "deduces down" from conceptual elaboration. Its practitioners try to build and to deduce at the same time, in the same process of study, and to do so by means of adequate formulation

and re-formulation of problems and of their adequate solutions. To practice such a policy . . . is to take up substantive problems on the historical level of reality; to state these problems in terms appropriate to them; and then, no matter how high the flight of theory, no matter how painstaking the crawl among detail, in the end of each completed act of study, to state the solution in the macroscopic terms of the problem. The classic focus, in short, is on substantive problems. (Mills, 1959b, p. 128)

The Human Variety and the Uses of History

In Chapters 7 and 8 of *The Sociological Imagination,* Mills discusses sociology's proper study—the "human variety"—and its uses of history in that endeavor. Sociology's focus on the human variety means that it engages in an orderly understanding of all the social worlds in which people have lived, are living, and might live their private and public lives. This includes the wide array of individual human beings imaginable: from an Indian Brahmin of 1850 to a pioneer farmer in Illinois; from a Chinese peasant of one hundred years ago and a feudal knight in France to a politician in Bolivia today and an English suffragette on a hunger strike in 1914. A full understanding of the human variety of individuals' lives requires that the sociologist consider the basic question, What varieties of men and women now prevail in this society and in this period? Without use of history and without a historical sense of the psychological matters that affect individuals, the sociologist cannot adequately state the kinds of problems that ought to be the orienting points of his or her studies.

Mills maintains that because people are social and historical actors, their biographies—their social psychology—must be understood with reference to the historical structures within which those biographies are enacted. Indeed, all of the features of an individual's character—his or her social roles, self-image, conscience, and mind—are best formulated as problems within specific historical social structures. It is in this way that the sociologist is able to properly understand the causes of individual conduct and feelings.

Answering the other, more macro question of the sociological imagination— Where does this society stand in human history?—requires practicing sociology as a historical, and a historically comparative, discipline. Without the historical comparative study of societies, the sociologist cannot expect to understand or explain the major phases through which any modern Western nation has passed, the salient trends it is experiencing, or the shape that it assumes today or may assume in the future. It is for this reason, declares Mills (1959b), that "all sociology worthy of the name is 'historical sociology'" (p. 146).

Rationality Without Reason

Mills then uses the sociological imagination to analyze his own postmodern period in history: the Fourth Epoch (so called by Mills because it follows, first, Antiquity; second, the Dark Ages; and third, the Modern Age). It is in the Fourth Epoch that the basic definitions of self and of society were being questioned. These definitions were premised on the two values inherited from the Enlightenment and that were now becoming contested: freedom and reason. Since about the 18th century, increased rationality had, in the Western world, been assumed to be the prime condition of increased freedom. But in the Fourth Epoch, with its dizzying bureaucratization of organizations and its proliferating division of labor (in the spheres of life, work, and leisure), it could no longer be assumed that increased rationality necessarily made for increased freedom. The problem was that the extreme complexity of the postmodern era made it so that ordinary people often could no longer reason about the great structural forces that affected their lives. The rationally arranged social setup of the Fourth Epoch did not lead to more freedom for the individual or for society; to the contrary, it generated greater tyranny and manipulation. This type of social structure, this mass society, creates individuals "with" rationality, but without the capacity to reason—that is, to formulate the available choices in life—and thus without the freedom to select from among those choices. It transforms individuals into cheerful robots who, on the one hand, are quite happy to be entertained and distracted—manipulated—by the mass media's machinery of amusement but, on the other hand, experience deep down an uneasy feeling of malaise and alienation, a sense of being trapped and powerless. In the opening lines of *The Sociological Imagination,* Mills (1959b) describes the situation thusly:

> Nowadays men often feel that their private lives are a series of traps. They sense that within their everyday worlds, they cannot overcome their troubles, and in this feeling, they are often quite correct: What ordinary men are directly aware of and what they try to do are bounded by the private orbits in which they live; their visions and their powers are limited to the close-up scenes of job, family, neighborhood; in other milieux, they move vicariously and remain spectators. And the more aware they become, however vaguely, of ambitions and of threats which transcend their immediate locales, the more trapped they seem to feel. (p. 3)

The Political Task of Sociology

The feeling of being trapped and powerless in turn creates apathy and political irresponsibility among the cheerful robots. By contrast, sociologists, given their ability to employ the sociological imagination and thus understand the interplay of the personal troubles of their milieus with problems of social structure, do not feel so trapped and are not so powerless. Indeed, they possesses an often fragile "means of power" as they address their work to three kinds of publics: (1) those individuals who have the power to act with much structural relevance and who are quite aware of the consequences of their actions, (2) those individuals who have the power to act but are unaware of the structural consequences of their actions, and (3) those individuals who cannot transcend their everyday milieus by their awareness of structure or effect structural change by any means of action available to them.

The political role of sociologists as regards the first public is to impute varying measures of responsibility for such structural consequences as they find in their work to be decisively influenced by the these individuals' decisions and lack of decisions. To the second public, sociologists direct whatever they have discovered about the consequences of the public's actions, attempt to educate this public, and again impute responsibility. Finally, as to the third public, which constitutes the majority of individuals in mass society, the political task of the sociologist in the United States is to make the social structure of the country, which is not altogether a democratic one, more democratic. The sociologist does this (usually in the role of professor) by continually translating

> personal troubles into public issues, and public issues into the terms of their human meaning for a variety of individuals. It is his task to display in his work—and, as an educator, in his life as well—this kind of sociological imagination. And it is his purpose to cultivate such habits of mind among the men and women who are publicly exposed to him. To secure these ends is to secure reason and individuality, and to make these the predominant values of a democratic society. (Mills, 1959b, pp. 187–188)

This political task of sociology—to define personal and social realities truthfully and in a publicly relevant way—in a mass society makes the sociologist a radical. To practice sociology in this way means to practice the politics of truth.

A Prophet of the New Left

One image of Mills that has persisted in the Millsian lore is that of a thinker without a political "home." No mere free-floating intellectual in the Mannheimian sense, Mills's political estrangement stemmed from his assiduous eschewal of all political parties (he never voted), ideologies (including liberalism and Marxism), and worker's movements (except for a vague sympathy with the Wobblies). Even more broadly, and in sharp contrast to most intellectuals of his time, he believed that the two predominant ideologies of the Western world— liberalism and Marxism—had become theoretically exhausted. And yet, despite, or perhaps because of his repudiation of the two doctrines, he was able to preserve certain left-wing ideals and thus, in this way, offer a radical critique of American politics and society at a time when it was most direly needed: at the height of the Age of Complacency.

However, while Mills always remained committed to challenging oppression, he nevertheless overlooked the social and political potential of women, the poor, and people of color—having candidly remarked about the latter, "I have never been interested in what is called the Negro problem. I have a feeling that if I did, it would turn out to be 'a white problem'—and I've enough of these on my hands just now" (as quoted in Gillam, 1966, p. 76). As a consequence, Mills could only be "a partial mentor" to the early student movement, concerned as it was with civil rights. "He wasn't God; all he was, was a prophet and prophets don't see everything," states Bob Ross, an early leader of the student movement. Mills's neglect of racism "was just a miss," continues Ross. "There were a lot of misses as a matter of fact, and that was good. We weren't good at hero worship. It's just as well" (Ross & Treviño, 1998, p. 268).

While it is doubtless regrettable that Mills overlooked the social and political potential of women, African Americans, and the poor at a time when he was so eagerly looking for agents of social change, he was nonetheless adroit enough to sense the prospect for an emerging agent of social change: the New Left made up of young revolutionaries based in third world countries, within the two power blocs, as well as in Great Britain. Because he most identified with the British New Left, it was within its circle of intellectuals—Ralph Miliband, E. P. Thompson, and Tom Bottomore, among others—that Mills, after a long, long journey, and only during the last 2 years of his life, was finally able to find new comrades. It was in fact to them that Mills, in 1960, addressed his famous "Letter to the New Left." And though there is no direct evidence that he ever participated in a political demonstration, in a memo in the FBI file on Mills dated April 25, 1961, a federal agent noted Mills's plan to speak against the U.S.-sponsored Bay of Pigs invasion of Cuba at a rally—not in New York or Washington, but in London (see Keene, 2003; K. Mills & Mills, 2000, p. 331). So comfortable did he feel in the British intellectual community that in 1961, Mills seriously considered permanently locating to the newly built red-brick University of Sussex. Ultimately, he turned down the university's offer, explaining that "[t]he decision has less to do with the many attractions of England than with the fact that my argument lies in America and has to be worked out there" (as quoted in Geary, 2009, p. 187).

So it is that despite his relatively brief life and career, Mills had a lasting influence on scores of leftist sociologists, in both the United States and the UK, throughout the 1960s and beyond. Indeed, shortly after his death, Mills came to be regarded as the "prophet of the powerless," a hero, an oracle, and a model of the radical intellectual for the New Left (Miller, 1987). He became the inspiration, albeit a tempered one, of young activists like Tom Hayden, Al Haber, Bob Ross, Dick Flacks, and other leaders of Students for a Democratic Society (SDS), the leading radical organization of the early 1960s, who closely studied Mills's writings a decade or so after they were written. The formation of the SDS and the release of its manifesto, the *Port Huron Statement*—which Tom Hayden had written and finished the day Mills died—heralded the emergence of the New Left in America. This New Left was much attracted to Mills's theory of power, his notion of the democratic society, and—most significant—it was inspired by the fact that Mills ultimately came to believe that it was not labor leaders who were to be the positive, radical agents of social transformation, or of arresting the main drift. Rather, it was to be an international New Left "young intelligentsia"—the students in South Korea, Cuba, Japan, Turkey, and even in the U.S. South. Indeed, Hayden (2006) has repeatedly made clear that the *Port Huron Statement* "was strongly influenced by C. Wright Mills's independent radicalism, especially his 'Letter to the New Left' in which he declared that 'the Age of Complacency is ending'" (p. 55).

In the end, however, it was perhaps Mills's penchant for sociological gloom and doom—his "disillusioned radicalism," as his recent biographer Daniel Geary would have it—that prevented the New Left from fully incorporating his theoretical ideas into their politics of "vision." In 1961, in his own "A Letter to the New (Young) Left," Hayden wrote frankly that "C. Wright Mills is appealing and dynamic in his expression of theory . . . but his pessimism yields us no formulas, no path out of the dark" (as quoted in Miller, 1987, p. 90). However that may be, Mills has, since the 1960s, been seen as a spokesman—as the impassioned voice of protest (Hayden, 2006)—for "the next generation." If his legacy survives the fads and fashions of American critical thought, his work will doubtless continue to inspire future generations of morally enraged and politically engaged intellectuals.

Conclusion

In the summer of 1954, Mills delivered a speech at the University of Toronto, which was also aired nationally by the Canadian Broadcasting Company, entitled "Are We Losing Our Sense of Belonging?" To his audience, who it is safe to assume consisted mostly of the informed community of publics, he said,

> You and I are among those who are asking serious questions and by that very fact I know that there is something to which you and I do belong. We belong to that minority that has carried on that big discourse of the rational mind; to the big discourse that has been going on—or off and on—since the Western society began some two thousand years ago in the small communities of Athens and Jerusalem. Maybe you think that is a pretty vague thing to which to belong; if you do think

that, you are mistaken. It is quite a thing to belong to the big discourse—even if as lesser participants—and, as I hope presently to make clear, it is the beginning of any "sense of belonging" that is worthwhile. It is the key to the only kind of belonging that free people in our time might have. And I think that to belong to it requires that we try to live up to what it demands of us.

What it demands of us, first of all, is that we maintain our sense of it. And, just now, at this point in human history, it is quite difficult. For we belong not only to the big discourse of the rational mind; we also belong—although we do not always feel that we do—to our own epoch; accordingly, since we are live people and not detached minds, we are trying to live in and with a certain set of feelings: the feelings of political people trying to be rational in an epoch of enormous irrationality. (as quoted in K. Mills & Mills, 2000, pp. 183–184)

In each of the three works examined in this chapter—*The Causes of World War Three*, *The Sociological Imagination*, and "Letter to the New Left"— Mills endeavored to arouse people out of their civic apathy and take political responsibility for their own lives and become revolutionizing agents. Regardless of whether he was addressing public intellectuals on whom he depended to prevail over the power elite's higher immorality and stop the drift toward war, sociologists and their students whom he admonished to cultivate the sociological imagination in order to develop reason and become active participants in history making, or the New Left young intelligentsia on whom he relied to promote participatory democracy, Mills's main concern was to utilize sociologically informed reason in the pursuit of a more humane and rational society. As such, perhaps to a greater degree than any other postwar figure in the human sciences, Mills believed that, in partaking in the big discourse of the rational mind, enlightened men and women could achieve human freedom in the Fourth Epoch of the postmodern period. Thus, compared to the received sociology of his time, particularly that which took the form of grand theory and abstracted empiricism, Mills's ideas were indeed radical. But he was a radical who was continually disillusioned, not only by events but, perhaps more vexing for him, by those in whom he placed his faith to bring about social change.

We leave this chapter with the following questions:

- What are Mills's main criticisms against the received sociology of his day?
- Why did he turn away from academic sociology and toward pamphleteering?
- Why is Mills today best remembered for his stratification trilogy, and not for his mass-market paperbacks?
- To what extent can it be said that *The Sociological Imagination* represents the defining statement of the discipline of sociology?
- In what ways is today's radical or activist social thought indebted to Mills?

8

Further Readings

C. Wright Mills's literary output—which includes books, monographs, pamphlets, articles, essays, introductions, reviews, commentaries, lectures, and letters, both published and unpublished—is prodigious, to say the least. Though much of it has been culled, compiled, edited, and translated into various languages, there are doubtless more pieces that have yet to be made available to an interested public. In his thorough bibliography of Mills's substantive writings, Horowitz (1963) puts the output number at a little over 200 publications. Summers (2008d) in a nearly exhaustive bibliography includes the writings previously listed by Horowitz, but also adds myriad other documents, from personal notes that Mills made in his journal as a teenager, to poems and papers he wrote as an undergraduate; from book notes which appeared in various journals, to sundry memoranda; and including addresses and interviews, which he gave throughout his career. Summers' list comes to nearly 380 items.

This last chapter considers some further readings by and on Mills. Examined are Mills's more substantial sociological works, but in particular those he left unfinished at the time of his death, those writings of his that have been organized and published posthumously, those retrospectives that have been written on Mills, and those studies that have endeavored to extend Mills's social and political ideas. In this context, the following questions may be asked: How forward-looking, or dated, are Mills's uncompleted projects? To what extent can Mills's statements about Soviet–U.S. relations be used to understand the politics and culture of the Cold War? What can Marxist social thought learn from Mills's ideas about Marxism and liberalism? In what directions can Mills's social thought be further extended? What is Mills's legacy half a century after his death?

The Unfinished Work

Much as he lived his life in general, Mills's style of writing was to "take it big" and in a hurry. He wrote fast and furiously, for as much as 6 hours a day, and "always juggled a number of ideas in various stages of formation" (Sawchuk, 2001, p. 46). What is more, he frequently borrowed, extended, and revised ideas from some of his books for use in several others on which he was working, thus making it difficult to distinguish one manuscript from the other. At the close of his career, it appears that Mills may have been working on three, or perhaps four, manuscripts in various stages of development. These constitute his unfinished work.

First there is the multivolume project tentatively titled *Comparative Sociology* that was intended as a highly ambitious work of global sociology. Indeed, it was to be nothing less than a historical comparative analysis of types of social structures found in 124 countries and territories. Mills regarded this bold and expansive project as "the sort of thing into which everything one does seems to fit. A sort of big framework that serves to orient and give point to smaller projects" (as quoted in K. Mills & Mills, 2000, pp. 274–275). In the end, he never got beyond producing a couple of segments of this proposed magnum opus.

Another manuscript, *Contacting the Enemy*, was supposed to be a volume consisting of a set of letters addressed to an imaginary Soviet colleague called Tovarich, the Russian word for comrade or friend. These letters, which Mills wrote to Tovarich between 1956 and 1960, at the height of the Cold War, were a political statement meant to go beyond *The Causes of World War Three* in endeavoring to foster dialogue and understanding—and ultimately, peace—between the intelligentsia of the United States and the Soviet Union. The letters, several of which are autobiographical in nature, were penned by Mills during his extensive travels outside of the United States. In the letter written from Sarajevo, in what was then Yugoslavia, during the winter of 1956–1957, Mills (in the self-assigned role of unattached American intellectual) explains to Tovarich, his Soviet counterpart, why he is writing to him:

> Tovarich, I am continually told that you are my enemy. Well, I am trying to get into contact with the enemy. I am trying to contact you—my opposite number in the Soviet Union. I want to bring you into a conversation so that we can make our own separate peace. In doing so I am of course assuming that there are—or that there will be soon—zones of real freedom in the Soviet Union. If they do not come soon I will have to wait; but when they come, I want these letters to be waiting for you. Tovarich, it's up to you and your society to identify the scope and quality of your freedom.

These letters should be some kind of combination answer to Lenin's question: "What is to be done?" and Tolstoy's: "How should we live?" Much of what I at least mean by politics and culture is indicated by these two questions, especially when you take them together. I want to write specifically and personally about culture and politics as they affect the ways you and I may be able to live for the rest of our lives—or even for how long. (as quoted in K. Mills & Mills, 2000, pp. 221–222)

The Politics of Truth

"Of all of Mills's late unfinished projects," writes Geary (2009), "the most important one was *The Cultural Apparatus*" (p. 189). What makes this book so important? Perhaps it is the fact that, unlike Mills's previous ones, it would at last strike a resonant note of optimism in giving hope to the notion that there could emerge a truly viable agency of left-wing change.

During the 1940s, at the time that he was researching *The New Men of Power*, Mills had viewed intellectuals as being quite impotent and irrelevant. They were powerless in controlling the uses made of them and of their work—their information and knowledge. Given that intellectuals were woefully ineffectual in influencing the conditions of their work setting, they had virtually no chance to contribute to progressive politics.

In one of his most intriguing and stinging essays, "The Powerless People: The Role of the Intellectual in Society" (1944/2008e), Mills laments the "organized irresponsibility" of contemporary society. He describes a world in which the average person—urgently experiencing a tragic sense of life and feeling frustrated, powerless, and helpless—had become dreadfully complacent and was only too willing to let a few powerful politicians make the decisions that affected their lives. Intellectuals, most of whom worked within controlling bureaucracies—in the film industry, the publishing houses, and the universities—were no different and no better. Owing to their compliance with the vacuous demands of a mass society of media markets, they too, Mills believed, had acquiesced to these stultifying influences. Thus, either through their own self-censorship or their silence, intellectuals had relinquished their moral responsibility to boldly communicate their unexpurgated knowledge and actively engage in a "politics of truth."

By the mid-1950s, Mills had arrived at a more sophisticated and nuanced understanding of the politics of truth—the critical voice of the intellectual that exposed *the* truth about the political power relations in U.S. society. He had become convinced that the power relationships in American life involved an important interplay between "the culture of politics" on the one hand and "the politics of culture" on the other. Thus, for Mills, understanding the culture of politics—the thought and actions that influence political decision making—also necessitated an understanding of the politics of culture—the determining influence of political decision making on the content of cultural work produced by intellectuals. As producers of cultural work, intellectuals—or to use the term that Mills (1958/2008d) later employed to encompass a larger stratum, "cultural workmen"—could have a hand in influencing the **cultural apparatus,** "all those organizations and milieux in which artistic, intellectual, and scientific work goes on" (p. 175). But these organizations and milieus—which included "schools and theatres, newspapers and census bureau, studios, laboratories, museums, little magazines, radio networks"—also defined "our standards of credibility, our definitions of reality, our modes of sensibility" (Mills, 1959/2008a, p. 204). Cultural workers—writers, editors, journalists, professors, artists, and scientists—were not powerless people; they had the power to shape images and ideas of reality. As producers of cultural work, leftward cultural workers could use the cultural apparatus to bring about cultural change. Mills (1959/2008c) admonished cultural workers on what they must now do:

> What we must do, in summary, is to define the reality of the human condition and to make our definitions public; to confront the new facts of history-making in our time, and their meanings for the problem of political responsibility; to release the human imagination, in order to explore all the alternatives now open to the human community, by transcending both the mere exhortation of grand principles and the mere opportunist reaction. (p. 222)

Intended as a book of about 11 chapters, to be published by Oxford University Press, *The Cultural Apparatus* was to be about the writers, scientists, and intellectuals in the United States, Western Europe, and the Soviet bloc. Although only five essays that were to be part of the book were ever published—"The Man in the Middle" (1958/2008d), "The Cultural Apparatus" (1959/2008a), "The Decline of the Left" (1959/2008c), "Culture and Politics" (1959/2008b), and "The New Left" (1960e)—Kim Sawchuk (2001) provides a synopsis of the volume based on a tentative outline housed in the archival documents, The Mills Papers, located at the Center for American History, University of Texas, Austin.

The book begins with a description of what is meant by the cultural apparatus and describes the means by which cultural work is made available to a variety of circles, publics, and masses. In the book's first section, Mills was to define the scope and variety of cultural activities and their place in society. He was to discuss the real, but not inevitable, split that existed between the intellectuals' cultural production and progressive politics. He also intended to compare the nature and position of the cultural apparatus in the United States with that of the USSR, Europe, and other nations.

Section two of the book would focus primarily on the place of the cultural apparatus within the social structure of American society as a whole. First, Mills would highlight four major positions for cultural workers in different world cultures. Then, he would look at the two industries—science and entertainment—that dominated the American cultural apparatus. Next, he would consider the institution of higher education and its production not only of cultural products, but also of cultural workers. He would conclude the section with a critique of the "end of ideology" thesis, discuss the development of the New Left and its consequences for politics and culture, and also examine the relation between the two.

In the book's third and final section, Mills would look at how culture and politics are indispensably related and outline the role of the ideal cultural apparatus. The book would conclude with a statement on the need for cultural workers to reclaim the cultural apparatus and use it for their own purposes. He would then offer suggestions on how to accomplish the repossession.

Had Mills lived to complete it, *The Cultural Apparatus* may well have been the book that put his critical social thought on a new trajectory. But in 1962, the year Mills died, any further discussion of a new trajectory—or of roads previously taken and not taken—would have to await the publication of his posthumous work.

The Posthumous Work

The Marxists (1962), published just 2 weeks after his death, is the only posthumous book fully completed by Mills. He wrote part of it in Mexico in early 1960, during the months he was giving a seminar on Marxism at the National University of Mexico. The low-priced paperback, which Mills called "a primer on Marxisms," is an anthology of 14 chapters. Seven of these, written by Mills, consist of extensive commentary in which he critiques all orthodoxies from left to right. The other seven chapters consist of selections from classic Marxist writings by Mao, Tito, Stalin, Lenin, Trotsky, and others. According to Horowitz (1983), the book's thesis is basically that "Marxists are important precisely because of their distinctive and different appraisals, whereas liberals are unimportant precisely because of the absence of such difference" (p. 195). Indeed, in the book Mills identifies and appraises three distinctive varieties of Marxism: vulgar Marxism, sophisticated Marxism, and plain Marxism.

The Three Marxisms

Vulgar Marxists seize upon certain ideological features of Marx's political philosophy and identify these aspects as the whole. They are usually apologists for the Soviet Union, exhibit a strong party allegiance, and operate within the strict confines of Marxism as a dogmatic ideological system. **Sophisticated Marxists,** by contrast, display greater flexibility as they are mainly concerned with Marxism as a model of society and with the theories developed with the aid of this model. They nonetheless remain loyal to a Marxist form of analysis and are unlikely to completely break away from that system. Finally, **plain Marxists**—among whom Mills numbered himself, along with Antonio Gramsci, Rosa Luxemburg, and Jean-Paul Sartre—utilize Marxism chiefly as a method of critical inquiry in an effort to advance current human concerns. According to Mills, plain Marxists emphasize the human being's freedom in the making of history, and they confront in Marx's work the unresolved tensions of humanism and determinism, of human freedom and historical necessity. Plain Marxists, therefore, take a critical stance toward other social theorists including Marx. While Mills does, to be sure, consider Marx to be a political thinker with whom social scientists have to come to grips, this does not preclude him from offering a trenchant critique of many of Marx's doctrinaire principles.

It is fair to say that Mills was not a "Marxist" except in the limited sense of being a plain Marxist. This tenuous affiliation with Marxism may explain why some socialists claimed him as a spokesman for their cause, while other socialists condemned him as a non-Marxist. In point of fact, Mills always resisted any complete identification with Marxism. As a plain Marxist, he rejects Marxism as ideological dogmatism and statist orthodoxy, but uses it very pragmatically as a "method of work," a working model. Even while revealing certain inadequacies in Marx's working model of society, Mills (1962) also praises him for providing social science with the basic tenets of the sociological imagination, which is to say, a master view of "(1) the structure of society in all its realms, (2) the mechanisms of the history of that society, and (3) the roles of individuals in all their psychological nuances" (p. 36). Mills holds that what is important is not the truth or falsity of the theories based upon the Marxian model, but the model itself. Marx's model could be used for constructing many different social theories as well as for correcting those made with its aid. Simply put, for Mills, Marx's model "is a signal and lasting contribution to the best sociological ways of reflection and inquiry available" (p. 129).

Anthologies

For many years, Irving Louis Horowitz was the only scholar to organize and make available the works produced by Mills. *Power, Politics, and People: The Collected Essays of C. Wright Mills,* edited and with an introduction by Horowitz, appeared in 1963. The collection consists of 41 major pieces—many previously unpublished—written by Mills. Of particular interest to Millsian scholars may be such difficult-to-obtain articles as "The Language and Ideas of Ancient China," which Mills wrote while a graduate student at Wisconsin. In this article he endeavors, along Weberian and pragmatist lines, to explain why scientific technology flourished in the West, but not in the East. As well there is "The Sociology of Mass Media and Public Opinion," which he completed in 1950 and intended for publication in the U.S. Department of State Russian-language journal *Amerika,* but whose publication was prohibited by Soviet authorities. The book also includes an invaluable comprehensive bibliography of Mills's writings.

A Spanish-language collection of Mills's papers, also edited by Horowitz, translated by Florentino M. Torner and published by the Siglo Veintiuno press in Mexico, is available as *De Hombres Sociales y Movimientos Políticos* (1969). According to Horowitz, the initial publication, in Spanish, of these essays was done to commemorate the profound affection that Mills had for Latin Americans in their struggle for self-determination, as well as to acknowledge the high regard in which Mills was held by many across the hemisphere. The 30 essays that comprise the volume, written over a period of two decades, are organized into three broad themes: Political Sociology and Sociological Politics, Ideals and the Intellectuals, and Social Scientists and Social Conscience. Twenty of the pieces had not previously been published in any form, nor have they been reprinted since. These consist of such rare and valuable pieces as "Types of Academic Men: Chicago Style Education," a memorandum that Mills produced under contract from 1947–1948 for the University of Chicago administration on its personnel in the social sciences and their practices. This essay is particularly representative of Mills's pragmatic temperament. Also included is a paper, "The Theory of Unionism of Selig Perlman," which Mills read in November 1955 at the conference on Sociology of Labor and Work held at Wayne State University. In "Consciousness of Epoch and Consciousness of Self," prepared in England in 1959 for oral presentation, Mills makes clear that sociology's role is to be truly helpful, and not just informative, to individuals who want to be helped.

In addition, Horowitz brought out Mills's PhD dissertation, in book form, as *Sociology and Pragmatism: The Higher Learning in America*

(1964). Here Mills analyzes the major concepts concerning higher learning of pragmatist philosophers Charles Sanders Peirce, William James, and John Dewey. This being very much a sociological (and not a philosophical) account of pragmatism, Mills situates his analysis in these philosophers' careers, reading publics, and sociohistorical context.

For a quarter-century, there existed no English-language collection of Mills's writings comparable to *Power, Politics, and People*—that is, until the appearance of John H. Summers's *The Politics of Truth: Selected Writings of C. Wright Mills* (2008d). This latter volume is an anthology of Mills's essays, interviews, speeches, and public lectures that together serve as a guiding commentary on his legacy. It contains such Mills classic pieces (many of which are available in the earlier Horowitz collection though with slightly different titles) as "On Intellectual Craftsmanship" and the 1954 article, "IBM Plus Reality Plus Humanism=Sociology," which marked Mills's disengagement from professional sociology and anticipated many of the arguments he later made in *The Sociological Imagination*. Also included are a few relatively more obscure pieces such as "The Man in the Middle" (an address Mills delivered before the International Design Conference in Aspen, Colorado, in June 1958) as well as "On Latin America, the Left, and the U.S." (one of the works on Latin Americans discussed in Chapter 5 of the present book, which was originally an interview with Mills drawn from a roundtable discussion held at the National University of Mexico, in March 1960). Also reprinted are the three University Lectures in Sociology that Mills gave, during January 1959, at the London School of Economics on the subject of culture and politics. As Summers reminds us, Mills drew the lecture series from the unfinished and never-published *The Cultural Apparatus*.

On Mills

The only book on Mills to appear during his lifetime was *The World of C. Wright Mills*, by the Marxist-Leninist historian, Herbert Aptheker (1960). This small volume, which basically consists of Aptheker's critiques of *The Power Elite, The Causes of World War Three*, and *The Sociological Imagination*, is generally a sympathetic assessment of them. The chapter on *The Power Elite*, where Aptheker endeavors to show some of the limitations of Mills's power elite concept as compared with the Marxian one of class struggle, had previously appeared as a book review in the left-leaning *Mainstream* magazine. Having read this review, as well as the one by Marxist economist Paul Sweezy (1956), Mills states rather nonchalantly, "Of course they're doctrinaire, but also no less so than all the liberal stuff and much more generous as well" (as quoted in K. Mills & Mills, 2000, p. 217). Aptheker ends the book by saying, "Mills is a writer with whom my disagreements, as I have striven to show, are profound; he is also, however, the kind of writer for whom one's respect grows as one's study continues" (p. 128).

As for collections written by others on Mills and his work, even before Mills's death, Horowitz had proposed a volume of essays on a series of studies and topics that Mills himself had opened up. Despite Mills's doubts that an appropriate and respectable group of scholars and intellectuals could be gathered for such a project, the contributors to the collection include such notables in social science as Pablo Gonzalez Casanova, Ralph Miliband, and Erich Fromm, as well as Ephraim H. Mizruchi, S. M. Miller, and Tom Bottomore. That volume, edited by Horowitz and titled *The New Sociology: Essays in Social Science and Social Theory in Honor of C. Wright Mills* (1964b), appeared just a couple of years after Mills's death. It contains some of the most penetrating commentaries on such Millsian topics as power, alienation, bureaucracy, social change, and nuclear war.

By far the most extensive collection of critical pieces written on Mills's social thought is Stanley Aronowitz's three-volume *C. Wright Mills* (2004) that contains 93 contributions originally published between 1948 and 2001. Included are reviews and reappraisals of *The New Men of Power, White Collar, The Power Elite, The Sociological Imagination,* and *The Marxists;* essays comparing Mills's thinking with that of John Dewey, Max Weber, Thorstein Veblen, Antonio Gramsci, Francis Fukuyama, and others; biographical statements on Mills; articles on the collaborative relationship between Gerth and Mills; and more.

Notwithstanding Mills's popularity with a variety of publics—students, sociologists, activists, journalists—full-fledged, serious intellectual biographies about him have been rare. Horowitz's highly entertaining *C. Wright Mills: An American Utopian* (1983), which provides a stark portrait of the man and a critical assessment of his work, stood for years as the only substantive account on record. This book is unique in that it provides a cross-section of opinion on Mills derived from papers, correspondence, and personal interviews conducted with individuals who knew Mills. Given that most of these individuals—some of whom were favorably, others negatively, predisposed to Mills—have since died (Clarence E. Ayres, Don Martindale, Richard Hofstadter, Robert K. Merton, Tom Bottomore, David Riesman), the biography offers a unique insight into Mills's life and thought.

Radical Ambition: C. Wright Mills, the Left, and American Social Thought (2009) by the social historian Daniel Geary now constitutes only the second such biographical effort. Geary frames the biography by situating Mills's life history in the shifting contours of radical politics in the United States on the one hand, and in the growing influence of sociological ideas within and outside the academy on the other. Accordingly, Geary demonstrates how Mills's mature social criticism was forged during the late 1930s and 1940s, the early part of his career that is relatively unfamiliar to most scholars and that, significantly, was marked by the collapse of the Stalinist Old Left. This Geary does in order to trace the origins of some of Mills's more distinctive themes and ideas—his search for radical agents of social change, his theory of power, what he saw as the poverty of liberalism and Marxism—that he most forcefully articulated in his influential writings of the 1950s and early 1960s and at the birth of the international New Left.

Less of a biography than a critical examination of two strikingly different intellectual styles and personalities, Oakes and Vidich's (1999) book examines the 13-year working relationship—at times greatly tormented and severely strained—between Mills and Hans Gerth. Here Mills is depicted severely as a careerist and an opportunist willing to do whatever was necessary—whether ethical or not—to get published and advance his ideas. Particularly helpful in constructing the story of the Gerth–Mills complex partnership were the letters exchanged between the two men as well as other items from Gerth's correspondence that were made available to Oakes and Vidich by Gerth's widow.

As for Mills's letters and correspondence, an immensely valuable collection was published by his two daughters, Kathryn and Pamela, as *C. Wright Mills: Letters and Autobiographical Writings* (2000). A treasure trove of material from Mills's point of view (often sarcastic and biting), providing great insight into his intellectual development, the book includes approximately 150 letters that Mills wrote to his parents, friends, and colleagues; several autobiographical essays; and other writings.

Research by students on Mills and his works has been ongoing since the early 1960s. One of the first and best executed of these efforts is Tom Hayden's master's thesis at the University of Michigan, which he wrote the year following Mills's death and during the time that Hayden was intensely engaged in the leadership of Students for a Democratic Society. Published 44 years later as *Radical Nomad: C. Wright Mills and His Times* (2006), Hayden's thesis is a balanced assessment of Mills's ideas about American society. Here, Hayden takes Mills to task for failing to attack the prevailing myth of the time: that poverty and discrimination were problems being confronted successfully. Hayden's judgment concerning Mills's disregard of poverty and racism is harsh indeed. Hayden argues that, as a consequence of this omission, Mills "fundamentally crippled his analysis of capitalist stabilization, the prospect for social change, and his own role as a radical" (pp. 147–148).

Another important early document is Robert J. S. Ross's senior honors thesis, *Power and the Intellect: American Democracy and the Theories of C. Wright Mills* (1963), written while Ross was an undergraduate at the University of Michigan and intensely involved with SDS. Like Hayden, Ross also critiques Mills for neglecting the potential of organizing power from the middle and bottom levels of society. Some social movements and some political elections, argues Ross, can be important factors in generating power—a fact that Mills regrettably failed to see.

A more recent dissertation-turned-book is *Postmodern Cowboy: C. Wright Mills and a New 21st-Century Sociology*, by Keith Kerr (2009). Its last two chapters are devoted to a discussion of Mills's foreshadowing of some current "postmodern" issues. Indeed, Mills is regarded as straddling both modernist and postmodernist claims. For example, on the one hand, he clearly understood, in a postmodern sense, that social life consists of a variety of competing social meanings. On the other hand, he was sufficiently modernist, being profoundly influenced by pragmatism, to also believe there is an objective reality—Truth with a capital "T"—behind these meanings.

The most thorough graduate school papers ever written on Mills's life and work are perhaps those by Richard A. Gillam. His master's thesis of 1966, *The Intellectual as Rebel: C. Wright Mills, 1916–1946*, examines the formative and early years. Gillam obtained important information on Mills's biography in interviews with Mills's relatives—Ruth Harper Mills (his second wife) and Yaroslava Mills (his widow)—and friends, William Goode, J. B. S. Hardman, and Harvey Swados. In addition, there is Gillam's doctoral dissertation of 1971, *C. Wright Mills: An Intellectual Biography, 1916–1948*, for which Gillam relied on a variety of sources including court records and personal interviews.

Extending Mills

Notwithstanding the myriad topics and themes that occupied Mills's attention throughout his 23-year career, it is disconcerting that only a limited number of empirical and conceptual studies have attempted to extend—critique and verify—his ideas.

Working from the premise that Mills's most provocative comments pertained to the structure of power in American society, particularly as presented in *The Power Elite*, G. William Domhoff and Hoyt B. Ballard compiled the "liberal," "radical," and "highbrow" reviews of that book in their *C. Wright Mills and The Power Elite* (1968). Indeed, not since Veblen's *The Theory of the Leisure Class* had there been a proper study of the upper reaches of American society, and Mills's *Power Elite* served to spawn a small cottage industry in the area. One of the earliest and most persistent contributors to this research area has been Domhoff himself. For example, inspired by the ideas of Mills (and several others), Domhoff, in *Who Rules America?* (1967), examines the controlling influence of the "governing class" (a national upper class) in U.S. society between the years 1932 and 1964. Marshalling a wide variety of empirical evidence—obtained from *Social Register* listings, private school attendance, club memberships, tax-exempt charity foundations, studies on wealth distribution, political campaign donations lists, lists of personnel heading the Department of Defense, and so on—Domhoff concludes that not only is there, in fact, a governing class in the United States, but that it manifests itself through what Mills called the power elite.

Later, in *The Higher Circles: The Governing Class in America*, Domhoff (1970) proposed utilizing three research methods—contingency analysis, the reputational method, and positional analysis—by which to further study, empirically, the upper class as a social entity. In the book, Domhoff also criticizes Mills for his treatment (based on sloppy research) of the "jet set"—the stars and celebrities that provide diversion and entertainment for the masses—as being a group apart from the power elite. Contrary to Mills, Domhoff shows that not only is jet-set society very much based in the social upper class, but many of its primary players also function as important businessmen and businesswomen. Why, then, was Mills so wrong about celebrity? Domhoff attributes it to the fact that Mills took too seriously and at face value his data sources, which mainly consisted of *Fortune* magazine and other writings by high society authors.

A more conceptual extension of Mills's ideas is Tilman's (2004) study of the political thought of Thorstein Veblen, John Dewey, and Mills. Though they come from quite distinct meta-theoretical positions, Tilman shows how a convergence of some of these three thinkers' ideas can produce an authentic, coherent, and original intellectual tradition of American critical science. In undertaking a comparative analysis and synthesis of their views on the business–industry distinction, feminism, and social aesthetics, Tilman endeavors to show how these three thinkers' radical tradition is relevant to postmodernism today.

A work that mixes both the empirical and the conceptual is by John D. Brewer (2003), who draws upon Mills's conception of the sociological imagination—which explicitly considers the intersection of biography, social structural conditions, and political power, all framed within a historical perspective—to empirically explain the emergence and progress of the peace processes in Northern Ireland and South Africa. As such, Brewer historically demonstrates how colonialism in these two countries instituted a social structure that had, since the 17th century, continuously reproduced cultural patterns of social cleavage (around race and religion) that made violent conflict endemic. Brewer further shows that in both countries, significant numbers of people had, by the 1990s, been mobilized to support the peace process through the political strategies of key leaders like Nelson Mandela, E. W. de Klerk, John Hume, Gerry Adams, and David Trimble, strategies that are rooted in these leaders' own biographical experiences (e.g., their prison experiences), their "spaces of selfhood" (Brewer, 2005). These leaders, Brewer asserts, were in turn simply responding to social structural conditions in the national and international political process, which included demographic shifts, economic changes, external intervention by third parties, and the development of civic culture and new lines of social differentiation in local milieus. These structural developments pushed militant leaders against armed struggle and persuaded political leaders to change. What is particularly intriguing about this study is that Brewer not only employs Mills's sociological imagination to explain the peace processes in Northern Ireland and South Africa, but he also uses the peace processes as a test of the utility of Mills's version of sociology when applied to issues of real political concern.

A Small but Pronounced Revival

Since 1964, the Society for the Study of Social Problems (SSSP) has each year given the C. Wright Mills Award to a book that is "consistent with Mills's dedication to a search for a sophisticated understanding of the individual and society." Below is a select list of some titles that the SSSP membership has, through the decades, singled out as being representative of the spirit of Mills's work:

Year of Award	Author and Book
2009	Mario L. Small, *Unanticipated Gains: Origins of Network Inequality in Everyday Life*
2008	Martín Sánchez-Jankowski, *Cracks in the Pavement: Social Change and Resilience in Poor Neighborhoods*
2000	Michéle Lamont, *The Dignity of Working Men: Morality and the Boundaries of Race, Class, and Immigration*
1990	Patricia Hill Collins, *Black Feminist Thought*
1987	William J. Wilson, *The Truly Disadvantaged: The Inner City, The Underclass, and Public Policy*
1982	Paul Starr, *The Social Transformation of American Medicine*
1979	Theda Skocpol, *States and Social Revolutions*
1974	Harry Braverman, *Labor and Monopoly Capital: The Degradation of Work in the Twentieth Century.*
1971	Frances Fox Piven and Richard A. Cloward, *Regulating the Poor: The Functions of Public Welfare*
1968	Gerald D. Suttles, *The Social Order of the Slum*
1964	David Matza, *Delinquency and Drift*

Notwithstanding the SSSP's long-time recognition of Mills's humanistic sociology and of writers who, like the above, have endeavored to follow in that tradition, Stanley Aronowitz, in 2003, was partly correct in saying that Mills's work had been "consigned to an academic purgatory for the last three decades of the twentieth century." Aronowitz's statement is only partly correct because the 1970s and 1980s saw the publication of at least four full-length monographs on Mills's social and political ideas: Scimecca (1977), Press (1978), Eldridge, (1983), and Tilman (1984). On the other hand, Aronowitz (2003) was quite right in claiming that in the first decade of the 21st century, Mills's work was beginning to experience "a small but pronounced revival" (n.p.). He cites in support of this revival the reissuance, between 2000 and 2002, of four of Mills's major books—*The New Men of Power, White Collar, The Power Elite,* and *The Sociological Imagination*—each released with new introductions written by prominent scholars. Since the publication of Aronowitz's article, there have appeared no fewer than six titles specifically devoted to Mills and his work—Brewer (2003), Tilman (2004), Hayden (2006), Summers (2008d), Kerr (2009), and Geary (2009)—with no doubt many more to come. As for recent, sustained research on Mills, the best and most productive representatives are John H. Summers (2006, 2007, 2008a, 2008b, 2008c) and Daniel Geary (2001, 2006, 2008).

Conclusion

In this small volume, we have examined the social thought of C. Wright Mills by appraising his major works—those of a distinct sociological stamp as well as those that are more expressly propagandistic. Clearly, the genius of Mills's critical approach lay in his scrutiny, first, of the morally irresponsible use—the monopolization and manipulation—of power by national elites, and second, of the ways that mass society molded the social psychological attributes, the character structure, of individuals in postwar America. His social thinking constituted a critical analysis of one of the essential characteristics that had, lamentably, become a master trend during the middle decades of the 20th century: employing rational means to achieve substantively irrational ends—the most disastrous result being the potential annihilation of the human species through thermonuclear war. In tandem with the likely extermination of humanity, there was the insidious corrosion of the human spirit that, through the mass media of amusement and distraction, was tragically transforming men and women into unreflecting automatons.

Always, however, Mills's radical critique was expressed within the framework of the "sociological imagination," or that quality of mind that allows people to get out of their civic apathy and political indifference—that unique way of thinking that assists individuals in better understanding the meaning of their own epoch for their own lives as well as helps them become active participants in history making. Moreover, even though Mills's taking-it-big approach was one of grappling with the larger problems of contemporary significance, he was at bottom motivated by the humanist concern, which meant connecting the social, personal, and historical dimensions of the disquieted lives of flesh-and-blood individuals.

In a retrospective article, Norman Birnbaum (2009) explains that today "Mills is half forgotten—perhaps because much of what he said is now taken for granted" (p. 36). It is my hope that this book will serve to remind readers of those aspects of the social thought of C. Wright Mills that we now take for granted—and that it will also serve to motivate a new generation of cultural workers to earnestly engage in the politics of responsibility and the politics of truth.

The volume ends with these questions:

- How does Mills's postmodern era, what he called the Fourth Epoch of the mid-20th century, differ from the postmodern era of the 21st century?
- Which of Mills's radical critiques are no longer relevant to contemporary U.S. society?
- Given today's increased globalization, how might Mills's approach of "taking it big" be extended to include an examination of various nation-states and multiple cultures in relation to each other?
- How is Mills's sociology for publics similar to and different from the various types of public sociology popular today?

Glossary

Abstracted empiricism. An approach that converts the pressing social issues of the day into mundane statistical assertions. In these assertions, there is a pronounced tendency to confuse whatever is to be studied with the set of methods suggested for its study.

Belongingness. The belief that the ultimate and most urgent need of individuals is to feel a part of a group.

Character structure. The relatively stabilized integration of the organism's psychic structure linked with the social roles of the person.

Cheerful robots. Apathetic individuals of a mass society who blindly and complacently accept their life-chances as being determined by fate.

Class. A grouping of people determined by wealth, property institutions, and the occupational roles operating within the economic institutional order. In its simplest objective sense, class has to do with the amount and source (property or work) of income as these affect the chances of people to obtain available valued resources.

Coincidence. When different structural principles or developments in various institutional orders result in their combined effects in the same, often unforeseen, outcome of unity for the whole society.

Community of publics. Scattered little circles of face-to-face citizens discussing their public business in the spirit of direct participatory democracy.

Convergence. When two or more institutional orders coincide to the point of fusion, thus becoming one institutional setup.

Coordination. The integration of a society by means of one or more institutional orders that become ascendant over other orders and direct them; thus, other orders are regulated and managed by the ascendant order or orders.

Corporate elite. The corporation chieftains who occupy the top command posts in the giant corporations.

Correspondence. When a social structure is unified because its several institutional orders share a common structural principle that operates in a parallel way in each.

Cross-classification. An analytical technique that uses charts, tables, or diagrams of a qualitative sort and, in systematic fashion, casts general notions as new types.

Cultural apparatus. All those organizations and milieus—such as schools and theaters, newspapers and census bureau, studios, laboratories, museums, little magazines, radio networks—in which artistic, intellectual, and scientific work goes on.

Cultural workers. Various intellectuals—such as writers, editors, journalists, professors, artists, and scientists—who, through the cultural apparatus, have the power to shape images and ideas of reality and bring about progressive cultural change.

Economic order. All those establishments by which people organize labor, resources, and technologies in order to produce and distribute goods and services.

Education. The sphere consisting of those institutions and activities concerned with the transmission of skills and values to those persons who have not acquired them.

End of ideology. A movement in the 1950s that asserted that Western civilization was no longer influenced by ideologies, "truth" ideas demanding a commitment to action, such as liberalism and Marxism.

Enormous file. An impersonal administrative hierarchy consisting of an army of clerks and a cadre of managers, divided according to specialized and standardized tasks performed in various divisions and units.

Fourth Epoch. A postmodern era where production, administration, and violence are centralized within bureaucracies and where reason and freedom are threatened. It is also a time that spawned previously unknown social groupings and trends.

Freedom. Involves people's chance to reason about the available choices, to argue over them—followed by the opportunity to choose.

Generalized other. The experience of the appraisals of those who are not immediately present but who are authoritatively significant to the person.

Globalization. The circulation of people, lifestyles, things, and ideas throughout the world.

Globalization of nothing. A consequence of globalization whereby societies worldwide are moving away from "something" (unique and distinctive indigenous social forms) and toward "nothing" (social forms that are centralized, dehumanized, and lacking in distinctive substantive content).

Grand theory. A general conceptual scheme for analyzing the structure and processes of social systems.

Great Celebration. The self-congratulatory trend that viewed the United States as the ideal contemporary manifestation of democracy.

Higher immorality. The thinking and behaviors of the power elite that involve the American system of organized irresponsibility that produced a general erosion of the old middle-class values and codes of uprightness.

Ideal type. An analytical model that allows the social scientist to talk generally and abstractly about some specific and concrete phenomenon. Serving as a yardstick that compares and contrasts empirical social phenomena, the ideal type helps to identify those cases that diverge or deviate from its stylized depiction.

Illiberal practicality. The idea that research is client-oriented and that social scientists have become mere technicians, co-opted by the powerful who buy their services and use their findings for bureaucratic and commercial purposes.

Inner-directed. A personality type characterized by conformity through internalized controls.

Institutional order. All those institutions within a social structure that have similar consequences and ends or that serve similar objective functions.

Institutions. Organizations of roles, one or more of which is understood to serve the maintenance of the total set of roles.

Intellectual craftsmanship. A reflective style of work that should guide sociologists' professional work as well as what they, as persons, observe and experience in their everyday lives.

Kinship order. All those institutions that regulate and facilitate legitimate sexual intercourse, procreation, and the early rearing of children.

Liberalism. An ideology, a political style of thinking, whose tenets emphasize individual freedom, egalitarianism, liberty, private property, fair competition, a laissez-faire market economy, and unlimited opportunities.

Main drift. The underlying forms and tendencies of the range of society in a particular time period. In the middle of the 20th century, historical and structural forces of the main drift were moving American society toward "rationality without reason," or the use of rational means in the service of substantively irrational ends.

Managerial demiurge. Those executives, "the new entrepreneurs," whose power is given and circumscribed by the hierarchical corporations for which they work.

Mass society. A highly bureaucratized and impersonal social structure whose culture is characterized by a uniformity and mediocrity—of goods, ideas, tastes, values, and lifestyles—that pave the way for the commercial and political manipulation of the mass of people.

McDonaldization. The process by which society takes on the principles of systematization, standardization, consistency, scientific management, and methodological operation that characterize the fast-food restaurant.

Military elite. The warlords of Washington who oversee the largest and most expensive feature of the U.S. government, the military order.

Military metaphysic. A way of thinking in which everything in the world situation is officially defined in terms of military necessity.

Military order. All those institutions in which people organize legitimate violence and supervise its use.

New middle class. Those propertyless white-collar workers involved primarily in sales and management and whose work situation was increasingly bureaucratized by the "command hierarchies" of business and government.

Occupation. A set of activities pursued more-or-less regularly as a major source of income.

Organism. The human being as a biological entity.

Organization man. The young man in the middle, the practical team player. He is the junior executive, the middle manager. Above all, he is conservative, since his inclination is to accept the status quo. Ruled by a spirit of acquiescence, he does not want to rebel; he wants to collaborate. The organization man does not question the "system"; he is not interested in ends but in means, or methodology.

Other-directed. A personality type with an overwhelming psychological need for approval and direction from contemporaries.

Overdeveloped society. An affluent industrial society where conspicuous production and consumption dominate and control the lifestyles of many individuals, but in particular those individuals of the middle classes.

Person. The human being as a player of roles that involve reference to emotions, perceptions, and purposes.

Plain Marxists. Those who espouse an ideology that utilizes Marxism chiefly as a method of critical inquiry in an effort to advance current human concerns.

Polar type. The methodological classification that contrasts opposites for the purpose of sorting their dimensions in terms of which comparisons are made.

Political elite. The political directorate that consists of higher politicians and key officials of government, but in particular the president, vice president, and the members of the cabinet. It also includes the White House staff as well as the most important appointed heads of major regulatory agencies and commissions.

Political order. All those institutions within which people acquire, wield, or influence the distribution of power and authority within social structures.

Politics of truth. The moral and political obligation that intellectuals have to tell the truth—to disclose the facts—about social reality, particularly as this reality is distorted by the stultifying culture of mass society and the manipulation of the mass media.

Power. Political influence; refers to the realization of one's will, even if this involves the resistance of others.

Power elite. A national group made up of a governing triumvirate—the corporate elite, the political elite, and the military elite—with tiers and ranges of wealth and power of which people in the rest of society know very little.

Pragmatism. An American philosophical tradition elaborated by Charles Sanders Peirce, William James, and John Dewey. The person most responsible for developing the pragmatic approach in social psychology was George Herbert Mead.

Primary public. Face-to-face groups of articulate individuals who have a shared interest in a public event or issue and express their opinions freely and publicly. They have the ability to resist those engaged in manipulating public opinion and manufacturing consent.

Private troubles. Those problems that individuals experience in the course of their daily lives and that tend to be limited to the specific milieus (home, workplace, neighborhood, etc.) in which they live their lives.

Properly developing society. A democratic order where troubles, issues, and problems are open to inquiry. It is a society that provides forums and other outlets through which all momentous decisions are made into public issues and openly debated by intellectuals before a community of free and knowledgeable publics.

Psychic structure. The integration of feelings, sensations, and impulses that are a fundamental part of the human organism.

Psychologism. The attempt to explain social phenomena in terms of the personal characteristics of individuals.

Public issues. Those problems of individuals that reside at the level of historically located social structure. As such, these problems are shared by many others and are not soluble by any one individual but by large-scale modifications of the entire social structure.

Publics. Various groups of politically alert and active people that, to one degree or another, have the power to influence political issues. They are aware of the issues' meaning and source. They can transform their personal troubles into public issues and see these issues' relevance for their community and their community's relevance for them.

Reason. The capacity of individuals to formulate available choices in life. Reason serves as a guide to freedom because it liberates individuals from the constraints of their social structure and allows them to achieve lucid summations of what is going on in the world and of what may be happening within themselves.

Religious order. All those institutions in which people organize and supervise the collective worship of God or deities, usually on regular occasions and at fixed places.

Roles. The units of conduct that by their recurrence stand out as regularities and that are oriented to the conduct of other actors.

Scientism. The practical part of the social ethic that involves a belief in the application of the methods of science to human relations in order to achieve "belongingness."

Significant others. Those intimates, encountered in a given institution, who matter most to us, to whom we pay attention, and whose appraisals—approbation and criticism—are reflected in our self-appraisals.

Social character. The more-or-less permanent socially and historically conditioned organization of an individual's drives and satisfaction.

Social ethic. An organization or a bureaucratic body of thought that morally legitimates the pressures of society against the individual and that places a high premium on scientism, belongingness, and togetherness.

Social structure. The interrelations of various institutions and the functions each performs.

Sociological imagination. A quality of mind that will help people use information and develop reason in order to achieve lucid summations of what is going on in the world and of what may be happening within themselves.

Sophisticated Marxists. Those who espouse an ideology mainly concerned with Marxism as a model of society and with the theories developed with the aid of this model.

Spheres. Those aspects of social conduct that characterize all institutional orders and that are rarely or never autonomous as to the ends they serve.

Status. The sphere consisting of agencies and means of distributing prestige, deference, or honor among the members of the social structure.

Strata. A grouping consisting of people who are characterized by an intersection of the dimensions of class, status, power, and occupation.

Symbols. Visual or acoustic signs, signals, emblems, ceremonials, language, music, or other arts used in understanding the conduct of human actors.

Technology. The implementation of conduct with tools, apparatuses, machines, instruments, and other physical devices and the skill employed in that conduct.

Togetherness. The belief that people want to belong together.

Tradition-directed. A personality type that possesses a conformist social character uncritically accepting of institutionalized roles that have endured for generations.

Vocabularies of motive. Those specific terminologies that individuals employ in given social situations to justify the past, sustain the present, or endorse intended future actions.

Vulgar Marxists. Those who espouse an ideology that seizes upon certain features of Marx's political philosophy and identifies these aspects as the whole.

Working model. A more-or-less systematic inventory of elements that is neither true nor false, but useful and adequate to varying degrees, and to which the social scientist must pay attention in order to understand something of social significance.

References

Aptheker, H. (1960). *The world of C. Wright Mills.* New York: Marzani & Munsell.

Aronowitz, S. (2003). A Mills revival? *Logos, 2*(3). Available at http://www.logos journal.com/aronowitz.htm

Aronowitz, S. (Ed.). (2004). *C. Wright Mills* (Vols. 1–3). Thousand Oaks, CA: Sage.

Bell, D. (1962). *The end of ideology: On the exhaustion of political ideas in the fifties* (Rev. ed.). New York: Free Press.

Birnbaum, N. (2009, March 30). The half-forgotten prophet: C. Wright Mills. *The Nation,* 34–36.

Brewer, J. D. (2003). *C. Wright Mills and the ending of violence.* Basingstoke, UK: Palgrave Macmillan.

Brewer, J. D. (2004). Imagining *The Sociological Imagination*: The biographical context of a classic. *British Journal of Sociology, 55*(3), 317–333.

Brewer, J. D. (2005). The public and private in C. Wright Mills's life and work. *Sociology, 39*(4), 661–677.

Chomsky, N. (1967). The responsibility of intellectuals. In N. Chomsky, *American power and the new mandarins: Historical and political essays* (pp. 323–366). New York: Pantheon Books.

Chomsky, N. (2003). *Hegemony or survival.* New York: Metropolitan Books.

Domhoff, G. W. (1967). *Who rules America?* Englewood Cliffs, NJ: Prentice Hall.

Domhoff, G. W. (1970). *The higher circles: The governing class in America.* New York: Random House.

Domhoff, G. W., & Ballard, H. B. (1968). *C. Wright Mills and the power elite.* Boston: Beacon Press.

Eldridge, J. E. T. (1983). *C. Wright Mills.* London: Tavistock.

Form, W. (1995). Mills at Maryland. *The American Sociologist, 26*(4), 40–67.

Fortune. (2010, May 3). Women CEOs. Available at http://money.cnn.com/magazines/ fortune/fortune500/2010/womenceos/

Fuentes, C. (1970). *Casa con dos puertas.* Mexico City, Mexico: Joaquin Mortiz.

Geary, D. (2001). The union of the power and intellect: C. Wright Mills and the labor movement. *Labor History, 42,* 327–345.

Geary, D. (2006). C. Wright Mills and American social science. In N. Lichtenstein (Ed.), *American capitalism: Social thought and political economy in the twentieth century* (pp. 135–156). Philadelphia: University of Pennsylvania Press.

Geary, D. (2008). Becoming international again: C. Wright Mills and the emergence of a global New Left. *Journal of American History, 95*(3), 711–736.

Geary, D. (2009). *Radical ambition: C. Wright Mills, the left, and American social thought.* Berkeley: University of California Press.

Gerth, H. H., & Mills, C. W. (1953). *Character and social structure: The psychology of social institutions.* New York: Harcourt, Brace & World.

Gillam, R. A. (1966). *The intellectual as rebel: C. Wright Mills, 1916–1946.* Unpublished master's thesis, Columbia University, New York.

Gillam, R. A. (1971). *C. Wright Mills: An intellectual biography, 1916–1948.* Unpublished doctoral dissertation, Stanford University, Stanford, CA.

Goffman, E. (1963). *Stigma: Notes on the management of spoiled identity.* New York: Simon & Schuster.

Goldsen, R. L. (1964). Mills and the profession of sociology. In I. L. Horowitz (Ed.), *The new sociology: Essays in social science and social theory in honor of C. Wright Mills* (pp. 88–93). New York: Oxford University Press.

Halberstam, D. (1993). *The fifties.* New York: Villard Books.

Hayden, T. (2006). *Radical nomad: C. Wright Mills and his times.* Boulder, CO: Paradigm.

Horowitz, I. L. (1963). An introduction to C. Wright Mills. In I. L. Horowitz (Ed.), *Power, politics, and people: The collected essays of C. Wright Mills* (pp. 1–20). New York: Oxford University Press.

Horowitz, I. L. (1964a). The intellectual genesis of C. Wright Mills. In C. W. Mills, *Sociology and pragmatism: The higher learning in America* (pp. 11–31). New York: Oxford University Press.

Horowitz, I. L. (Ed.). (1964b). *The new sociology: Essays in social science and social theory in honor of C. Wright Mills.* New York: Oxford University Press.

Horowitz, I. L. (1983). *C. Wright Mills: An American utopian.* New York: Free Press.

Jamison, A., & Eyerman, R. (1994). *Seeds of the sixties.* Berkeley: University of California Press.

Jones, D. (2009, Jan. 2). Women CEOs slowly gain on corporate America. *USA Today.* Available at http://www.usatoday.com/money/companies/management/2009-01 01-women-ceos-increase_N.htm

Katz, E., & Lazarsfeld, P. F. (1955). *Personal influence: The part played by people in the flow of mass communication.* Glencoe, IL: Free Press.

Keene, M. F. (2003). *Stalking sociologists: J. Edgar Hoover's FBI surveillance of American sociology.* New Brunswick, NJ: Transaction.

Kerr, K. (2009). *Postmodern cowboy: C. Wright Mills and a new 21st-century sociology.* Boulder, CO: Paradigm.

Landau, S. (1965, August). C. Wright Mills: The last six months. *Ramparts, 4,* 46–54.

Lee, A. M. (1973). *Toward humanist sociology.* Englewood Cliffs, NJ: Prentice Hall.

Mannheim, K. (1968). *Ideology and utopia: An introduction to the sociology of knowledge* (L. Wirth & E. Shils, Trans.). New York: Harcourt, Brace & World. (Original work published 1936)

Martindale, D. (1975). *Prominent sociologists since World War II.* Columbus, OH: Charles E. Merrill.

Mazón, M. (1984). *The zoot-suit riots: The psychology of symbolic assimilation.* Austin: University of Texas Press.

Menendez, R. (2010). *Corporate diversity report.* Available at http://menendez.senate .gov/imo/media/doc/CorporateDiversityReport2.pdf

Miller, J. (1987). *"Democracy is in the streets": From Port Huron to the siege of Chicago.* New York: Simon & Schuster.

Mills, C. W. (1939). Language, logic, and culture. *American Sociological Review, 4*(5), 670–680.

Mills, C. W. (1940a). Methodological consequences of the sociology of knowledge. *America Journal of Sociology, 46*(3), 316–330.

Mills, C. W. (1940b). Situated actions and vocabularies of motive. *American Sociological Review, 5*(6), 904–913.

Mills, C. W. (1942). *A sociological account of pragmatism: An essay on the sociology of knowledge.* Unpublished doctoral dissertation, University of Wisconsin, Madison.

Mills, C. W. (1943a). The professional ideology of social pathologists. *American Journal of Sociology, 49*(2), 165–180.

Mills, C. W. (1943b). The sailor, sex market, and Mexican. *The New Leader, 26* 5–7.

Mills, C. W. (1948). *The new men of power: America's labor leaders.* New York: Harcourt, Brace.

Mills, C. W. (1951). *White collar: The American middle classes.* New York: Oxford University Press.

Mills, C. W. (1953). Two styles of research in current social studies. *Philosophy of Science, 20*(4), 266–275.

Mills, C. W. (1954). IBM plus reality plus humanism = sociology. *Saturday Review, 37*(18), 22–23, 54–56.

Mills, C. W. (1956). *The power elite.* New York: Oxford University Press.

Mills, C. W. (1958). *The causes of World War Three.* New York: Simon & Schuster.

Mills, C. W. (1959a). On intellectual craftsmanship. In L. Gross (Ed.), *Symposium on sociological theory* (pp. 25–53). Evanston, IL: Row, Peterson and Company.

Mills, C. W. (1959b). *The sociological imagination.* New York: Oxford University Press.

Mills, C. W. (1960a). *Images of man: The classic tradition in sociological thinking.* New York: George Braziller.

Mills, C. W. (1960b, September-October). Letter to the New Left. *New Left Review, 5,* 18–23.

Mills, C. W. (1960c, December). Listen, Yankee: The Cuban case against the United States. *Harpers Magazine, 222,* 31–37.

Mills, C. W. (1960d). *Listen, Yankee: The revolution in Cuba.* New York: Ballantine Books.

Mills, C. W. (1960e). The New Left. In I. L. Horowitz (Ed.), *Power, politics, and people: The collected essays of C. Wright Mills* (pp. 247–259). New York: Oxford University Press.

Mills, C. W. (1961). On Latin America, the left, and the U.S. *Evergreen Review, 5*(16), 110–122.

Mills, C. W. (1962). *The Marxists.* New York: Dell.

Mills, C. W. (1963a). *Power, politics, and people: The collected essays of C. Wright Mills* (I. L. Horowitz, Ed.). New York: Oxford University Press.

Mills, C. W. (1963b). The sociology of mass media and public opinion. In I. L. Horowitz (Ed.), *Power, politics, and people: The collected essays of C. Wright Mills* (pp. 577–598). New York: Oxford University Press.

Mills, C. W. (1964). *Sociology and pragmatism: The higher learning in America.* I. L. Horowitz (Ed.). New York: Oxford University Press.

Mills, C. W. (1969). *De hombres sociales y movimientos politicos* (I. L. Horowitz, Ed.; F. del Torner, Trans.). Mexico City, Mexico: Siglo Vientiuno.

Mills, C. W. (2008a). The cultural apparatus. In J. H. Summers (Ed.), *The politics of truth: Selected writings of C. Wright Mills* (pp. 203–212). New York: Oxford University Press. (Original work published 1959)

Mills, C. W. (2008b). Culture and politics. In J. H. Summers (Ed.), *The politics of truth: Selected writings of C. Wright Mills* (pp. 193–201). New York: Oxford University Press. (Original work published 1959)

Mills, C. W. (2008c). The decline of the left. In J. H. Summers (Ed.), *The politics of truth: Selected writings of C. Wright Mills* (pp. 213–222). New York: Oxford University Press. (Original work published 1959)

Mills, C. W. (2008d). The man in the middle. In J. H. Summers (Ed.), *The politics of truth: Selected writings of C. Wright Mills* (pp. 173–183). New York: Oxford University Press. (Original work published 1958)

Mills, C. W. (2008e). The powerless people: The role of the intellectual in society. In J. H. Summers (Ed.), *The politics of truth: Selected writings of C. Wright Mills* (pp. 13–23). New York: Oxford University Press. (Original work published 1944)

Mills, C. W., Senior, C., & Goldsen, R. K. (1950). *The Puerto Rican journey: New York's newest migrants.* New York: Harper & Brothers.

Mills, K., & Mills, P. (Eds.). (2000). *C. Wright Mills: Letters and autobiographical writings.* Berkeley: University of California Press.

Morley, C. (1939). *Kitty Foyle: The natural history of a woman.* Philadelphia: J.B. Lippincott.

Mumford, L. (1961). *The city in history: Its origins, its transformations, and its prospects.* New York: Harcourt, Brace & World.

Oakes, G., & Vidich, A. J. (1999). *Collaboration, reputation, and ethics in American academic life: Hans H. Gerth and C. Wright Mills.* Urbana and Chicago: University of Illinois Press.

Office of History and Preservation, Office of the Clerk. (2010a). *Black Americans in Congress, 1870–2007.* Washington, DC: U.S. Government Printing Office. Available at http://baic.house.gov/historical-data/representatives-senators-by-congress.html?congress=111

Office of History and Preservation, Office of the Clerk. (2010b). *Women in Congress, 1917–2006.* Washington, DC: U.S. Government Printing Office. Available at http://womenincongress.house.gov/historical-data/representatives-senators-by-congress.html?congress=111

Parsons, T. (1951). *The social system.* New York: Free Press.

Pew Research Center for the People & the Press. (2004, June 8). *Media consumption and believability study.* Available at http://people-press.org/reports/pdf/215.pdf

Press, H. (1978). *C. Wright Mills.* Boston: Twayne.

Pursell, C. W. (Ed.). (1972). *The military-industrial complex.* New York: Harper & Row.

Riesman, D. (1950). *The lonely crowd: A study of the changing American character.* New Haven, CT: Yale University Press.

Ritzer, G. (2007). *The globalization of nothing* (Second ed.). Thousand Oaks, CA: Pine Forge Press.

Ritzer, G. (2010). *The McDonaldization of society* (Sixth ed.). Thousand Oaks, CA: Pine Forge Press.

Ross, R. J. S. (1963). *Power and the intellect: American democracy and the theories of C. Wright Mills.* Unpublished senior honors thesis, University of Michigan, Ann Arbor.

Ross, R. J. S., & Treviño, A. J. (1998). The influence of C. Wright Mills on students for a democratic society. *Humanity and Society, 22*(3), 260–277.

Sawchuk, K. (2001). The cultural apparatus: C. Wright Mills's unfinished work. *The American Sociologist, 32*(1), 27–49.

Schickel, R. (1991). *Brando: A life in our times.* New York: Atheneum.

Schmal, J. P. (2009, May 18). Hispanics in the U.S. military. *LatinoLA.* Available at http://latinola.com/story.php?story=7475

Scimecca, J. A. (1977). *The sociological theory of C. Wright Mills.* Port Washington, NY: Kennikat Press.

Scott, R. F. (1970). The zoot-suit riots. In M. P. Servin (Ed.), *The Mexican Americans: An awakening minority* (pp. 116–124). Beverly Hills, CA: Glencoe Press.

Summers, J. H. (2006). Perpetual revelations: C. Wright Mills and Paul Lazarsfeld. *Annals of the American Academy of Political and Social Science, 608,* 25–40.

Summers, J. H. (2007). James Agee and C. Wright Mills: Sociological poetry. In M. Lofaro (Ed.), *Agee agonistes: Essays on the life, legend, and works of James Agee* (pp. 199–216). Knoxville: University of Tennessee Press.

Summers, J. H. (2008a). The cultural break: C. Wright Mills and the Polish October. *Intellectual History Review, 18*(2), 259–273.

Summers, J. H. (2008b). The epigone's embrace, Part II: C. Wright Mills and the New Left. *Left History, 13,* 94–127.

Summers, J. H. (2008c). No-man's land: C. Wright Mills in England. In W. R. Louis (Ed.), *Penultimate adventures with Britannia: Personalities, politics, and culture in Britain* (pp. 185–199). London: I.B. Tauris.

Summers, J. H. (Ed.). (2008d). *The politics of truth: Selected writings of C. Wright Mills.* New York: Oxford University Press.

Swados, H. (1963). C. Wright Mills: A personal memoir. *Dissent, 10*(1), 35–42.

Swarnes, R. L. (2008, June 30). Commanding a role for women in the military. *New York Times.* Available at http://www.nytimes.com/2008/06/30/washington/30general.html?_r=1

Sweezy, P. (1956, September). Power elite or ruling class? *Monthly Review, 8,* 138–150.

Tilman, R. (1984). *C. Wright Mills: A native radical and his American intellectual roots*. University Park, PA: The Pennsylvania State University Press.

Tilman, R. (2004). *Thorstein Veblen, John Dewey, C. Wright Mills and the generic ends of life*. Lanham, MD: Rowman & Littlefield.

Wakefield, D. (1971). Taking it big: A memoir of C. Wright Mills. *The Atlantic, 228*(3), 65–71.

Wallerstein, I. (1968). C. Wright Mills. In D. L. Sills (Ed.), *International encyclopedia of the social sciences* (vol. 10, pp. 362–364). New York: Macmillan/Free Press.

Weber, M. (1946). *From Max Weber: Essays in sociology* (H. H. Gerth & C. W. Mills, Eds.). New York: Oxford University Press.

Weber, M. (1978). *Economy and society* (G. Roth & C. Wittich, Eds.). Berkeley: University of California Press.

Whyte, W. H., Jr. (1956). *The organization man*. Garden City: Doubleday.

Wilson, S. (1955). *The man in the gray flannel suit*. New York: Simon & Schuster.

Zweigenhaft, R. L., & Domhoff, G. W. (2006). *Diversity in the power elite: How it happened, why it matters*. Lanham, MD: Rowman & Littlefield.

Index

About the Author

A. Javier Treviño is the author or editor of several books including *The Sociology of Law; Talcott Parsons Today: His Theory and Legacy in Contemporary Sociology;* and *George C. Homans: History, Theory, and Method.* He was a Research Fellow in Sociology at the University of Sussex, England (2006), and a Fulbright Scholar to the Republic of Moldova (2009). He has served as president of the Justice Studies Association (2000–2002) and of the Society for the Study of Social Problems (2010–2011).